Personal Best

Personal Best

THE AUTOBIOGRAPHY OF BERYL BURTON, O.B.E.

BERYL BURTON WITH COLIN KIRBY

To Charlie, without whom none of this
would have been possible.

BB

Published by Springfield Books Limited, Norman Road,
Denby Dale, Huddersfield HD8 8TH, West Yorkshire, England

First edition 1986

British Library Cataloguing in Publication Data

Burton, Beryl
Personal Best: the autobiography of Beryl Burton.
1. Burton, Beryl 2. Cyclists—England—Biography
I. Title
796.6'2'0924   GV1051.B/

Re-printed 2009 with the kind permission of the Burton family by:

Mercian Manuals Ltd
353 Kenilworth Road
Balsall Common
Coventry, CV7 7DL.
www.mercianmanuals.co.uk

ISBN: 978 1 903088 470

CONTENTS

Acknowledgements

The author and publishers are grateful to the following for
kind permission to reproduce copyright material:
Associated Press
Camera Press/John Drysdale
Cycling Magazine
Fred Fisher
Press Association
Publifoto, Milan
Gunter Rowell
Wolfgang Ruprecht
Bernard Thompson
United Press International
Yorkshire Post Newspapers

The photograph on the front cover was taken by Derek Reynolds
and the portrait of Beryl on the jacket flap is by Fred Fisher

We should also like to express our
gratitude to Ken Evans and Edgar Whiteley
for making archive material available for our research,
and to Martin Ayres, editor of *Cycling*, for his permission
and encouragement to quote from the magazine.

A Frenchman once wrote with great perception, 'If Beryl Burton had been French, Joan of Arc would have to take second place.'

In spite of the mainly indifferent attitude of the British sporting press to cycling sport (although in recent years the situation has improved a little), B.B., as she is affectionately known within the fraternity, could not be altogether ignored. In 1967 she was the *Daily Express* Sportswoman of the Year. The same year, and perhaps more importantly, she topped the Sportswriters poll. Most of them never wrote a word about her but, to give them credit, they knew her worth, and the esteem in which she was held in other parts of the world.

The following year Beryl was honoured with an O.B.E. following the M.B.E. she had been awarded in 1964. Somewhere among the corridors of the people who ordain these matters it had been realised what an amazing sportswoman the country possessed. No such award could have been more richly deserved.

Beryl was and remains an ordinary Yorkshire lass. From a humble background and as a delicate schoolgirl seemingly destined never to take part in physical sport, her iron will has overcome many setbacks that would have brought an instant end to other sporting careers. Her twenty-five successive years as the British Best All-rounder must be a feat without parallel; nobody else has dominated a sport for so long.

She has been known to give a wry smile and comment that if she had been a tennis player or born in France she would have become a millionairess. There is no bitterness about this: it is a fact of life which she accepts. For many years Beryl and her husband Charlie have made sacrifices from an ordinary working class income to help make it possible. No Sports Council or municipal grants, which in other sports almost seem to be the norm for those who have yet to prove their worth, have arrived at the Burton household.

If behind every successful man there is the helping hand of a woman, the reverse can also be true. In the case of Beryl Burton it was supplied by her husband Charlie, chauffeur, mechanic and helpmate, always in the background, but there when needed. But even here Beryl is not conventional. She has always been her 'own woman', riding the races she thought she should and in the way she should. On occasion an ear turned to advice from those who knew her well may have brought dividends, but this woman pedalled her way to the top on her own ability and desire to win. No coach advising her and supervising training; no Svengali behind the scenes; simply a housewife who still rides prodigious distances on a bike 'because I like cycling', and who beats girls and men half her age in a most demanding, physical and competitive sport.

It has been my privilege to assist Beryl in writing her story. In parts she makes what she considers honest and valid criticism of individuals who no doubt were acting for the best as they saw matters at the time. She admits where, in retrospect, she now thinks she was wrong. The saga continues in spite of advancing years and her fair share of misfortunes. I am pleased that she asked me. I am delighted that she, Charlie and Denise are my friends.

COLIN KIRBY, MORLEY, *December 1985*

I was born in May, 1937. I have a sister fifteen months older than me, and a brother nine years younger. We had a fairly strict upbringing; perhaps, by the standards of today, very strict. Maureen and I had to help with various domestic chores each evening. The idea was that we should both help each day, but after a time we decided that we would take each evening in turn; that way we would each have a full evening to ourselves at least every second day.

I attended Coldcotes Junior School in Leeds. Maureen and I could not stay to school dinners. I think they could only manage a certain number and we were not on the list. We had to run all the way home, eat our lunch, and then run all the way back to be in time for the afternoon lessons.

I played quite a lot by myself. In those days girls would play by completing a set of 'exercises' throwing a tennis ball against a wall. I would set a target of twenty, bouncing the ball hard, catching it and throwing it against the wall again. It was probably a little more difficult than it sounds and I would often miss the rebound. If I failed to complete twenty without a mistake I would be filled with an inner rage. I think even then I was setting myself exacting standards. After twenty would come twenty-five, and so on, each failure resulting in an inward 'ticking off'. I would even bite the ball with frustration and annoyance. I would then play the same game with two balls, always setting myself a target that had to be beaten before I increased it. I would try the same at skipping. Just me, playing alone, trying to beat myself!

Later I lived with my grandmother in Armley, a district of West Leeds. I attended school there and became interested in swimming. My competitive nature came to the fore and I began to be modestly successful, winning a few certificates. I recall that I was very good at swimming under water.

I enjoyed school, even the subjects at which I was not particularly good, and I had no qualms about taking the eleven-plus examination which children sat to decide their academic future. Possibly psychiatrists and educationalists may read something into what happened to me. Came the day – and I completely froze. Even papers in the examinations which should not have caused me any great problem might just as well have been printed in Urdu. I was an abject failure! Shattered, my childish ego bruised beyond belief, I developed a high fever and was rushed to St James Hospital in Leeds, where the doctors diagnosed chorea, in plain terms a kind of St Vitus Dance with rheumatic fever thrown in for good measure! Anyway, I believe it stems from the nervous system – and I blame it on that eleven-plus exam.

I missed my sister and brother very much, particularly Jeffrey. It was the first time that somebody's absence really worried me. We three were quite close, and the fact that Jeffrey was much younger did not make any difference. From a window in Ward 19 I would watch the main gate for the family at visiting time. Round the corner would come Jeffrey, waving, and I would wave excitedly back. But this was later, when I began to feel a little better. At the beginning I was in quite a state. Unable to speak properly, I became paralysed down one side and this persisted for a long time. Even when the fever subsided and I was allowed to visit the bathroom I had to hop on one leg, and for months I could only use one hand. In the early days it was considered vital that I be kept warm at all times, and I was smothered in blankets, so much so that I found it impossible to sleep. I sweated until the sheets were wet through, and the nurses were not allowed to change them in case I caught a chill which would have done the rheumatic fever no good at all. During the night I would work a leg from under the blankets and stick it out of the bed to obtain a little relief from the heat. Then the night sister came along, tut-tutting as she thrust my leg firmly under the blankets again. Sleeping pills had been prescribed but one night I rebelled and refused to take them. After cajoling and then threats from the night sister the doctor was sent for. His blandishments were just as fruitless. In exasperation he agreed that I could do without if that was what I wanted. Looking back now I shiver at my temerity – eleven-year-old Beryl Charnock against the medical establishment! Later in my life I always refused to seek what might decorously be called 'assistance' with my racing!

I was nine months in hospital. There followed a period of convalescence, fifteen months in all, making a total of some two years away from school, and hanging over me the stricture that I must take matters easily for the rest of my life. From hospital I was sent to a convalescent home at Southport which was run by an order of nuns, and I have happy memories of this. Every morning we had to go to church and then the nuns would take us for a walk. The incense that was used during the mass made me sick, so after a time I was excused attending the services.

Eventually it was all over. I was declared fit enough to resume my schooling and back I went. I felt that my whole future had been placed in jeopardy by a silly examination thought up by people who had long since forgotten their own schooldays. I knew that I was quite bright, and I had had good school reports before my illness. I determined there and then that somehow I would make my mark.

The family were now living in the Moortown district of Leeds, and I attended Stainbeck Secondary School. I enjoyed my time there. It was a pretty good school. I worked hard to catch up, and my school reports were quite good.

When I left school I started work in the office at Sir Montague Burton Ltd, the multiple tailor who in those days had men's shops in every High Street, and a large factory in Leeds employing thousands. One day a bronzed-looking chap came into the office and attracted my attention immediately. I eyed him from top to bottom without, I hoped, making it too obvious. When my eyes alighted on his feet I thought 'Oh dear, the poor chap must have something wrong with them.' In fact he was wearing cycling shoes, which I had never seen before. What Charles Burton was doing wearing them at work I don't know but, peculiar shoes or not, I was attracted to him.

At this time cycling had no part in my life. I had an old roadster, but regarded it purely as a means of transport. I don't think I knew about cycling as a sport, about cycling clubs and people actually racing on bikes. The first inkling came one Sunday morning. To earn a little extra money I had a Sunday job at a wealthy household at Alwoodley. They entertained on Saturday evenings, and on Sundays I went to clear up from the previous night and generally clean. While I was on my way there one morning a cyclist, resplendent in his club colours, shot past my plodding roadster and disappeared down the road, and I recall being impressed.

I was soon on chatting terms with Charlie and quickly learned of his interest in cycling. Soon he loaned me a lightweight and persuaded me to take up club cycling. He was a member of the Morley Road Club, and this was the beginning of my association with a wonderful town which has had my allegiance ever since, although I have not lived there for a number of years now. Morley is now part of the Metropolitan District of Leeds, formed during the local government changes in the early seventies, but until that time it was a borough in its own right, with a Mayor and Council and municipal services. I feel much was lost when towns such as Morley had to sink into large conurbations, but Morley is still there, a few miles south-west of what I think of as Leeds, and most Morleians consider themselves as belonging to Morley and not to Leeds.

The Morley R.C. generally met on a Sunday morning outside the G.P.O. in Leeds City Square, a convenient meeting point for rides to the Yorkshire Dales or the Vale of York, or west into Lancashire. From Moortown into the centre of Leeds it was mostly downhill, and that part of the day was easy. The rest of the day usually remained a blank. I would return home absolutely whacked. For weeks mother would ask me on my return home where I had been and usually I had no idea. I would see Charlie during the week, of course, but had no contact with other club members except on Sundays. As I left them on Sunday evening I would manage to gasp 'See you next week.' I am sure they were quite surprised when I kept turning out Sunday after Sunday and managing somehow, with Charlie's help, to hang on. It could not have been easy for him as he did not want to lose me but, as any club cyclist will understand, there was never any question of him giving up his sport. Neither was there any doubt about my hanging on. As even experienced West Yorkshire cyclists will tell you, a day in the Dales can be pretty tough indeed, and whether I actually enjoyed myself I can't recall. What I do remember is that I was not going to be beaten by anything – and this demanded my turning up week after week. I know there were occasions Charlie had to give me some help by pushing because it was an unwritten rule that the club never left anybody behind. Sadly, club riding, outside the Cyclists' Touring Club sections, seems to have diminished, and there is now more and more emphasis on racing. However, I have never lost my love of cycling for its own sake, and most years Charlie and I still manage some touring and youth hostelling.

The many social activities of cycling clubs have dwindled too. Morley R.C. held Christmas parties, and everyone would help. The yardstick for the cakes the girls baked would be the number of members expected to attend multiplied by the size of the piece of cake they would expect. Tins of fruit and other items were brought in abundance. There was always too much even for cyclists' large appetites, and what was left would be raffled, with the proceeds going into club funds.

I began my club cycling with a bike borrowed from Charlie while I saved to buy a machine of my own. Eventually I was able to purchase an Armstrong Moth sports, which was an improvement on the roadster of my pre-club days. Later I had a frame built by John Hutchins of Morley. It cost me £7-15s (£7.75). For many years we used to go to John's shop and root through the cardboard boxes of parts he kept upstairs. Finding something we needed, or thought we might need in the future, we would ask him 'How much for this, John?' and a bargain would be struck. Cycling owed a lot to establishments like John Hutchins', and there are a few like it still around today. We paid him half-a-crown (12½p) a week all the year round, and usually just managed to stay on the credit side!

By now I had left Montague Burton and was working at the Rose Foregrove Co., who made packaging machinery. I had also become aware that there was such a thing as competition on bikes. During the week the club ran 10-mile time trials on the Bradford Road near Morley and I would ride over straight from work to watch. One evening one of the club lads suggested I should have a try. The thought of going all-out for ten miles frightend me, but my built-in determination not to be beaten did not allow me to refuse. Afraid that I might make a spectacle of myself, I set off on that first ten miles sitting 'on the tops' instead of crouching down and appearing to be racing. My idea was that any casual onlooker who noticed me would think I was not really trying to go as hard as I could! I rode my first three or four evening '10s' in this fashion. Eventually it was gently suggested to me that I should 'get down on the drops' and that way I might move a bit faster. I completed my first event in just under 33 minutes. Most novice club girls now would consider that a very slow time.

Charlie and I married when I was a month short of my eighteenth birthday at St John's Church, Moortown. It was thought to be very young in those days. Charlie is eight years older than me, and I doubt whether I would have married so young if he had been about my age. For two months we lived with Charlie's mother in Morley, but then we found a place of our own – a little one up and one down, back-to-back house, one of thousands built in the last century to accommodate factory workers as industrial Britain began to boom. We lived in that house in Cross Street for about four years. About this time I had a medical in connection with work, and the doctor was aghast at my cycling. He told me to take it easy, and always walk up hills as he was sure the others would wait! I did not tell him about my racing.

I improved my evening '10s' a little and became interested in the Heavy Woollen Combine events. The Combine is, as the title suggests, a combination of the cycling clubs in the area of the woollen mills of the West Riding, and they held races among themselves in keen but friendly rivalry. However, I still had no intention of widening my racing activities, although I had ridden my first open event at 25 miles. In 1955 my daughter Denise was on the way; she was born in the following January and I carried on with my racing until the previous July. For the last few races I had to raise the handlebars a little to accommodate her!

I was happy at the prospect of becoming a mother, but a little disappointed that I would not be able to carry on with my racing, because I was beginning to make my mark locally. However, soon after Denise was born we fixed a sidecar to Charlie's bike and resumed club cycling. My first race outside my own area was in Lancashire; I rode back afterwards and Charlie brought Denise out to me about halfway. My racing career was back into its stride. I was fortunate, not only at this time but throughout Denise's childhood, that when it was not practical to have her with us my mother-in-law was always happy to look after her. It was a good solution to what could have been a difficulty, and I was relaxed knowing that my daughter was in good hands. I have always been grateful to Charlie's mum, for she played an important part in helping with my cycling career, albeit off-stage.

One of my earliest successes was in a 25-mile time trial promoted by the White Rose Ladies club near York. I rode over on the Saturday to stay the night at the Carlton House Café, and shared a room with Iris Miles. That year, and also the following year, Iris was British Best All-rounder, as well as the winner of the 50- and 100-mile championships. Iris, who rode for the Scala Wheelers club in South Yorkshire, was a formidable opponent and I realised that this was my biggest test to date. Iris knew, of course, of my growing reputation and that I would be aiming to beat her. Each uneasily aware of the other's presence, neither of us slept much that night. The next day victory was mine by two slender seconds, and I began to think that perhaps I was pretty good. I had come some way from riding the club '10s' 'on the tops', and a long way from the paralysed child who had been told to 'always take things easy'.

Among our club members was Nim Carline, a farmer in the Morley area and well known as a rhubarb-grower. He was a rider with great stamina who later won seven national championship victories in the 12- and 24-hour events. I had begun training with him and I am sure that his advice and the hard miles he put me through brought out any talent I have. He was such a hard taskmaster that I would wait in the house before a training run wishing that there was some way I could avoid it. I was in and out of the lavatory and perspiring even before I sat on the bike. There was no question of simply following him. I had to match him side by side, although toward the end of the stint I just had to follow his wheel, tears in my eyes, but determined that I would not drop behind.

I had left my previous job to have Denise, and by this time had started to work on Nim's farm. I would push Denise there in the pram, except when I was going to do some tractor work, when I could not keep an eye on her. Then, I would leave her at Charlie's parents' house, pushing her there with bike in one hand and pram in the other, running up Fountain Street to take her to her grandmother's, and then it was on the bike to the farm. After work, the process in reverse. Even though Nim was a fellow club member, working for him was no cushy number – entirely the opposite. Nim had a business to run and there were no passengers. I worked alongside young men, lifting heavy boxes on and off vehicles, digging holes for the roots of whatever was being planted, ten at a time, and you had to be finished by the time the lorry arrived with more. Carrying, lifting, bending, digging, all day long in all weathers until my back ached, my arms ached, my shoulders ached, my legs ached. I was determined not to let up but to match the others in everything. Then at the end of the working day, most nights were spent out training, sometimes with Nim, who was as relentless on the bike as off it. It was the old determination not to be beaten, to keep going however fatigued I may have felt; the benefit of all this I have reaped in later years. It was not only crops I was planting but the seed of my future success.

Maybe there is a lesson here for young sportsmen and women of today. I set about toughening my body and my will without coaches, facilities or grants, and for no other reason than I wanted to win for my club and, later, for my country. I was in a sport that in Britain would not bring me any riches and, relatively speaking, not too much glory. The great Reg Harris climbed to the top ploughing a similar lone furrow, although he was able to capitalise on his rich talent in the world's velodromes as a professional rider.

There were occasions when I felt that I would have liked to follow a 'proper' career. It was quite impossible if I was to continue cycling at the level I was engaged in, so my jobs with the Post Office, the Yorkshire Electricity Board and as a temporary civil servant were all relatively low-key, with no point in pushing myself forward for advancement. It had to be work which I could perform conscientiously but whose main purpose was additional income, mainly used to support my cycling activities.

In spite of my victory over Iris, I did not consider that I had any more natural ability than anyone else. I just tried my hardest to win. I trained hard and conscientiously, whatever the weather; it was part of my discipline. I had no idea what training the other girls did. If I missed training I felt uneasy because already the competition bug had bitten deep. There was no coaching in today's sense; it was hard slog and the development of a will not to be beaten. Other scraps of advice would be picked up from older club members.

Iris Miles had obviously been stung by her defeat in the White Rose event. Two weeks later she beat me soundly in the Goole Wheelers 25-mile by 1 minute 21 seconds. We met again two weeks later in the Doncaster Wheelers '25' with Iris seeking a fast time for the Best All-rounder and, with Millie Robinson also entered, it promised to be a keen tussle. However, Millie did not ride that day and it appeared to be a Miles–Burton battle. I was leading until very near the finish when Iris pulled out a little bit extra and won by three seconds.

So my first serious season came to a close. I had accomplished the 14th fastest time in the country at 10 miles, the 5th at 15 miles, the 13th at 25 miles and the 14th at 50 miles.

I continued riding throughout the winter. If the weather was reasonable the whole family was out, with Denise in the sidecar. I think it was the first time Morley had seen an infant being towed around in a sidecar attached to a bike and we became very well known in the area. On one occasion as we rode through Leeds she was wide awake and, as we passed the Town Hall, stood up and let out whooping sounds at the top of her voice. I thought she gave a good imitation of a Roman charioteer! After that we strapped her in. One day Charlie's mother called at the house, very anxious because somebody had said that all the bumping around would affect Denise's spine. But Denise always seemed most comfortable and spent most of the time asleep, and I felt she was better sleeping in the country air than at home. And we were happy as a family, involving Denise in our activities.

I looked forward eagerly to the 1957 season, and when Iris Miles and I clashed again on May 3rd in the Yorkshire Cycling Federation 15-mile we had a battle royal. Iris was reigning British Best All-rounder champion, and I was delighted to tie with her in a time of 40–48. I was particularly pleased with this achievement because I still could not afford 'real' racing wheels and tyres, and was riding on Michelin high pressures, which were the next best thing in those days. I also felt at a slight disadvantage among the top racing girls in that I was the only one with a full-time job and a youngster to look after. It was hard work fitting in training with all these other commitments.

The week following my tussle with Iris we were both entered in the Clifton C.C. 15-mile and it produced a record. Mary Dawson of the Tees-side Clarion set new national figures with a scorching ride of 37–59, beating Iris by nineteen seconds and I was a disappointed third, a further 1 minute 29 seconds behind.

I felt it was time to spread my wings and entered for the national 25-mile championship near Grantham. We could not afford rail fares so I rode down to the event with Charlie on the Saturday, staying overnight with a clubman who, in the great spirit of the cycling fraternity, gave us a night's lodging.

I was very nervous – it was only a short time since I had found out that there were such things as national championships – and perhaps I should not have been so disappointed by my sixth placing in an event won by the great Millie Robinson, who was lifting that particular title for the third time.

I suppose that I still had something to learn when riding in the highest class with a championship at stake, because a few weeks later I finished 'only' eighth in the 50-mile title clash held in Lancashire. On this occasion Iris Miles showed that she was the best in the country at this distance, beating Millie Robinson into second place.

I trained hard for the 100-mile championship held a few weeks later. Everything seemed to go well although I found the rain in the early part troublesome. Riding cautiously at the beginning I was not in contention at twenty-five miles, had improved a little by halfway, and then began to come good. Miles, Robinson and others who were among the favourites began to slip back in the hard going and with about twenty miles to go Nim Carline, at the roadside taking time-checks, indicated I was in the lead. Unfortunately nobody had been taking notice of an outsider, Roma Clarke of Leicestershire R.C. Riding in her own area she improved by seven and a half minutes on her previous best and kept the title from me by 1 minute 31 seconds. It was a disappointment, but I had increased my racing knowledge along the way and gained my first medal, albeit the silver and not the gold I wanted. I hope it will not seem immodest of me to say so, but quite honestly I have lost count of all the medals I have won in my career. The pleasure of cycling has always been the basic motivation of my competition. True, I have always set out to win, and been disappointed when I have not – the determination to succeed at something following that set-back during my childhood made sure of that. But winning any race meant, for me, the attaining of that particular goal and was not something to be gloated over afterwards. I simply pushed it into the background and looked forward to the next challenge. Thinking about the '100' championship later I began to see the true worth of my second place. I had beaten all the 'names' in the country and felt quietly satisfied about that. But Roma Clarke showed me that there would always be an outsider who could spring a surprise.

In September the Morley R.C. held its Open 25-mile and I had the satisfaction of beating Iris Miles with a time of 1–5–7 against her 1–5–59. Bad weather prevented a faster time and, as the report in *Cycling* stated, I needed something better to improve on my fifth position in the British Best All-rounder competition. An interesting sidelight on our Morley race is that twenty-one riders failed to start because of the Asian flu epidemic. I think that will stir the memory of some readers.

At this stage I should briefly describe the Best All-rounder (B.A.R.) competition to which I have previously referred. The competition is based on m.p.h. at three distances – 25, 50, and 100 miles. A rider's fastest time in open events at each of the three distances throughout the season is calculated in terms of m.p.h. to three decimal places and the average taken of the three. The men, of course, have a separate competition and this is based on 50 miles, 100 miles and 12 hours. At the season's end the winner can really claim to be a true champion. *Cycling* magazine publishes the positions from about half-way through the season and out comes the pencil and paper (or, these days, the calculator!) for A to decide that he or she needs to improve by, say, 0.015 m.p.h. next week to move up a place over B, provided B does not also make an improvement. I don't want to put any other sport down but I know of no other which makes such demands upon its adherents. To reach even a modest standard and then maintain it demands complete dedication. You can't really 'play' at cycling in a true competitive sense. It's training, training, miles and yet more miles. A week off the bike can set you back a month or more, although there are exceptional individuals who manage good performances with a minimum of training. With a fraction of the effort, a young lad can still pick up a medal playing for his local football team and enjoy a much better social life during the season. I think that as a nation we are basically rather lazy, and who wants to spend hours training after work in all weathers to improve in a time trial by ten seconds and still finish sixty-first in a field of

120? Well, some do, and they are the salt of the earth. An untold number come into the sport each year and I would hazard about one in ten stick it out. Those who do find a way of life which transcends everything else – a kind of freemasonry.

My first season in serious competition, 1957, had, I thought, been pretty good. I had finished second in the 100-mile championship and fifth in the B.A.R. and had won the Yorkshire B.A.R., and I was determined to do even better the following year. I felt I was getting stronger, but how I needed to! Coping with a young daughter, domestic chores and a heavy job as well as all the training would tax all my resources. If I felt this put me at a disadvantage, I kept it to myself and never drew attention to it. One can't alter life to even things up.

A final memory of 1957, showing how naive Charlie and I were in those days, relates to the Best All-rounder concert and prize presentation in London. It was held at the Albert Hall, and Charlie made some enquiries about what we should wear. It was a big occasion for me, and to appear on stage to receive my silver medal for the 100-mile championship was rather awe-inspiring. We booked into one hotel for our accommodation, but the dinner which was held for prize-winners and officials of the controlling body, the Road Time Trials Council, was at another. We had been advised to dress informally for the dinner, and Charlie wore a sports suit and I a plain dress. When we arrived, to our consternation everyone else was in formal wear – dress suits and evening dresses. After dinner we rushed back to our hotel by tube to change into more formal wear for the presentation, only to discover when we got to the Albert Hall that the people who had been at the dinner had also changed – back into informal clothes!

Chapter 2
National titles and a record – Robinson–Burton duels –
My first world championships

At the end of the 1957 season the Morley Road Club and the Morley Wheelers amalgamated and became the Morley Cycling Club, because there was really only room for one club in a town the size of Morley. Thus I became a member of the Morley C.C., and I have carried their turquoise, white and black colours ever since.

There followed, in 1958, a season-long duel with the great Millie Robinson. Millie, an Irish girl who lived on the Isle of Man, was a happy character, always ready with a joke, but on the bike she turned to grim determination. We first clashed in April in the Goole Wheelers 25-mile, and she beat me by nearly three minutes, although I did finish second. For the next few weeks I rode locally, my mind on the 25-mile title race and hoped-for revenge on Millie. Came the 12th June and I was at the start in Surrey. I was aware that Yorkshire cyclists had pinned their hopes on me but that I was still a relative newcomer to the top flight. I had set a schedule of 1–3 for a difficult course, and hoped that would see me through. It was calm but very cold for June, and at halfway Millie was leading me by eleven seconds. This season I had increased my gear to 84-inch and I was still slow at getting into my stride. In later years I used much higher derailleur gears, in common with everyone else, but at this period of my career I rode fixed-wheel. I nearly managed my schedule, winning in 1–3–51, beating Millie by seventeen seconds. My first national championship and my first gold medal. My private vow to succeed after the cruel circumstances of my eleven-plus failure had at last come true. But I was determined to achieve even more.

The following week I raced in the Tees-side C.A. 100-mile in good conditions. The road seemed to fly under my wheels, and near the end I realised that I had a chance of beating the record as well as winning. I poured everything into the final miles, finishing in 4–33–26, beating the record Mary Dawson had held for three years by thirty-seven seconds. Already I was being tipped as the winner of the B.A.R. for 1958, but a week later I was made to realise what a hard task it would be. In the Preston Wheelers 50-mile I was beaten into second place by Mary Dawson who had finished fourth in my record-breaking '100', while on the same day Millie Robinson cracked the 25-mile record in winning the De Montfort Ladies event. Millie brought the record down to 1–1–49, the first 24 m.p.h. to be recorded in women's open time trials, and already the cycling world was beginning to think that the first 25 m.p.h. win was on the horizon.

Shortly afterwards I tried track racing on my first visit to London's Herne Hill track. This was the venue for the men's 4,000 metres pursuit championship, and among the men's events there was some women's racing. I think my road speed was attracting the attention of international selectors with a view to my inclusion as a track pursuiter, and I was matched against an experienced girl, Val Garrett of Silchester Wheelers, who had finished third in the national '25' championship. I won easily enough, and enjoyed it as an outing more than anything else. My main recollection is of Denise playing happily in a sandpit that was there for the youngsters, and of the late and great Tom Simpson winning the pursuit title and being hailed at the age of twenty as a future world champion.

The 50-mile championship north of Oxford brought a savage day, strong south-west winds and heavy rain with the last fifteen miles into the wind, but my strength told. I added the 50-mile title to my '25' with a time of 2–13–20 and Millie was nearly two minutes behind.

With the fastest hundred miles ever and two title wins I was riding high, and looked forward to the next meeting with Millie which came in the Clifton '50' in Yorkshire. She started before me and stormed round the course to set up a new record of 2–9–17. But I, too, was going well. I had scheduled for a 2–10 ride and, in spite of a troublesome wind over the final miles, came in to beat Millie by a second. Poor Millie! It must have been a keen disappointment for her to lose both the race and a new record by a paltry second. An extra bonus for me was that team-mate Sheila Briggs and I won the team prize for Morley.

By this time there was discussion as to whether Millie or I would be the first to break the magical 4–30 barrier at a hundred miles, and whether I would be the first rider to accomplish three title wins in one season – the 25, the 50 and the 100.

Charlie, Denise and I then went away on our first family cycling tour – to Eire. Unfortunately, the weather did not match up to the charm of the Irish people and we spent most of the time in our capes. During the tour we saw in a copy of *Cycling* that Millie Robinson had broken my '100' record with 4–32–7. Millie had thrown down the gauntlet in no uncertain terms and it seemed a great battle lay ahead for the Best All-rounder title.

We followed our planned itinerary back through North Wales and the Peak District to Yorkshire, hoping that the weather would improve. Travelling through Wales, I think in Conway, I trapped my wheels in some tramlines and came a cropper. I was helped into a nearby shop to sit and recover, and Charlie tried to bring Denise in to me but she positively refused to budge.

Mummy had to be brought out to her to convince her that I was all right. Continuing over Holme Moss and nearing home the little man in the sky who presses the button which makes it rain on cyclists had a final fling, with a cloudburst which turned the steep road into a river. Finding a shed at the roadside we took refuge and completely stripped Denise to dry her and put on fresh clothes. In the next village people were frantically sweeping and mopping to keep the rain from their homes, such had been the downpour.

As with all cycle touring, it had been fun whatever the weather, and I returned ready to respond to Millie's challenge. On August 21st the 100-mile championship was held in the Midlands. My rival was racing better than at any time in her great career. She had been left out of the Great Britain team for the world championships in Paris the following month when many thought her strength and stamina would suit her for the track pursuit. I had no road racing as against time trialling experience, and my track record was virtually nil, so I don't suppose I was even considered. I should explain for those who may be puzzled that road racing is different from the time trialling I had been doing. Everyone starts together and the first across the line is the winner. It sounds simple enough, but tactics can play a big part, whereas time trialling is supremely a test of speed and fitness over a given distance. The European cyclists call trialling the 'test of truth' and even hardened professionals indulge very sparingly during the course of a season. They think we are mad to compete in them week after week and run a season-long competition based on results. Unfortunately, there is no women's world championship in time trialling and I had to win world titles in track pursuits and in road racing, but that comes later in my story.

Millie's answer to the international selectors came on the Tuesday before the championship '100' when she went to Manchester's Fallowfield track and unofficially beat the world hour record by nine yards. Too modestly, she had scheduled an attack on the British record only and captured that by 612 yards. The world record stood to Renée Vissac of France on the much faster Vigorelli track in Milan.

Millie and I battled grimly for the '100' title and for the rest it was no more than a ride for third place. It was cool, with intermittent drizzle, and again I rode fixed-wheel on 84-inch gear, 2 inches higher than Millie. I don't recall it being mentioned at the time, but I have to be fair and consider that she may not have recovered from her great ride at Fallowfield. However, I won, beating her by 1 minute 59 seconds, in a record 4-29-21, the first woman inside four and a half hours. I was jubilant as I returned to Yorkshire, for I had accomplished the women's bike-racing equivalent of Bannister's four-minute mile and, if it passed almost unnoticed in the general press, the cycling world knew its worth. It was Millie's record that I had broken, and she had beaten her own record in finishing second.

I gradually wound down my season. Robinson's wonderful '25' record time earlier in the year meant that she was on top of the B.A.R. table by 0.179 m.p.h., and I needed a considerable improvement at this distance to wrest from her a title she richly deserved. It had been a great year for both of us and we both had our rewards. I was now at the pinnacle of my sport, and I could not believe that I had arrived there so quickly. I was reminded about the doctor who had said I should walk up hills and be careful not to exert myself –. and I wondered if he had heard about my success.

Charlie and I entered into the social round beloved of the cycling world, club dinners, socials and pea-and-pie suppers, being invited to many of them because of my title wins. We cycled everywhere across Yorkshire and into Lancashire in the depths of winter, arriving home in time to meet the milkman. After one dinner in Lancashire we were riding down Fountain Street in Morley when out of the shadows a policeman jumped into the road and called upon us to halt. He was a bit surprised and suspicious to see a couple out on bikes in the early hours of a winter Sunday morning, and then incredulous when Charlie told him we had been to a dinner in Lancashire and ridden back to Morley. The dinners at clubs in the Leeds area were always hilarious affairs, with some of the Morley lads going along with us. Usually I had been presented with a bouquet during the evening and I would ride back to Morley with it stuffed down the back of my jacket so that it was sticking out above my head – I looked like a flower-pot on wheels! Some of the lads would start telling jokes and after a time I would become helpless with laughter and the whole convoy would stop while I stood at the roadside to compose myself. There were some damn good bike-riders in the club but a few of them were even better comedians!

I began the 1959 season with a few wins in short time trials and my first 25-mile was the Goole Wheelers at the end of April, which I won with a time of 1–6–18 from a girl whose racing career has matched mine, Joan Kershaw of Liverpool Eagle (now Prescot Eagle). For years Joan and I have battled it out all over the country. It is nothing short of amazing how such a tough sport as bike-racing seems to breed a species who go on racing, often in the top flight, year after year.

I beat Joan by 2 minutes 18 seconds, and looked forward to my first clash of the season with Millie Robinson in the Loughborough College road race. Both of us had an eye on that year's world road championship, and we provided a good race. Ken Bowden reported in *Cycling* that he had never seen a finer girls' road race, even though it was really only between Millie and me after one and a half laps. Entering the last lap Millie was just behind me, and as I looked round to see if she was coming through to take a turn at setting the pace, she appeared not to have much left. Worried in case the chasing group should catch us I stayed at the front. With 150 yards to go Millie came smartly round me and pipped me to the line. It was a lesson learned. A few weeks later it was brought home to me that I was not going to have things all my own way even when Millie was not around when I was beaten into fourth place in the Women's Cycle Racing Association road championship by the late Sheila Holmes.

My first main goal of the season was to retain my 25-mile championship in North Nottinghamshire, but prior to that I rode in a three-stage race held over two days in Northamptonshire. I won the first stage almost four minutes clear. In the second I broke clear, but nobody seemed able or willing to work with me, so I drifted back to the bunch and then won the sprint. I have never been known as a sprinter, but in my earlier days I could find a useful finish when I had to. The last stage was over thirty-three hilly miles and, again, there were no takers when I tried to form a useful break, and I won in a sprint finish from Sheila Holmes.

I repeated my 25-mile win of the previous year in a championship record of 1–3–44, beating Millie Robinson by 1 minute 17 seconds and, to make it a really good day, Morley won the team race with me, Pat Clayton and Kath Mitchell breaking the four-year Silchester hold and clipping eighteen seconds from an eighteen-year-old team record.

I also repeated my 50-mile championship win in 2–6–38, and again Morley won the team award. I was beginning to look forward to duplicating my 1958 success of three championships, but before the '100' there were the world championships in Belgium and I had hopes of being chosen. My track experience was still rather light, but in a pursuit I had beaten one of the contenders for a place, and on my day I was as good as anyone in the country in a road race, having in fact collected the road championship among my other wins. However, I was named only as a non-travelling reserve and I was very disappointed indeed. It seemed incredible! Later, I was promoted to travelling with the team and went to Belgium, not certain that I would get a ride. I was a bit miffed by all this, as I genuinely felt that I had done enough to warrant outright selection.

Even so, it was a big occasion; except for my trip to Ireland I had never before been abroad and, as Charlie was to come along (at his own expense), it seemed almost like a holiday. Here let me say at once that I had no intention of not trying my damnedest if I got a ride; there was no possibility of my wearing a Great Britain jersey and doing anything else. I mention it particularly, though, because in some years British riders have been accused of gaining selection for international events abroad and then treating it as a chance for a pleasure trip and failing dismally in competition. For me, particularly, it was a break, because I was able to leave behind, for a time, my domestic chores, my work and looking after Denise – a welcome opportunity to concentrate on my cycling.

We travelled over by boat and in Tom Feargreaves' old scout car – there was no luxury travel in those days. On arrival Charlie set about preparing my one and only pair of racing wheels. Track tyres are sealed to the rim with shellac rather than the ordinary rim cement used for the road. Something of a novice at this, Charlie set out into Liège looking for a shop where he could buy the ingredients for shellac. Since he had no foreign languages his difficulty can be imagined, but eventually, by dint of a lot of arm-waving and the help of a proprietor who spoke some English, he returned to the hotel with the shellac.

The hotel was in the centre of Liège near the bottom of a very steep, cobbled hill which had to be climbed to reach the track at Rocourt and I have a memory of the track boys riding down the cobbles in the rain with one hand and holding large umbrellas in the other.

I don't recall the circumstances now, but I was selected to ride and we arrived at the track for the pursuit championships – my first taste of international competition. I was very nervous. Somebody asked me where my best wheels were, and I had to admit that I only possessed one pair and they were already in the bike! Eventually Millie Robinson lent me a pair which were much better.

My memories of those world championships are rather hazy – I was so excited and nervous about everything. I rode well throughout the series of pursuits (over 3,000 metres) and if memory serves me right I beat the Russian girl Shchogina in the semi-final while in the other semi-final Elsy Jacobs of Luxembourg won against the other Russian, Kotchetova. Came the final and I knew that, whatever happened, I had won at least a silver medal for myself and my country – and Morley! It was very hot and, sitting under the track tunnel, Tom Feargreaves tried to keep me calm; he peeled an orange for me but my hands were shaking so much that I could hardly put it to my mouth. I put on my cycling shoes but my fingers could not manage the laces and Charlie had to tie them for me. On edge, I berated him for not doing it right, and then consigned him from the track centre out into the area for paying spectators. It was the first and almost the only time he has not been at the trackside for my world or national pursuit rides. He is virtually a non-smoker, but on this occasion went through a packet of cigarettes like the proverbial mill-chimney, hardly able to find his mouth with the cigarette! We were both really in quite a state but, somehow, in that final ride I settled down and the adrenalin began to flow. My competitive urge came to the top and I sought some kind of retribution against the gods for that damned eleven-plus and the childhood ill-health. I cannot recall the times but I beat Jacobs by something like two-tenths of a second, and I was champion of the world! We returned to the hotel in jubilant mood and the proprietors hung my world's jersey in the centre of the restaurant for all to see as we tucked into their speciality of mussels and chips. I should explain for those who may not know that, in addition to the gold medal and sash, a world champion is presented with a 'rainbow jersey' which is put on at the medal-giving ceremony; it is white with blue, red, black, yellow and green bands. While on the subject of clothes, I remember that I could not afford at that time to buy a smart-looking track-suit, which even then was *de rigueur* and at the trackside I wore a pair of plaid trousers and a green cycling jacket. (Later the trousers were cut down to make use of the material for other things, among which was a small shoe bag for Denise to use at school. She still has the bag to this day!)

One other little matter before I leave the story of Liège. The riders paid their own way to and from London and we were given £2 a day toward our board and lodging at the hotel. Things were cheaper then, but even so it was meagre in the extreme; I had learned that British cyclists had to dig deep into their own pockets to win medals for their country.

Before returning home I rode with the team in the road race. It was on a course which hardly suited me, but I think I managed fifth place behind Yvonne Reynders, the Belgian girl, who provided a popular home victory, and who subsequently played an important part in my cycling career.

Millie, Kay Ray and I did not return straight home but accepted an invitation to ride the track in Luxembourg and some road races in France. We were well looked after and there never seemed to be a shortage of money for this purpose. I was learning that cycling in world terms is a top sport, arguably 'the' top sport, and if that surprises many readers it is only because they have been directed a certain way by our sporting press. It was a thrill to be part of all this and to realise that I, a girl from Yorkshire with a small club, was a world champion recognised beyond Britain.

It came home to me just what the title was worth in Great Britain, outside cycling circles, when I arrived at Leeds City station late one night, just a girl with a couple of bikes and some luggage, and no one took any notice. To be fair, my exact time of arrival was not known because of my racing in France, but the contrast was marked. Charlie was at home looking after Denise, and I set off to walk to Morley, pushing the bikes. When I arrived at the bottom of Churwell Hill a lorry gave me a lift into Morley, and it was back to work and reality with a bump. Back to the domesticity, looking after Denise with training to fit in during the evening. I prepared to meet my next challenge, the 100-mile championship.

The race was held in Essex, and Charlie and I set out on our bikes the previous Wednesday to ride down in stages. We had no transport other than our bikes. The story of my ride in that 100-miles is best summed up by *Cycling* reporter Ken Bowden who started his report '. . . I'm no longer dizzy, dazzled and dumbfounded. But I can still hardly believe it . . .' Bowden went on to write ' . . . you just can't believe it until it has been done, that a woman will ride a '100' covering the first 25 miles in 1–5–8, the second in 1–4–52, the third in 1–6–53, and the fourth, the critical vital fourth in 1–3–11. Can you?. . . . The most perfect combination of style and power in a woman I've ever seen . . . at the finish this incredible Yorkshire lass said she'd enjoyed her ride 'except for the last two miles', and then *ran* down the road to greet Millie Robinson.'

I had started fifteen minutes behind Millie, caught her three and a half miles from the finish and dropped her by another 1 minute and 21 seconds to the line. My time for the '100' was 4–20–4, beating my own record by 9 minutes 17 seconds. Millie had to be content with third place (Joan Kershaw taking the silver medal) nearly twelve minutes behind me, but took this defeat as graciously and sportingly as she did her many victories. The tail-piece to Bowden's report was that during my short career I had already won everything worth winning except the 12-hour race, which is something of a speciality for a woman rider, but that even more intriguing was the possibility of an attack on the world hour record.

By this time we had left the little house in Cross Street and moved to a larger one in Bridge Street. The main advantage was that it had a bathroom and after training I could now bathe in comfort! I decided to try my hand at real long-distance riding. If something over four hours at racing speed for a woman seems formidable to those not versed in cycling, twelve hours in the saddle must seem like madness. Obviously the m.p.h. is lower, but this length of time at even fast touring speed is not a light undertaking. The record at the time stood to Chris Watts of the Addiscombe C.C., a noted long-distance rider, with 237.91 miles and I hoped that given reasonable conditions I could beat it. In a matter of weeks I went from riding pursuits on the track, which takes something over four minutes, to cycling a hundred miles in something over four hours, and then to twelve hours' non-stop cycling. I wonder what an Olympic sprinter would think if he were asked to run the 100 metres, the 1,500 metres and then the marathon, all in a few weeks!

The event was the Yorkshire Cycling Federation promotion on a bitterly cold autumn morning. It was more like January but at least it was dry, and the rain held off throughout a grey day. The previous Sunday I had again been riding in France in a kermesse, on a circuit round the town of Roanne with prizes at given points, which the French call 'primes'. I won every 'prime' as well as being the first to finish. A few days earlier I had raced at Dijon and crashed but still managed to finish second to Elsy Jacobs. I carry the scar of that crash to this day.

But back to the 12-hour. I finished with a distance of 250.37 miles, taking the record by about thirteen miles and averaging close on 21 m.p.h. *Cycling* pointed out that only two men in the concurrent men's event had greater mileages. I had lost about five minutes with a puncture, but had captured the record so clearly it really did not make much difference. One press report was kind enough to call it 'incredible . . . amazing . . . a record to end all records', but even so the national press generally and, more importantly to me, the papers in my own region, gave it scant regard, as indeed they had my world title, and sadly I had to accept that the press 'play' the favoured, and cyclists are generally not among them in this country. I did not mind so much for myself, but I felt it keenly for my sport.

However, I was gaining *some* recognition. I had a big day out in London when I was one of six sportswomen honoured by the Sportswriters Association – I was number six. The next day I gave my first major speech, at the Pedal Club Luncheon, a function which takes place monthly for representatives from all sections of the cycling world: manufacturers, tourists, competitors, officials, cycling press, etc. I told them that Charlie had given me a schedule for 250 miles in the 12-hour and I had just not dared fall behind it!

The year was drawing to a close, but there were still a few highlights to come. I had won the first of my B.A.R. championships at an average speed of 23.724 m.p.h., with Millie Robinson in second place. The Mayor and Council of Morley gave me a civic reception at the Town Hall, the Mayor that year being Alderman R. W. Pumphrey, B.E.M. It was a marvellous evening with my family and friends and Morley club members, and I was presented with two framed pictures by the Mayor on behalf of the people of Morley.

Following this came the big night of the year for the cycling fraternity – the Best All-rounder prize presentation at the Albert Hall. That night there were 4,238 clubfolk there to honour the champions, and I had a new pink dress and white stole for the occasion. It was a tremendous moment for me as I stepped forward to receive the trophy. 'The greatest woman rider cycling sport has ever known . . . national champion at every distance', was the accolade, and I felt very proud and near to tears. Dear Charlie was a bit overcome too. In spite of all my own efforts, I don't think it would have been possible without his whole-hearted support and help in so many ways.

Perhaps I should say a word or two about the great yearly gathering of cyclists, which in recent years has been held at the Assembly Rooms in Derby. It is a tremendous occasion and no other sport has anything like it. Often the Guest of Honour is a person who has made their mark in some other sport, and they are always amazed at the size and scope of the whole affair, which is organised, rather remarkably, entirely by amateur officials. Those from outside the sport can be somewhat overcome by the great feeling of *bonhomie* that the amateur sport of time trialling engenders and the fact that it is exemplified in such a professional way. There still exists a feeling in some quarters that a get-together of cyclists must signify a collection of baggy-shorted individuals meeting in a village hall, and not the mixture of sophistication and jollity that is a B.B.A.R. concert.

I wondered what 1960 would hold for me. I could still hardly believe that I was a world champion, receiving civic recognition in my home town and within the sport. Hundreds of small-town cycling clubs hold a dinner every winter and honour their club champions and those who may, perhaps, have made a mark nationally. This year Morley had a world champion, and not many clubs can savour that distinction, so their dinner in February was a very special occasion – and extra special for me: George Pearson, the then editor of *Cycling*, the weekly magazine which was founded in 1891 and is still going strong to this day, came to Yorkshire, bringing with him the famous Golden Book of Cycling, and I was invited to sign the illuminated page setting out my achievements. I seemed to have come such a long way in a short time. The citation read:

'Beryl Burton, of Morley, came to national prominence in 1958 when she won all three women's time trial championships, also achieving that year competition records at 50 and 100 miles. But it is 1959 that will always be remembered as the Beryl Burton year. In the short space of four months she produced a series of performances without equal in the annals of women's cycle racing – performances bordering on the incredible, equal as they were to those of all but the best male riders of the day. Mrs Burton began her grand slam by winning the 25-mile championship on June 14th. On June 28th she broke the 25-mile competition record with 1–1–27. On July 12th she won the 50-mile title with another record ride, 2–6–38. On July 19th she outsprinted her friend and rival Millie Robinson to win the British Cycling Federation road race championship. On July 26th she became the first woman to win a world championship for Britain when she beat the reigning women's world road champion Elsy Jacobs for the track pursuit title in Belgium. On August 23rd she won the 100-mile time trial championship with a staggering ride of 4–20–4 that reduced her own record by 9 minutes 17 seconds.

She won the 1959 British Best All-rounder Competition with a record 25, 50 and 100 mile average of 23.724 m.p.h.

On September 27th she completed her fantastic saga with a record ride of 250.37 miles in the Yorkshire C.F. women's 12-hour time trial, adding 12.46 miles to the half-day record. Club, Morley C.C. Age 22.'

The next highlight of that social season was receiving the Bidlake Memorial

Plaque at the Heavy Woollen Combine Dinner on February 12th. F.T.
Bidlake was the father of time-trial sport in that he was instrumental in
organising the first time trial, over 50 miles, on October 5th, 1895. A great
racing cyclist, he was also a leading official in the cycling world of those far-off
days, and his memory is revered by a memorial at Girtford Bridge in
Bedfordshire. It gave me particular satisfaction to receive this prestigious
award in the district in which I had learned my cycling, and it was very
heart-warming to receive a telegram of congratulation from Millie Robinson.

Unexpectedly, I received an invitation to join a Great Britain team to ride in
East Berlin, under the management of Arthur Maxfield, on the Werner
Seelenbinder indoor velodrome. The prospect of competition before our own
season had opened was an exciting one. Among the men in the team was a
young nineteen-year-old, Barry Hoban of Wakefield Clarion, who went on to
achieve great things in later years as a professional roadman on the continent.
The men were all hopefuls for an Olympic place that year, and the other girl
with me was Jean Dunn, a sprinter who won five world championship bronze
medals in her career and, in my view, is undoubtedly the best girl sprinter we
have ever produced in Britain. If anyone is wondering why the Olympic
Games do not figure in my story it is because women's cycling was not
included in the Games until 1984 at Los Angeles, when a women's road race
was held. Its inclusion was largely due to strenous efforts over many years by
Mrs Eileen Gray, a noted track rider in the late forties and now President of
the British Cycling Federation. I think that my world championship successes
might well have had more attention paid to them in this country if I had won
Olympic as opposed to world medals. For myself, I cannot see any lessening of
their value by comparison: if you take on the best in the world at any given
time and win a medal, what's the difference?

The fact that we were travelling behind the 'Iron Curtain' added an extra
spice to the trip, and I wondered a little uneasily what awaited us. East
German officials met us and we were transported some way outside Berlin to
the sports university where we wasted no time admiring our extremely
comfortable quarters – training on the track began immediately! One of the
team members was Lloyd Binch, the British sprint champion at that time and
arguably the best sprinter Britain has ever produced (Reg Harris apart),
winning many Grand Prix and other international races. Unfortunately, he
never seemed able to turn on his best form in world championships. Lloyd
took me aside and told me to change and wait for him outside the ladies'
changing rooms. 'On no account go into the hall and see the track until I go
with you,' he warned me. Lloyd went with me into the magnificent
velodrome, and I was aghast when I saw the track. Fallowfield in Manchester
had seemed frightening enough when I had seen it for the first time; I think it

has a banking of about 30°. This indoor track had bankings of about 60° and looked like the veritable 'wall of death'.

It's amazing, really, when you come to think of it, that our track cyclists have to make do with one world-standard track – Leicester – which in those days did not exist anyway. My own city of Leeds came near to building a super bike stadium some years ago, and spent £50,000 of the rate-payers' money on the preliminaries, only to chicken out at the last moment. They would be reaping the benefit of it now. They have also never fulfilled their promise of 1947 to build a modest track at Lockwood Farm in South Leeds – but all that is another story!

Lloyd told me to follow him around the track, and we began to circle slowly along the bottom. Gradually he moved higher, and then a little higher, telling me all the time to push slightly harder round the banking as we rose from the inside of the track towards the rim, saying that wherever he went I could go too. Soon I was circling round away from Lloyd, going faster and faster, becoming more and more confident until, in the end, I was like a child who had discovered a new toy. They had to nearly drag me away when the training session was over. I shall always be grateful to Lloyd Binch for schooling me on a very steep banking, and I used the same technique with my daughter, Denise, when I introduced her to a banked track. If I had gone on to the track without Lloyd, I would probably have tumbled and lost my nerve.

The East Germans had, of course, been racing throughout the winter on that track and others like it, whereas we had really only begun to think about serious training for the following season. We had spent the winter on the training rollers we had recently acquired and installed in a room above the local 'Co-op' back in Morley or riding, when we could, on the dark wet roads of Britain. During training this lack of preparation affected us all in the form of cramped muscles at first.

Our opening meeting was on a Saturday night, and I felt very nervous appearing before the huge crowd who had paid to see the racing. It was a far cry from the grass circuit at Roundhay Park in Leeds or the Morley 'Co-op'. Among all the fanfares, the roar of the crowd as we were introduced and the glamour and excitement, I wondered if I was going to do myself justice.

In the sprint Jean Dunn beat Stiecher and I managed third place, and was quite happy with that, sprinting not being my forte. The following night I won two longer races, Jean finishing second in one of them, so we made up for the showing of the men, who were having only moderate success.

The following Saturday I won a 2,000 metres pursuit, establishing a new track record of 2–46.2, beating Andrea Elle into second place. The following night I was beaten by Roatzsch in a 200 metre flying start time trial, tying for second place with Elle and, at the last meeting the following Wednesday, I finished second again in the flying start one lap with a time of twelve seconds. As these sprint time trials were not exactly what I was supposed to shine at, I thought I did rather well.

Altogether it was a wonderful trip, for me anyway. Every night, after the evening's racing, there would be a big reception where tables groaned under the weight of beautifully presented food. It was such a contrast with what was available in the shops that you felt slightly guilty tucking in, but it brought home to me that, in East Germany, racing cyclists were very important people indeed. I have always enjoyed my food, and friends pull my leg that years later I can recall something I had to eat following some important race but little of the event itself.

Jean and I got along very well with the East German girls away from the track, and I made a particular friend of Andrea Elle, probably because I discovered that she had a daughter about the same age as Denise. She was unmarried and her daughter was looked after in a state nursery. Andrea usually spent two days a week with her and the rest of her time was taken up with training and racing, with everything else taken care of. My thoughts kept returning to the mound of washing awaiting my return to Morley!

However, not everything was sweetness and light. Jean and I managed several times to visit the city of East Berlin, and very quickly we realised that we were being followed by large men in dark overcoats. After a time we devised a game of trying to lose our shadows, and Jean would dash into a shop and I would scoot off in another direction. Our amateur efforts at playing 'spies' never succeeded, and perhaps they were a little foolish. Shades of John Le Carré!

Among the prizes I won were beautiful items of cut glass and racing tyres and, for me, the tyres were much more important as they represented a saving on the costly business of bike-racing. The German girls were interested to know if we had any spare talcum powder, etc., but, since this was my first trip to Eastern Europe, I was a novice at the game of bartering. Some of the lads who knew the ropes had taken across jars of coffee and other things in short supply to trade for the very good German bike equipment.

One unusual experience that I had on that trip occurred during a training session when our boys and many of the German lads filled the track, with more coming on. Soon the track was completely filled, with hardly enough room to squeeze another rider on, and we were all going round at a fair rate. If anyone had fallen, there would have been carnage, but everyone was an experienced 'trackie' and knew what to do. In spite of the 'block' we circled round and round which resulted in a strange feeling, almost like being on an endless belt, with the cyclists motionless and the track moving under our wheels. I was very happy to be accepted in training among the men, because riders of this standard can often be very tetchy if a woman or less experienced male wants to join a training stint.

Back in England I rode on the track at Fallowfield, Manchester, in April, winning the point to point (sprinting again!) and then took on seven other riders in a six-lap pursuit. I cleared the track – catching my last opponent, Dorothy Whitwham, the national pursuit champion when she was lying second.

A month later the speed was still in my legs when I won the Doncaster Wheelers 10-mile in a record 24–35, twenty-five seconds better than the record of Jo Bowers of Rosslyn Ladies a week earlier. Then it was time to start defending my titles, the first being the 25-mile held in Nottinghamshire in mid-June on a very windy day. Jo Bowers was considered to be my greatest threat as she had been 'flying' in the weeks before the championship but, in the end, it was Joan Kershaw who came nearest – thirty-one seconds behind my winning time of 1–4–40, with Jo Bowers in third place. The following week I was at Welwyn Stadium riding in the national 3,000 metres pursuit championship, which I won by beating Kay Ray in the final with 4–17.7, with my old friend Jean Dunn retaining her sprint title. Next day I rode in the Midlands in a 50-mile trial, winning that in 2–7–21 – 3 minutes 21 seconds faster than Joan Kershaw.

That weekend was typical of this demanding sport: you go out and give your all two or three times a week, week after week. No question of riding a warming-up race as part of your training and then 'peaking' for one important race. It is these demands, quite likely in different disciplines of the sport which, in my opinion, make it hard for British cyclists to shine internationally when they come up against 'shamateurs' or 'state professionals' of other countries who have been groomed for months for a particular event.

Next, it was the Isle of Man cycling week, a festival of racing which is still going strong, and I won two or three time trials and then the Ben-my-Chree road race, twenty-two seconds ahead of Sheila Holmes. Charlie and Denise had come along to the island to make it a family holiday, and were delighted when I made a clean sweep of everything I raced in by winning two sprints at the Onchan track. Our joy was marred somewhat by Charlie crashing off his bike and taking a tumble which cut his face, resulting in hospital treatment.

Following this was a road race at Amersham which had an East German team, including their road champion, Hansel, among the riders. The course included a long steep hill which suited me, and on the first lap I sprinted away and left the field to win by 2 minutes 40 seconds.

Then the 50-mile championship – another title to defend. I have realised, if anyone has, what it is like to be a defending champion, there to be shot at by the rest of the field! The 50-mile that year was held in Northamptonshire on a wet but calm morning, and the headline in *Cycling* a few days later simply said 'Berylized!' I retained my championship with a time of 2–5–45 – a new competition record – beating second-placed Joan Kershaw by 5 minutes 21 seconds.

To illustrate what I have already written about 'mixing' the competition, a week later I tried my hand at the half-mile grass championship at the Harworth track in South Yorkshire in which I was a close second to Valerie Rainbow, who was a specialist at that type of racing. I think it's worth my recalling events like that because, in later years, young cyclists who were not even born in those days have commented that I could only go fast on dual carriageway courses.

The team for the world championships to be held in Leipzig had been chosen, and I had been named for both the pursuit and the road events. Unfortunately, if I was to defend my '100' title I could not travel out with the girls to East Germany. The British Cycling Federation hummed and hawed about it but when they realised I was determined to ride the 100-mile they relented enough to allow me to fly out immediately after it – provided I paid my own fare. The '100' was held on a course west of London, and it was a fairly tough hundred miles, made a little more difficult for me in that I had to ride Charlie's bike – adapted to suit me – since my own bikes had travelled with Charlie and the rest of the team to East Germany. Eighty miles covered and everything was going smoothly – I knew I was 'on a ride' and, barring accidents, I would retain my title in, possibly, a new competition record time. Well, the accident nearly happened! I tried to slow to avoid a car that had pulled up in front of me – and nothing happened! At the last moment I managed to swerve and avoid the car and, glancing down, realised that my brake-cable had slipped from the brake lever. I pounded on, ever watchful for corners and hazards which normally would have needed a touch of the brake lever, fretful in case I should run into difficulties. Twenty miles to go and a record in sight if I managed to keep out of trouble. I came through unscathed in a new competition record of 4–18–19, 11 minutes 19 seconds clear of Joan Kershaw in second place. Six hours later I boarded the plane for East Berlin.

The Great Britain team had by this time arrived in Leipzig, and Charlie, without a word of German, and not much experience of foreign travel in those days, bravely set about catching a train from Leipzig to East Berlin to meet me. The plane was late, so we missed the train back to Leipzig with no other until the following day. To be stranded at night in East Berlin is not the cosiest of situations to contemplate, and we wandered round the city thinking about obtaining a night's lodging, deserted streets, I might add, making our surroundings seem more eerie than ever. About midnight we came across a building which appeared to be a police-station and went in to explain our plight, eventually getting across to the officials who we were and why we happened to be in East Berlin. They sat us in a bleak waiting room while they set about contacting somebody who could help. Eventually things started to hum. We could hear numerous phone calls taking place in the next room, and the tone of the officer making the calls seemed to us, even with our lack of German, to become ever more deferential. Eventually, instructions were given right from the top – the East German Minister for Sport no less – to take us to a hotel. By now it was two o'clock in the morning and, thankfully, we sank into bed and welcome sleep. The next day we were asked if we wanted breakfast but, taking into consideration our meagre ration of money, we declined the offer and went hungry. As it happened, the night's lodging was by courtesy of the East German government and breakfast would have cost us nothing! The lot of innocents abroad, for that is what we were in those days, can be hard indeed, particularly if you don't understand the language.

Charlie then had a bright idea. His money was in English currency, and he had heard that it was possible to exchange five East German marks for one of West German, so we took the overhead railway and crossed the frontier to the Zoo Gardens station in West Berlin. Hunting round we found a place to exchange currency where he exchanged his English money into West German marks and, at another place, he exchanged these for East German marks. For about £25 we came away with the East German equivalent of £90, so it may be that Charlie was not such an innocent traveller after all! Back over the frontier into East Berlin and to the station for the Leipzig train. After a time armed police came round the train checking everybody's papers, and we felt a little apprehensive when they checked our passports, but all was well.

Leipzig seemed alive for the championships. They were proud that their city was hosting this great world sporting event, and bunting and flags were everywhere, with the road leading to the stadium a mass of colour, very different from the rest of East Germany.

The velodrome was packed and, as I went to the line for the first round of the 3,000 metres pursuit, I felt everybody's eyes upon me. I was the defending champion – a hot favourite for the title – and I felt very nervous. I was drawn against Elsy Jacobs of Luxembourg, the girl I had beaten in the previous year's final, and she started fast and had a length on me after the first lap. I stepped up the pace as, vaguely aware of the crowd roaring and cheering, my legs began to flow and the wheels hummed over the track. By two laps we were level, by three I was nearly a second and a half in front and, as storm clouds gathered and rain loomed, I gained more and more ground to finish in a championship record time of 4–12.9. Shchogina of Russia qualified for the following round in 4–20.6, the next fastest time to me. Our other girl in this event, Kay Ray, just squeezed through with a time of 4–26.

The following day it rained hard, and we had to wait until the next morning before racing was resumed under a warm sun. I came up against Kotchetova, the other Russian, who gained a slight lead over me in the early stages. I thought of the evening '10s' on the Morley–Bradford road, the room over Morley 'Co-op', and all the British cyclists back home, and placed all that in my mind against the might of the Russian sports machine. 'Yorkshire for ever!' I thought. 'I'll show 'em!' I let everything rip. Poor Kotchetova never stood a chance and I zoomed to an all-time world best of 4–10.4 against her 4–22.6

Kay Ray turned out what was probably the best pursuit of her career in going down by only a few metres to Shchogina and, meantime, Jean Dunn had made it to the semi-final of the sprint.

At last I came to the 'semi' against my old friend Andrea Elle. I almost hated doing it, but I crushed her in front of her own crowd to cruise into the final. Marie-Thérèse Naessens of Belgium had surprisingly beaten Shchogina in the other semi-final in 4–11.7, and with a time like that I knew she must be a formidable adversary for the final.

I had some time to spare before my final, and Charlie and I took a tram into the centre of Leipzig to look around and take my mind off the coming battle. They had some system of boarding at one end of the tram and alighting at the other, and people seemed to pay with discs rather than money. We never did fathom all this out, but it didn't matter because, when they realised who I was, they let us off paying. We had another adventure here, too. We went into a shop to buy something and, because we were foreign, we had to show, in our passports, the record of the East German marks which had been officially issued. Charlie proferred his passport and then realised too late that it had no such entry. The man studied it for a moment and then went into the back of the shop from where we heard him making a phone call. Fortunately, he had not thought to take the passport with him and, in a panic, Charlie picked it up and off we went, leaving our intended purchase on the counter. The phone call may not have been as sinister as we thought, but we were taking no chances.

In the changing rooms before the pursuit final I sized up Naessens. She spoke some English and we chatted amicably, both of us aware of the supreme test that awaited us and trying to appear nonchalant and confident. Naessens was very bronzed, with a slim boyish figure, and had the look of a finely-honed athlete. I knew that coming from Belgium, that hotbed of cycling, she would not lack the best of coaching and advice. Here was a human machine turned out by the Belgians for one particular task – to win the world pursuit championship. And here was I, an ordinary British club girl, who rode in just about every type of race going, coached and assisted by nobody except

Charlie and the encouragement of our uttetly amateur set-up back home.

The stadium officially held something over 20,000 but I think there were nearer 25,000 there that day. With flags everywhere, the band playing and a crowd who knew its cycling, the atmosphere as Naessens and I took to the track (a beautifully-designed 333–metre with 46° bankings) for our final was something I shall never forget and was almost overwhelming. The fact that two West Europeans were the gladiators seemed not to diminish their appetite one little bit. It may seem strange to those who are reading this but, in fact, I can remember hardly anything of that particular final – I don't think I have ever ridden in such a cacophony. But, if one had the nerve to try and blot the noise out and concentrate on the job in hand, the reception of the East German spectators was wonderful. Do you know I can't even recall what Naessens' time was or by how much I won! I know that the records show that I won with a time of 4–6.1, easily a world record time. It was a marvellous championship series at Leipzig – made special for me, of course, because of my success – and I still retain an overall impression of the place, even if time has dimmed some of the actual details a little.

It had been a reasonably successful track series for Great Britain; Jean Dunn had taken a bronze in the women's sprint, and Dave Handley had also won a bronze in the men's sprint, so it was in a good frame of mind that we went out to the Sachsenring circuit for the road race. I already had a gold and, whatever happened on the road, that was safely 'in the bag'. Even so, there was a certain amount of pressure: I knew that the girls from all the other nations were sizing me up as their main adversary.

The Sachsenring circuit is nearly five miles long, and it had to be covered eight times for the race. With me in the British team were Joan Kershaw, Sheila Holmes, Valerie Baxendine, Ann Sturgess and Kay Ray, and among others we had against us were Yvonne Reynders of Belgium who had won the previous year, Naessens, and the might of Russia and East Germany. It was cold for August, which suited me, and the field set out at a fair rate. The Sachsenring, quite a hilly circuit, had a crowd estimated at 65,000 and, as at the velodrome, there was an ambience of great excitement.

A roar preceded the field, inspiring in its volume and giving the impression that the whole world had its eyes on this group of women cyclists, each striving to become a world champion. With some of the favourites I stayed near the front, and we forced a hot pace, but the field was still mostly together when, on the fourth lap, Elsy Jacobs of Luxembourg attacked. I made an instant decision to go with her. For a minute or so I thought we had formed a 'break' together which would keep us away, for Elsy was a powerful and experienced rider but, as I glanced back, waiting for her to come through and take her turn at the front, she shook her head, and her expression told me in an instant that she could not stay with me. Another quick decision had to be made. I decided to press on, knowing that I had the world's finest women riders in pursuit, making the pace for each other, sheltering each other, while I, a lone breakaway with nearly twenty miles to the finish, had to plough on by myself. I put my head down and tried to imagine I was riding a 25-mile time trial. At the end of that lap I had a lead of six seconds, not very much for a lone rider with a long way to go. Later, reading accounts of the race, I learned that Joan Kershaw was well up near the head of the field, trying tactically to slow down the pace to give me a better chance. On the fifth lap Sels of Belgium and Pouronen of Russia made a great effort to close the gap, but I gained a further minute. My wheels were flying, the East Germans roared their applause and, at the end of the sixth lap, my lead was up to over three minutes. The official race car carrying spare machines and wheels came in behind me, and I was still going away from the rest, with my last lap something of a lap of honour. I felt tremendous. I knew I was licking the world's best out of sight, and I had a fleeting thought of the doctors who had told me to take things easy for the rest of my life. The German crowd thundered their applause around the final five miles, and I crossed the line over three and a half minutes before Sels of Belgium took the silver in a sprint from the East German, Kleinhans.

Later Sels, Kleinhans and I were driven round the full circuit in a huge black open car in ceremonial triumph, holding our enormous bouquets of gladioli. During this lap of honour an old man darted from the crowd, evading police lining the route, and stood in front of the car, forcing it to stop. He thrust into my hands an engraved plate. I cannot read the inscription, but I think it is from either a village or a factory, and presumably the old gentleman had been deputed to present it to the winner by hook or by crook! Well, he managed it, and from that day to this that piece of plate has hung upon the wall of wherever my home has been. Somehow it seems more important to me than the gold medal. It represents one of the greatest periods of my life, when I was received so wonderfully and sportingly by the people of East Germany.

A final word about that day. The rest of the British girls, especially Joan Kershaw, rode wonderfully as a team, probably as well as they have ever done in the sense of riding for each other, and for me especially. For the record, Joan finished thirteenth in spite of crashing on the last lap, Valerie twenty-first, Ann twenty-second and Kay twenty-fifth. They can all be proud, I think, of riding for their country on the Sachsenring that day.

They had to leave for home within hours of the race finish, but I was persuaded by our East German hosts to stay on for a further night to receive my trophies at a reception. When I prepared to return to England on the Sunday I noticed a small sliver of glass embedded in one of my tyres. By good fortune it had not worked through to the inner casing, otherwise I should have had a puncture. If that had happened late in the race I would probably still have survived with a wheel-change, but if it had happened in the first few laps the field would have attacked whilst I was delayed, and I would have had some chasing to do!

Into Heathrow where I was just a girl loaded with bike equipment, and back home to Morley and the council flat at Elmfield Court. The local Morley weekly paper printed a short piece about me in their next edition and the three Yorkshire daily papers printed in Leeds gave my success a cursory mention. National papers managed varying degrees of short reports on their sports pages. I was not seeking personal adulation, but a little more recognition would not have come amiss. I was a double world champion in an international sport and it might as well have been the ladies' darts final down at the local as far as Britain was concerned.

Chapter 4
The 'Hour' record attempt – Racing trip to Ghent – I lose my world titles –
A disturbing experience

I did not rest on my international laurels but plunged straight into defending my British B.A.R. title by riding in the Altrincham Ravens 25-mile. Joan Kershaw was there as well, and she won the race in a time of 1-3-16. As for me – well, I crashed at a roundabout with about fives miles to go and, though not injured, did not finish. I had been riding very smooth tyres and the bike swept from under me. For years afterwards I always rode tyres with some tread on them.

Next came a track meeting at Welwyn, where Jean Dunn easily won the sprint and I won the six-lap pursuit. Jean was at her peak at this time as a sprinter, and her great efforts were, perhaps, unfortunately rather overshadowed by my successes. She was a bundle of nerves during a sprint series, so much so that other girls hardly dared sit near her. She warned everyone in advance that she was going to be like that, and when competition was finished she would apologise to everyone for being so 'stroppy'!

However, greater things were now afoot. The world hour record had been in my mind for some time and everyone felt that I was capable of taking it on the superfast Vigorelli track in Milan. The record stood to Elsy Jacobs with a distance in imperial terms of 25 miles 1,207 yards. Finance was the problem for us, since the cost of travel to Italy, accommodation, track fees and the services of the necessary timekeepers and officials was obviously beyond Charlie and me. The Mayor of Morley at that time, Councillor Mrs Annie Clayton, opened a fund and, on a more private basis, the late Charles Rice also started one. Charlie and I had budgeted for about £300 to see us through and both funds soon began to swell. Norman Grattage, manager of the Fallowfield track, had drawn up a schedule for me, and special tyres were being prepared in Milan. The famous Reg Harris had his name linked also with the attempt, although, in fact, he was never actually part of our preparations or plans. We flew from a cool, autumn England to what we expected to be a warm, but not too hot, Milan – the ideal conditions, in fact, for a record attempt on what was then the fastest track in the world.

In fact, it was a wet and cold Milan when we arrived and settled into a small *pensione* with two bikes and spares, hardly believing that the uncharacteristic weather could be anything other than a slight climatic aberration. In fact it snowed! It hardly seemed possible that the worst October weather in Italian memory could have coincided with our visit, but there it was, and we awaited the expected rapid change. Reg Harris turned up and proffered advice and assistance. His great knowledge of the continental cycling scene and his intimacy with Italian officials and people at the track were an invaluable help. The weather never relented. It was not only damp, but windy, and I really never had any chance of taking the record. But there we were, in Milan, financed by the numerous club-folk and people in Morley who had given donations to my fund. I just had to try, and on October 5th I made my first attempt.

Unlike athletic records, cycling records have to be set on the track by the rider alone, with no obliging pacemakers or cheering crowd. Fastest in competition is one thing, but only riders who have scheduled for an attempt and then broken the record get their names in the cycling record books. The track has to be booked, the official timekeepers and other officials have to be paid, and the whole thing set out to conform to the regulations of the Union Cycliste Internationale. For a professional backed by his sponsors there is no problem. No problem, either, for amateur riders in the major cycling countries, who may be financed by their own Federation or private sponsorship. My attempt on the record had to be made on a shoe-string, with nothing at the end of it but the glory, which I knew in advance would be minimal in Britain outside cycling circles.

The outlook was dismal. The weather was damp, there was a gusting wind, and the huge velodrome was empty except for a handful of officials. There was no atmosphere to lift me although I think I could have overcome that in decent conditions.

After about thirty minutes I had to call it a day. I was down on schedule, and, clearly, to carry on would have been pointless. We retired to our small hotel, deeply conscious that the project had only been made possible by the contributions of individuals whom I did not want to let down. We decided to stay in Milan for a few more days in the hope that the weather would relent, before making one more attempt, after which we would have to head for home. Neither I nor Charlie could hang about indefinitely waiting for better weather.

An amusing recollection of mine from this period involved my partiality for boiled eggs for breakfast, which we took in a snack-bar attached to the hotel. The chap running it had never heard of this method of cooking eggs and he thought we were crazy as we tried to explain the seemingly simple process to him. He dipped the egg in the water he was boiling for coffee and when it was broken open it was just a raw, runny mess. We never did get across to him that an immersion of three and a half minutes in the water would be better.

We collected the officials together and off I went again on my second attempt. I think I felt in my heart that everything was against me from the beginning, but I tried my damnedest as I always have done. I hovered about the record mark for some time and, at twenty kilometres, established new world record figures of 28–58.4, beating Elsy Jacobs' record by 3.8 seconds. From then on it was a losing battle and, as the hour expired, I was about 500 metres short of the record. It was a bitter disappointment.

Sadly Charlie and I returned home and looked at the remaining funds. Surprisingly we had over £100 left, and it seemed worthwhile for me to have another try. I travelled out alone since there was not enough money left to cover Charlie's fare as well but, in any case, he had his job to think of and could not have accompanied me.

Schedules for records have to be placed giving forty-eight hours' notice, and on that second trip there was one day when conditions seemed ideal, but my schedule was not for an attempt on that day – a frustrating experience! Reg Harris was on hand again, and he placed me with a family he knew and looked after the details. I remember that he always wanted me to take absolute rest after training, something which I found irksome as I was used to being so active between my races in England with all the domestic chores and work I had to attend to.

My wretched luck with the weather continued, and I could only train on the track when it had dried out sufficiently, trying, alternately, an 89-inch gear which seemed too high and an 88 which seemed too small and thinking a 90 would have been better. Clearly another attempt was just not 'on'. It was suggested to me that perhaps I could try for a few indoor records on Milan's indoor track, but funds were beginning to run low, and I felt that the donations that had made the two trips possible had been given for a specific purpose and that it would not have been correct for me to attempt anything other than the outdoor record. So I came home, very disappointed both for myself and for all the people who had pinned such high hopes on my taking the record and, in spite of the wonderful season that I had just been through, my morale was dented a little.

Following the world championships, Oscar Daemers, the manager of the renowned indoor track at Ghent in Belgium, had suggested to me that perhaps I would like to appear there during the winter in a 'revenge' match against Naessens. I had told him that I would be interested, providing it would not be too late in the winter – having no indoor tracks in Britain I would not be properly fit and I would be at a disadvantage anyway, not being able to train indoors. (I did not try to explain about the set of rollers over Morley 'Co-op', the idea of which, I think, would have been incomprehensible to him. I don't think he could have imagined a civilised country not having at least one indoor velodrome.) With all the business of Milan I had forgotten about his suggestion until an invitation arrived from him to appear in a 3,000-metre pursuit match with Naessens prior to the famous Ghent six-day race in late November. I had been riding the rollers during the evenings, and riding club runs at the weekend, but that was simply a way of keeping in some sort of shape before serious training at the end of the winter when the weather improved and the days started to lengthen. It is hard to convey the difference between that background and the atmosphere of an indoor velodrome packed with thousands of excited fans, but that is what I had to face against a Naessens who had had the use of the track for training. A small track, only 160 metres, ideally suited for the six-day Madisons (or relays), it did not suit my normal, comparatively slow start. Naessens wiped the floor with me, catching me in 3 minutes 34 seconds, her fast start on that small track being more than I could contain. Kay Ray had also made the trip with me, and the other Belgian girl involved was the famous Yvonne Reynders. The four of us rode a twenty-lap point-to-point, and they beat us 20 points to 16. Reynders beat Kay in a sprint match and then we had a two-up pursuit. Neither Kay nor I had ever ridden this type of race before, and it was pretty obvious that the Belgian girls had trained together on the track to 'nick' together as a team. In the circumstances I think we did pretty well to be beaten by only 0.2 of a second.

Again I should mention the excitement of racing in a 'cycling' country, and the prestige that being a world champion means among the other European nations. It meant adjustments, on my part, when travelling from England where, if you like, I was a minor sporting personality, to countries where I was well known. There is something in the Bible about prophets in their own country being of no account. Perhaps it is not quite apt, but it gives the drift of what I felt on those trips.

Back home I was runner-up to Anita Lonsborough, the swimmer, as *Daily Express* Sportswoman of the Year. Anita had won an Olympic gold in Rome, and this worthy success had made her a certainty for the award; I was rather surprised that I had made even second place.

It was another hectic end of the year for me following the trip to Ghent. The Cycle Industries Association made a wonderful gesture to Charlie and me by presenting us with a three-wheeled car, a modest enough vehicle perhaps, but at that time it seemed to us almost like owning a Rolls-Royce. Charlie learned to drive very quickly. It opened up a new world of travel to races, even if it was a little cramped with the bike and wheels, and it meant I could leave home for events much later and with much less hassle.

I was given another civic reception by the Mayor of Morley, Alderman Mrs Annie Clayton, and I stood on the Town Hall steps feeling rather queen-like waving to the local people. It was a moving experience to be acknowledged by the townsfolk and something I shall never forget.

In early December came the British Best-allrounder concert at the Albert Hall, attended by over 5,000 cyclists from the length and breadth of Great Britain. A sparkling variety concert, with Tommy Trinder acting as M.C., preceded the presentation. Bryan Wiltcher, who was the men's Best All-rounder for a second year, and myself, were the principal prize-winners and in addition to all my trophies I was presented with an extra one – the Bidlake Plaque, which I had been awarded for the second time. Only the great Reg Harris had previously won it twice.

So, another great year came to an end amid rumours that I was to turn professional for a cycle firm with a view to attacking the various place-to-place road records on the list of the Women's Road Record Association, culminating with the famous Lands End to John o'Groats.

Eventually a representative arrived at the Burton home to discuss the matter. Charlie and I leafed through the mass of paperwork which he brought with him and were wryly amused at the long list of 'thou shalt nots' and the way they wanted to hedge my life around with 'do's and dont's'. There was one curious clause which stated that, if a record then standing on the books was broken before I attempted it and I was successful, I would be paid less than if I broke the record existing at the time I signed. It seemed logical to me that the breaking of a newer record should be worth more, not less. The sum offered seemed very modest in view of what would be entailed on my part – making promotional appearances in between training and actually going for records. At the time I was working in machine accounting, and Charlie and I worked it out that, at the end of the day, I would be little better off financially than if I stayed amateur. Another thing about it which did not appeal to me was the proposed three-year term and the probability that at the end of that period I would not be re-signed. My competition career would be at an end, and I planned to go on for longer than that. Today a professional can be re-instated following a period out of the sport, but that was not the position in those days. The Raleigh representative made numerous visits trying to persuade me to sign for them, but I consistently declined. It is a decision I have never regretted.

In May 1961 I won the Beacon R.C. 10-mile in a record 24–27, beating my own record by eight seconds, and then had mixed fortunes over the Whitsun week-end. On the Saturday, in the Women's Cycle Racing Association championships at Welwyn I won every prime in the course-des-primes, a sprint race, and then slashed seven seconds off the best time recorded in Britain by winning the 3,000 metres pursuit with 4–10.1. It was a cool, breezy day and lowering the record by such a big margin was not a bad effort. The next day I was shown in no uncertain way by Jo Bowers of the Roamer club that I was not infallible, when she beat me soundly in the Hounslow 25-mile by almost a minute. It was the third successive year that I had finished second in this particular race, so it seemed jinxed. I raced again the next day in the W.C.R.A. road championship, breaking away in the third lap with Cynthia Carey of the East Anglian C.C. We worked well together and left the bunch and then, with a few miles remaining, I thought it was time to make my own move and leave her behind. This proved more difficult than I expected and Cynthia, who had been amongst the outsiders, could not be shaken off until the final hill three miles from the line when I succeeded in dropping her to win by fifteen seconds. Another busy weekend with three days of hard racing and travelling – and some of our highly-paid footballers complain if they have to play more than two matches in a week!

Two weeks later in the Goole Wheelers 25-mile I came within fifteen seconds of my record with 1–1–42, and my clubmates Freda Drayton and Pat Clayton filled second and third places. Between us we knocked nineteen seconds from the team record which the Roamer club had established only two weeks previously. The national title in June was promoted by the Phoenix C.C., a Liverpool club, on a rainy day with a strong breeze which I overcame to take my fourth successive 25-mile title with a time of 1–2–45. Observers considered that I would have become the first woman to beat 'the hour' on a better day but, in any event, I had forty-four seconds in hand over Jo Bowers. My old adversary Joan Kershaw was temporarily out of the racing scene awaiting a happy event, and it is yet another sign of continuity in cycling families that Joan's daughter, Louise, is today one of the country's most promising young riders. The battle between Morley and Roamer was an exciting one, with the southern girls taking the team title in another new record, beating Morley by 1 minute 14 seconds.

There followed another trip to the Isle of Man, where I won the Ellan Vannin 25-mile, beating the record I had set the previous year by 1 minute 54 seconds, and then the 30-mile road race, with a tussle between Sheila Holmes and me over the last ten miles. I beat her in the sprint for the line by a length.

Riding in the Isle of Man at this time had a special significance because the women's world championships were to be held on the island during August, and already I was beginning to feel keyed up about defending my titles in front of a home crowd. One race I did lose during that week was the pram race, which was part of the gymkhana when all kinds of fun events were held. I teamed up with my old friend Lloyd Binch who did the pushing and frequently jolted me out onto the ground. Lloyd could not push a pram as well as he rode his bike!

At the end of the month I was able to renew my acquaintance with Andrea Elle as she was a member of an East German team racing at the Herne Hill track. The weather was very hot indeed, and it seemed to affect Jean Dunn more than it did me, for she lost in the semi-final of the sprint, and Elle won the series from her compatriot, Stuwe. A Belgian team containing Naessens and Rosa Sels also competed so the competition was fierce, but I won the course-des-primes and the pursuit and Great Britain were the overall winners.

Next day it was back to the road at Great Missenden. With twelve miles to the finish I was two minutes down on Jo Bowers: the result of a puncture. I had to ride about two miles on a flat tyre before picking up a spare wheel and forcing my way back to the leaders. Then it was Jo's turn to puncture! I caught and passed Sheila Holmes and Rosa Sels, then Bowers who crashed, and I raced on alone to win, 4 minutes 24 seconds clear of Sels.

I successfuly defended my 50-mile title early in July, winning in 2–6–3 with Jo Bowers second, but the Roamer girls won the team title and also took another Morley competition record.

Later in the month Jo Bowers beat me in the road championship, held in the Chilterns. On the first climb Jo broke away and I went with her and we put our heads down with the intention of dropping the rest of the field early. We nearly managed it but not quite! A young girl who was fairly new to top-class racing, Janet Smith of Long Eaton C.C., stayed with us rather to our surprise. We worked well together, and Janet showed no sign of flagging and deserved to be 'in at the death'. Jo jumped and I followed, coming round on the line. It was desperately close, and I thought I had just made it, but the verdict went to Jo by inches, with Janet a length down.

Now came the centre-piece of the year – the women's world championships on the Isle of Man. It is history now that I lost both my titles, taking second place in the pursuit and the road race behind the great Belgian, Yvonne Reynders. In the qualifying time trial of the pursuit, for some strange reason I had to ride first as the reigning champion, instead of the reverse. That meant I had to set up a time for the others to aim at, and Reynders went off knowing what she had to do. I completed the seven laps in 4–7.5, and I should point out that the distance covered was actually 2,830 metres and not the full 3,000 championship distance. The track at Onchan was slow, and had not been designed for world championships, so, to fit in the start and finish with the electrical timing, seven laps it had to be. My time was reasonable, and I had obviously made it into the next round when the match racing would begin.

Savina of Russia had come closest to me with 4–12.8 by the time Reynders went to the line, and it was soon evident that the Belgian girl was really 'flying'. She had already won the national crown in her own country, beating Naessens, and would qualify for the later rounds comfortably but Oscar Daemers, the Belgian team manager, wanted no doubt about Reynders' form, and he signalled for an all-out last lap. Reynders responded, seeking a psychological advantage over me. Her time was a magnificent 4–1.1.

I knew that I was not at the top of my form. Good enough for a medal – yes. Enough for the gold? I had my doubts when I considered the form of the Belgian. For a few weeks before the 'worlds' I had been on edge, although only Charlie knew it. The reason was that, in what I thought was a friendly conversation with a woman official from outside my own area, I had been rebuked for not giving other riders a chance and told that it was about time I retired. This had wounded me deeply, and I brooded over it in the weeks before the championships. I was in my mid-twenties and could see no earthly reason why I should give up the competitive side of cycling simply because I was successful, but it nagged me that perhaps others were thinking along similar lines to that official. Probably the remark was not intended as seriously as it had sounded to me at the time, but my exterior calmness hides a temperament that can be deeply hurt. I mention all this not as an excuse for losing my titles to Reynders, for there can be no doubt that she was the top girl of the championships, but to illustrate how a sportsman or woman can have their peace of mind destroyed in a few seconds in the build-up to a big event by a casual or thoughtless few words.

Andrea Elle was still holding her place in the East German team, and in the next round I beat her by over five seconds while, in her match, Reynders disposed of a French girl. Jo Bowers also went out in this round to the Russian, Valentina Savina, by only 0.06 of a second, and I felt very sorry for her. Success and comparative failure are so often separated by only a fleeting moment of time.

The semi-final had Burton v Naessens and Reynders v Savina. The evening was very cool for August, but calm and good for pursuiting, and I tried to relax while Reynders and Savina were on the track battling for a final place. Charlie kept me cheerful with his horrendous stories of camping in the rain for, as usual, the Burton budget was stretched and he was saving the expense of a boarding house. Reynders had no difficulty with Savina, 3–59.6 against 4–7.2, and then came my fight with Naessens, a repeat of the previous year's final.

It was a continual battle to halfway, but then I forged ahead, Naessens unable to contain my pressure, and I kept on relentlessly, winning with 3–59.2 against 4–6.4. Perhaps I should have eased a little toward the end in view of the following day's final, but I wanted to pressurise Reynders as well. It was the fastest time of the championship and put me in a better frame of mind.

It rained heavily that night and throughout the next morning, and it seemed at one time that the final might have to be postponed, but racing did start on schedule, although the track was still damp and I felt extremely uneasy about it as we took our starting positions.

I made a fast start and quickly gained a few lengths, but Reynders reacted in the second lap and went ahead and, by the third, had a lead of about six lengths. To the crowd it may have appeared that at that stage I had already 'cracked'. I was not going to surrender my title that easily, but I realised that I was against a well-prepared girl in world championship form. I pulled out everything I could summon, and by halfway had reduced my deficit to two lengths, but she was matching everything I could muster. Her lead was reducing – but not enough! With two laps to go she still had a length or so advantage. Could I pull it back? I was striving with everything I had. She seemed to be wavering, and for a fleeting moment I thought I had overcome her, but there she was coming back at me again. One lap to go and the crowd was roaring its encouragement, the sound going over my head and falling behind me like a backdrop to glory – or failure. I put in my final assault and I thought I was going to succeed – but Reynders was responding once more! A few metres to go, and then we seemed to cross our respective finishing lines together. She had put in a wonderful last half-lap. Had I retained my title? Result: Reynders 4–0.7; Burton 4–0.8. I had to be content with the silver.

Had the damp track unsettled me all that much? Yes, I would have preferred it completely dry. Had the previous mental upset taken off some of my edge during the weeks preceding the championships? Yes, it had. Could I have ridden a better line? Yes, I should have, but I blame the damp track. Should I have saved a little from the Naessens semi-final? Yes. Would the result have been different if the race had been held over the full 3,000 metres? Perhaps.

But there really is only one answer at the end of the day. You lost the race – to a great opponent. You did your best and the record books will show for evermore what the result was. No amount of recrimination against yourself or anyone else and no number of 'what might have beens' or 'if onlies' will alter that fact. Nobody except your nearest and dearest understands the anguish. So I was second-best in the world. Still not a bad thing to say about yourself, but rather bitter-sweet when you have already been the best.

Two days later came the road race on the Willaston circuit, nearly forty miles, some of them hilly, under a warm sun. I was out for revenge over Reynders, and determined to retain my road title. Its forty corners required plenty of braking action, particularly the corner in Onchan which I never liked; it needed a fast approach, followed by vicious braking, then immediately a hill. It was a killer on the legs, and called for some slick gear-changing. The fourth time over this climb the main field was all together, with me setting the pace, but a few riders had already been dropped. The fifth lap, and Elsy Jacobs of Luxembourg, a former champion, was trying for a break. The Belgians and I responded, the field stretched and chased her past the grandstand at halfway. Next time round and I, with Jacobs, Reynders and the Russians, Lukshina and Pouronen, opened a gap; the field brought us back, but already we were softening them up. With fourteen miles to go Jacobs was away again and I countered; so did the Russians. In the bunch Reynders, having just changed her machine in the pits, was caught momentarily adrift. Alive to the danger, in an instant she forced her way up to us – a superb piece of riding. We had riders in that bunch and, as the *Cycling* report of the time stated, at least one of them should have been on Reynders' wheel: 'Our champion has been a one-woman band too long, and it was to persist, on this occasion, to the end.'

Reynders and Jacobs were now working together. I knew they were friends, riding the continental circuit together, and they had plenty at stake. To go back on to the continental mainland with a medal would not only enhance their prestige but would be financially remunerative. For me, with actually only a handful of road races each season among my time trials, a victory would bring no cash, and little kudos outside cycling circles.

On the next hill Jacobs – what a gutsy rider – tried again and succeeded in breaking up the five. The Russians went off the back and three previous world champion road girls were left to fight out the finish. I felt good, the hills were no trouble, I thought I had their measure and, perhaps, if I had attacked then . . .? Well, who knows? The speed went up, hurtling down the hill to Willaston at 45 m.p.h. and the last corner. It was all on the final sprint on an uphill finishing straight. Jacobs led, Reynders second. Jacobs weakened a fraction with less than 200 metres to go, Reynders stormed past her and I also passed Jacobs and tried to hold Reynders, but to no avail.

Again it was the silver. Taking two second places seemed small consolation because I had dearly wanted to retain those golds on British soil. There had been many holiday-makers new to cycling on the Isle of Man watching the racing, and it would have been satisfying to give them the fillip of at least one British victory. Jean Dunn had taken another third in the sprint, so we had not fared too badly against European might.

Recalling those days on the Isle of Man I remember the relative freedom which the Russians and the East Europeans enjoyed, in contrast to the constrictions of world championships in other West European cities; they went through all the shops in their free time and photographed everything and everybody. I don't think they had ever enjoyed themselves so much.

At the reception which opened the championships Charlie and I had made the acquaintance of one of the Russian girls through an interpreter, and expressed an interest in the shoe-plates they had on their racing shoes since they were deeper-cut than those we could obtain in this country. At the dinner and final get-together for riders and officials the girl (I think she was one of their road team) sidled up to us and produced from under her skirt a pair of these shoe plates. For a moment we were a little taken aback and then Charlie, not wanting to accept them without giving something in return, tried to explain this. The girl backed away, more frightened than embarrassed I think, and one of the minders that always accompanied the Russian teams came seemingly from nowhere, grabbed hold of her and hustled her away from the proceedings before the dinner began. Charlie was left holding the shoe plates and we felt terrible. It ruined the evening for us, but that was of small importance compared with any retribution that may have been taken against that poor girl for an act of friendliness. Perhaps the plates were the property of the mighty Russian state, but if that great empire cannot afford the price, maybe someone in Moscow will kindly inform me of the cost and I will reimburse them. I later attached the plates to a pair of red cycling shoes and the Russian girl rode with me in spirit over many racing miles. Such is the true friendship international sport can foster if the sportsmen and women are allowed to get on with it. I never saw that poor girl again at any international competition, and that incident has haunted Charlie and me from that day.

I put the disappointments of the Isle of Man behind me and resumed my time trialling, the next big event for me being the defence of my 100-mile title in the North Midlands promotion held in Nottinghamshire. I really slammed the field that day, winning with a time of 4–23–1, a win by nearly seventeen minutes over Pat Pepper of Roamer. To round off the day the Morley club took the team award with Pat Clayton and sixteen-year-old Pauline Hunter backing me. With that victory I had won all twelve championships over four seasons.

Early in September I met Reynders again at Herne Hill in what was billed as a 'revenge' match in the University Athletic Union meeting. We raced in a 3,000 metres pursuit. I tried chatting to her in the dressing rooms, but she was her normal, aloof self – not antagonistic but merely not willing to talk. Later she walked past me with a glazed expression as though I wasn't there.

Well, I took my revenge, if that is what it was, beating her with a time of 4–10.7, very fast for Herne Hill, to 4–13.9, and it gave me a certain amount of satisfaction, although it was a one-off match and not the final to a series under international conditions.

The 1961 season was now drawing to a close, and I had won the British Best All-rounder title again. At the end of September I put in a schedule to attack the W.R.R.A 25-mile record which stood to Joan Kershaw. I took Joan's record by 1 minute 8 seconds in a time of 1–0–31 on the road between Goole and Hull late on a Saturday afternoon. I was a little disappointed that I had not managed to beat the magical 'hour' on this ride. Road records are distinct from records achieved in competition, as I have previously explained: a rider puts in a schedule to attack a particular record on a certain course on a given day, and there are strict rules, as in all cycling records, to ensure that the rider has no pacing or cars following behind, etc.

At the B.A.R. concert which followed at the end of December, I was thrilled at meeting my idol, Jacques Anquetil, the great French cyclist and master time triallist. The world has not seen before, or since, such a rider against the watch. His skill and talent made him five times a winner of the Tour de France and nine times the winner of the Grand Prix des Nations, the most prestigious time trial of them all. I did not know it at the time, but the 'Nations' was subsequently to play a part in my career also. Jacques travelled from his Normandy home with his wife to present all the championship prizes for the year to the British time triallists, and it was one of the highlights of my life to receive the B.A.R. Trophy and medals from his hands. I presented a bouquet to Madame Anquetil, and *La Marseillaise*, followed by *Auld Lang Syne* brought a tremendous evening to a close.

There was one further distinction to round off the year. The great Yorkshire cycling official and co-founder of the Yorkshire Cycling Federation, Charles Arthur Rhodes, had died the previous year, and the Federation had instituted an annual C.A. Rhodes Award for outstanding merit in services to Yorkshire cycling in his memory and honour. The first Award was presented at the seventieth dinner of the Yorkshire Road Club, C.A. Rhodes' only club, and I was the proud recipient of the Memorial Volume and Certificate.

Altogether it was not a bad way to finish what had been a successful year, even if my world title defeats still rankled – at least a little bit!

Chapter 5
A bad crash – World champion again – My first 'under the hour' ride – Rocourt –
A poignant memory

My first race of 1962 was something of a lark – a mudlark in fact. My club promoted a ladies' cyclo-cross at Tingley over an 8-mile course, and I won it from Val Rainbow by nearly three minutes. It was good fun, and a happy augury for the coming season.

I rode a few early-season time trials and track races with my eye on the first big race of the year, the 25-mile championship. There had been heavy rain before the start of the race, and it was still chilly before my ride, but I managed to retain my title with a new championship record of 1–1–51, more than two minutes in front of Jo Bowers. Again the Roamer girls beat Morley for the team shield.

Thinking about the world championships to come, I was doing more track work, and a week before Whitsun I rode at Doncaster and won a four-lap pursuit and then a ten-lap scratch race before travelling to Herne Hill for the holiday Saturday and a pursuit series. Young Pauline Hunter joined me and reached the semi-final. In the final I met Joan Kershaw and recorded 4–14.8. to Joan's 4–28.2. I also tried my hand in the sprint and came second to Jean Dunn. In this earlier part of my career (although by now, I had been around for a few years!) I rode everything and anything. I feel that those in the sport with short memories or lack of knowledge sometimes need to be reminded about this.

I rode the Hounslow 25-mile on the Sunday – the event which had previously seemed to have a jinx on me. This time I made no mistake and won in 1–2–35, with Kershaw and Bowers the runners-up. The following day it was the W.C.R.A. road championship over forty-five miles and Pat Pepper and Cynthia Carey really made me work to win this one – it was all down to the sprint at the end.

I was now hitting my top form and the following week I broke my competition record in the Long Eaton C.C. 25-mile with 1–1–10. Charlie and I stayed the previous night at Southwell Youth Hostel; we are still active hostellers, particularly at Christmas, when we like to go hiking in the Lake District. I lowered my record of 1959 by seventeen seconds and, in view of what I had since accomplished, it was rather surprising that it had stood so long, as Jo Bowers and Joan Kershaw were always likely to hit a good morning. Young Pauline also improved to a '1-7' and helped me to win the team prize for Morley and, in addition, I won an extra prize for breaking the record – I wonder what Reynders and company would have thought about collecting a cycle-shop voucher worth £3 for a morning's work!

Then I hit a low spot with what these days is referred to as a traumatic event. At the end of the month I was competing at a track meeting at Manchester's Fallowfield track, in the national sprint championship and almost made it to the last four, going down to the late Christine Rowbotham in the repechage heat, with the rising star of British sprinting at that time, Val Rushworth (née Rainbow), taking Jean Dunn's title from her. In the points race later in the meeting four of us were sprinting hard, when Christine Rowbotham suddenly switched across. I tried to avoid her, but four of us came down. The others seemed uninjured, but I was in considerable pain and almost fainted. I had skidded across the track, ripping my jersey and taking most of the skin off my back in the process. I was taken to Manchester Royal Infirmary where a nurse, seeing my tattered racing colours and short hair referred to me as a 'he'. I managed to overcome the pain sufficiently to claim indignantly that I was a 'she'!

The hospital discharged me later that day and Charlie managed to get me back to Morley, still in great pain. To make matters worse my bike had been badly damaged in the crash so it had been an expensive as well as unpleasant trip. I had daily hospital treatment in Leeds because I had given my hip a nasty knock in the crash, and my back was very painful too. I moped about the house wearing a loose-fitting dressing gown because any clothing touching me was so painful.

At this time I was working for the G.P.O. in Leeds, and received no pay for my time off work with this injury. Later, when I had to ask for time off to travel abroad to world championships, I had to fill in a large form stating the reason for my request. They never refused, but were always at pains to point out that I could not expect to be paid while I was away and permission was given only grudgingly. Well, maybe they had a point, but I leave it to the reader to contrast my lot with that of present-day amateur stars. I wonder if I would have received a more amicable response if I had been representing Great Britain in certain other sports and not cycling. Later the Post Office relented a little and said they would allow me half-pay on the days I was actually in competition in world championships.

You would think over the years that you would get used to crashing on a bike, but you never do – or at least, I never have. It happens so quickly that you have no time to try to cushion your fall, and if you're racing your feet are strapped in, so you can't get them out either.

But it is all part and parcel of the sport. Luckily I hardly ever fall as such – usually someone else knocks me off. I fall mostly on black ice when I'm riding to work in the winter. I fell off twice in a few yards once, before I realised what the trouble was. But on ice you tend to slide, and don't hurt yourself.

For ten days I did not touch a bike, nor did I have much sleep as lying down was so painful. Consequently, I felt that the 50-mile championship, to be held near Lincoln two weeks after my crash, would come too soon for me to have any chance of defending it. However, I decided to 'have a go'. I started slowly but managed to quicken the tempo after about ten miles. By this time I was well down, as far as the favourites were concerned anyway, but managed to claw something back as the miles went by. Feeling wretched, I gritted my teeth and tried to put the pain in my hip out of my mind. At the halfway point I had pulled up to third place, and with about ten miles to the finish I was second, twenty-five seconds behind Joan Kershaw. Try as I might I could only manage a few more seconds against her in the final miles, and Joan was the worthy new champion at 50 miles in a time of 2–9–45, beating me by twenty-two seconds.

The day before the '50' I had also surrendered my 3,000 metres pursuit national title at Fallowfield to Jo Bowers, so the accident in a minor track race had cost me dearly. My week-end earned me two second place national medals and a rocket from the hospital when they learned that not only had I been out on my bike, but I had been racing into the bargain. I felt the effects of that accident for many, many years.

I was not the only one winning medals for Morley at this time, for Nim Carline won the 24-hour national championship at the end of July. This was his first title win, and he accomplished it with a distance of 471.05 miles in windy and wet conditions in the south of England. Nim had ridden this event as he did all his long-distance races – charging off from the start at a great rate of knots, building up a big lead and then using his courage and strength to hang on to it. This is against all the tenets of distance racing, but Nim is an individualist like me and does things his own way.

At the beginning of August I had a very successful Bank Holiday riding the Dragon R.C. 100-mile on the Sunday and the Nene Valley 25-mile the following day. Four times previously I had broken the competition record at the century distance, and I managed it a fifth time in the Dragon race with a time of 4–14–29, lowering my own figures by nearly four minutes. The conditions had been near-perfect, my back and hip had not troubled me too much during more than four hours of effort, and I had beaten the second girl by over eleven minutes. The next day in the '25' I came up against a Jo Bowers who was in top form. She had not raced in the '100' the previous day and, perhaps because I had this effort still in my legs, Jo was leading me at halfway by nearly a minute and seemed to be on a record ride. Such a deficit seemed too much to pull back against a rider like Jo who was obviously going so well, but I was determined I was not going to be beaten. I flew over the second half feeling sure that I was reducing the deficit but all the time wondering by how much. I could tell that I was on a beating of my own record – but what had Bowers, who finished before me, accomplished? Jo recorded 1–1–9, a one-second beating of my old record. I must have really been flying from halfway, finishing with 1–0–34 and beating her record by thirty-five seconds and my own by thirty-six. That magical 'inside the hour' seemed to be creeping closer!

Jo Bowers and I were selected for the world pursuit championship and as part of the road team while Val Rushworth and Jean Dunn were selected for the sprint. We flew to Milan on the 22nd August accompanied by Eileen Sheridan as our chaperone. That seems an old-fashioned appointment, doesn't it? But as recently as the early sixties the Federation thought it wise to have somebody outside the team management as such to take on that task for, in those matters, we came under the jurisdiction of the overall British team manager. Eileen Sheridan was the leading amateur girl cyclist in the years after the war, and then turned professional to capture all twenty-one W.R.R.A. records, the climax being one ride which captured the Lands End–John o' Groats and 1,000 miles figures. In later years the diminutive Eileen has become renowned as a glass engraver, and I have two specimens of her work at home.

I was feeling well and was obviously fit, but I worried about the lack of international competition. The strip of water, the English Channel, seemed to make a lot of difference to everything, and I felt that we were rusty in tactics and technique. I knew that both the West and East Europeans had regular international competition within their own spheres and were used to racing at the highest level, whereas I think we were sometimes a little overwhelmed by it all. We had no system of coaching at this time, for practising the start of a pursuit, for example, on the track; no get-together as a road team to discuss tactics. Indeed, we knew little of these anyway. It was the usual genuine amateur approach to things, which did not win any sympathy when we failed, and not all that much wonderment when, as sometimes happened, we succeeded.

Charlie travelled to Milan on the back of club-mate Dick Hudson's scooter, together with a small tent and other camping gear, amazingly. He has a vivid recollection of them setting fire to the tent on the first night. Later, crossing the Simplon Pass in the dark, they had a 'blow-out'. They managed to stick a patch over it and limp into the next town where they were able to buy a replacement tyre. Before this they had spent the night sleeping in a graveyard. The British cycling scene demands a lot from its supporters as well as those who actually race! Of course, they were late arriving and poor Charlie met an irate Beryl who angrily demanded where he had been all that time. My anger was really concealing concern for him and Dick. The latter was suffering from mosquito bites, and his face was so puffed up that his eyes looked like mere slits. I felt I should give such devoted followers something to cheer about.

Charlie has always said that, unlike some other promising sportsmen and women who never give of their best 'when the chips are down', I can rise to the important occasion. So it was to prove in Milan, although I always felt very nervous when appearing before a large continental crowd.

If Italy is one of the hotbeds of cycling, Milan in particular is white-hot with enthusiasm for the sport. The two favourites for the professional sprint title were both Italian: Antonio Maspes, the reigning champion, and Giuseppe Gaiardoni. I think Gaiardoni must have been a local because the streets near the Vigorelli track were festooned with flags and banners bearing his name – in addition, of course, to all the razzmatazz to be found at these world gatherings. We have had two world championship series in recent times in this country and, marvellous as the track events were at Leicester and however brilliantly organised, I think they were rather low-key in terms of what they meant to the people of that city.

I had the honour of meeting Maspes, and it really was like meeting royalty, such was his standing in Italy. Before one of his sprint heats he was actually carried in a chair to the trackside, presumably so that he would not waste any energy in walking! Then his acolytes put on his shoes for him and prepared him for the battle ahead. Maspes went on to retain his title, beating Gaiardoni, and the Italians also provided the winner of the amateur road race, so it was a good championship series for them.

I also met the great Signor Masi, who had a workshop under the Vigorelli track and was a frame builder for all the greats of Italian cycling, including the 'Campionissimo', the one and only Fausto Coppi. I let him check over my equipment, and Charlie's care of my machines met with his expert approval.

How the atmosphere then at Vigorelli contrasted with the time I had attempted the hour record. Flags flying, a great crowd, bands playing, and the whole of Milan seething with excitement. Again, I could not help comparing this with my usual racing, early on Sunday mornings, with just a handful of club-folk supporting us at the finish of some event. We were like Daniels going into the lions' den. I knew I was good, though, and that all the coaching, all the know-how and support of the continental nations could be balanced by Yorkshire grit and determination.

In the preliminary round Reynders pulled out a superb 4–6.5 and another well-known adversary, Pouronen of Russia, recorded 4–9.2 to my 4–9.8. Jo Bowers was sixth in this round with 4–12.2, and we all awaited the next round, wondering about Reynders' ability to maintain this form and whether or not the Russians were holding back a little.

The quarter-finals were scheduled for after eleven o'clock on Sunday night. If this surprises anyone, that is the way it goes. Championships go on all day, which is why they can be so exhausting for competitors, hanging around the track, keyed up and wondering what to eat or when to eat, whether to go for a spin on the road, or whether to rest or even try to sleep. The mental strain, as well as the physical, is colossal. Winning a world championship at cycling takes every ounce of nerve, equilibrium and confidence that you can muster.

Reynders clocked a 4–5 easing up against the French girl, and I was on against another old rival, Naessens. 'Right,' I thought. 'Watch this, Reynders!' I slammed Naessens with a 4–1.7 ride, the Belgian pulling out quite a respectable time with 4–10.5. Poor Jo Bowers went down to the Russian, Tikhomirova, 4–7.1 to 4–10, but, nevertheless, I don't think Jo ever rode a finer pursuit.

Pouronen, the other Russian, came through beating a Czechoslovakian girl, and the four survivors contemplated the semi-final draw. It was Reynders v Pouronen, Burton v Tikhomirova. Yvonne dealt with her Russian without great difficulty, 4–12.6 to 4–18.8 – an easy 'semi' for her, I thought, as I faced the other Russian. Tikhomirova was a new name to me. The Russians had a habit of producing new world-class riders in their search for gold, and I wondered about her. I started fast but the Russian countered and drew ahead. I came back at her in the third lap, went ahead and put on the screw. I went further ahead, but Tikhomirova did not give in easily. She tried to come back at me and I had to keep up the pressure to maintain my lead. The red and green track-lights which signal which rider is ahead became a focal point. I had to reach my light before hers flashed. This was going to be another Morley victory over Russia if I had anything to do with it. The Russian went down, fighting to the last. A good time – 4–7.3 – but mine was better – 4–2.0 – and again, it was to be a Burton–Reynders final. My Russian, Tikhomirova, beat Reynders' Russian in the ride-off for the bronze, and then it was on to the final against the old enemy. I had to wipe away the memory of the Isle of Man. I thought of the accolade Reynders would receive in Belgium if she won, in comparison with what I would receive if I did, and of the hard-earned cash it had cost Charlie and me for us both to be there. He had, as usual, wangled his way to the trackside – on the back of a scooter with a colour-blind club-mate who could not tell whether he should stop or go at Italian traffic lights! What a set-up! What the hell was I doing here anyway? I wanted to be at home in Yorkshire, not having thousands of bike-mad Italian fans staring at me as I took my place on the line. Who in Britain, at 11 p.m. on a Monday evening, knew that I was carrying their colours in a world final in Milan? 'It doesn't matter,' I thought. 'I'm riding for Charlie and Denise and the lads and lasses in Morley Cycling Club.'

It really was tense. There was a delay as Reynders and I went to the wrong starting lines – I had to start in the back straight – and this seemed to upset Reynders more than me. I had asked our team manager, Tommy Godwin, why I was in the back straight. 'Because you'll finish in the home straight in front of the best seats and all the officials, and they expect you to win.' Tommy knew a thing or two about pursuiting and pursuiters. He had taken the bronze medal in the London Olympics back in 1948.

'Right, no messing about,' I told myself. 'Hit her with everything from the start.' Then we were away on seven and a half laps plus twenty-two metres of perhaps the most famous cycling velodrome in the world. I knew she expected to start faster than me, and then to hold me. I pounded my 89-inch gear as though my life depended on it. Within the first half lap I was an amazing three lengths up on her and I held it. I expected a counter attack. It didn't come. I was feeling good and increased the pressure and my lead shot up to eight lengths. Reynders, at last realising her title was slipping away, put in an attack but I held her and she began to crack. My lead increased and I kept up the pressure to the end, steadily drawing away.

I regained my title in the best possible way. A new world record time in competition, 3–59.4. The first ride inside four minutes. I had set a new milestone in pursuit racing. *Cycling* magazine described it as the greatest ride ever in the history of the women's pursuit.

For the record Reynders' time was 4–7.3, not a bad time in itself, but I had slammed her by about 100 metres. My time has, of course, been broken on a number of occasions over the years. Indeed, a world-class woman pursuiter, given reasonable conditions, needs to be able to break four minutes with something to spare on a decent track these days. But at the time it was considered to be phenomenal. Performances in athletic sports improve all the time, and I feel that sometimes the champions of the past do not get their just desserts when comparisons are made. But at any particular time in history champions beat the standards and the opponents of their era, pushing the barriers back just that little bit further, setting the example for others to follow. In Milan I think I did just that, racing for the track-lights to make sure that my opponent's light did not appear before mine, blinking in the flashlights of the trackside photographers, hazily aware of the roar that accompanies you round the track, and finally, with tears in my eyes, standing on the podium to receive a world champion's jersey and sash, and the gold medal. The National Anthem has never sounded so sweet.

I received a telegram from Morley and it read: 'I send you warmest congratulations on behalf of your fellow townspeople on your magnificent achievement. All here are delighted with your success. Signed, Cyril N. Akeroyd, Mayor of Morley.' I went to bed that night feeling utterly drained physically and mentally and thought back to those early days in St James Hospital and, more recently, to the doctor who was so appalled that I was even riding a bike so soon after my Fallowfield crash. My hip ached and I could not sleep – but tucked under my pillow was a world champion's gold medal.

The road race took place on the shores of Lake Garda at Salo, and was a disappointment for the British team – everyone was swamped by the superb team riding of the Belgians. A group, including myself and Jo Bowers, were away in front on the circuit's long climb when, at the Tormini hairpin, Gaillard went away. On the fast descent she increased her lead. Reynders and Naessens were skilfully countering our moves, and we were caught in the classic dilemma of whether to lead a chase and give Reynders and Naessens an 'armchair ride' for some miles, or to hang back hoping that Gaillard would not keep up the pace on her own. Our other girls were behind and they could not bridge the gap, the pace was so high, and Jo and I faltered. When they felt Gaillard was safe Naessens and Reynders put on the pressure, and Jo managed to stay with them. It was a Belgian one–two–three at the line – Gaillard, Reynders, Naessens, with Jo Bowers fifth and me eighth. Their tactics exemplified the essence of team riding: they rode for a Belgian victory, no matter which of them took the gold.

There was a rather muted postscript to this Italian venture. Charlie and I stayed on in Milan for a few days for me to have another attempt at the hour record. I suppose I was, frankly, rather half-hearted about it, but the track was there, I was there – so why not? I was down on what was needed at half-way and I gave up shortly after, realising that the record was not 'on'. Again, the weather had changed but, while it was by no means as bad as for my previous attempts, I think my pursuit victory had also taken my edge a little.

Three weeks after winning my world title I was riding in the Y.C.F. 12-hour. What a contrast between racing 3,000 metres on the track before an excited Italian crowd and pounding around the Yorkshire lanes for twelve hours all on my own. I think I can truthfully claim to be an all-rounder. I had scheduled for 255 miles to beat my own record of 250.37, and for some time it seemed 'on', but it was a cold day and I had yet another spill taking a feeding bottle which unsettled me. Eventually I ran out the winner with 244.99 miles, a distance which would have placed me seventh in the men's event which was being run at the same time. In this a club-mate, Dave Robertson, finished a fine fourth with over 250 miles.

I was again the winner, for the fourth successive year, of the British Best All-rounder competition with an average speed of 24.036 m.p.h. – the first over-24 m.p.h. average, and nearly one mile per hour faster than Joan Kershaw in second place – and I began to look forward to the B.A.R. concert and the social season. In October I was given a civic reception by the Mayor of

Morley, the third time in four years that I had been so honoured, and the mayors from the two previous occasions were there for an informal evening in the Mayor's parlour. The sport had another great night at the Albert Hall where Tommy Simpson was the Guest of Honour. He had won a stage of the Tour de France that year and led the race for a time and when he appeared, wearing the yellow jersey of Tour leader that he had worn in that great race, it brought down the house.

Sponsored amateur clubs were beginning to make news at this time and it seemed that there could be a split in the club-world between those who welcomed the idea and those who wanted things to remain as they were. In my speech of thanks accepting my prizes that year I made a plea for moderation before the taking up of entrenched positions, and stressed that unity in the sport was more important. Sponsored clubs are still with us, and it is still a matter of debate whether they are good for the sport or not. My own club has survived without any help outside its membership, but it could also be argued that it would be bigger and better with financial help from an outside source.

The beginning of 1963 brought more awards, as I had been voted fourth in the Sportswriters Association poll and also fourth in the *Daily Express* Sportswoman of the year for 1962. Both these awards were won by Anita Lonsborough the swimmer, who later married Hugh Porter, four times the world professional pursuit champion.

I had a bad winter, probably as a result of my Fallowfield spill, with constant back trouble putting me in bed for several weeks, while I worried about the coming season and wondered if my racing career was at an end. At last the pain appeared to ease – perhaps resting my back had done it some good – and I started training as spring approached with no miles in my legs and feeling very unfit from a cycling viewpoint.

Early that season the Women's Cycle Racing Association held a training week-end at Loughborough Technical College, and fifty girls attended. I think everyone was particularly enthusiastic because it was the girls' own Association that had organised it and not the British Cycling Federation, who did not seem willing to help our girls prepare for international competition.

Late in May came the ride I had long dreamed about. I was seeking a good early-season 25-mile for the B.A.R., and I travelled down to the Southend Road, the famous E.3. course, to ride in the Easterly R.C. event. There was a rising headwind to the turn at about halfway, which I reached in about thirty-two minutes and, feeling good, began 'flying' over the second half. I smashed my own record with a time of 59–25, the first 'under the hour' ride, and another milestone in cycling history. It was akin to my 'under four minutes' in the Milan pursuit, although to be seen in purely British terms. I must have really been on form that day because the record was a 1 minute 9 seconds improvement, no mean feat at the 25-mile distance. Moreover I beat Jo Bowers, who finished second, by 2 minutes 34 seconds, a big margin over a rider of her class. In achieving this 'under the hour' ride, I also won a special gold medal that *Cycling* had offered four years previously to the first woman to ride 'out and home' in less than sixty minutes.

A week later I won the W.C.R.A. road championship by seven and a half minutes on a 45-mile course at Chobham, with Cynthia Carey in second place. I broke away after five miles and time trialled to the finish. Usually I did not consciously try to force a break; it was simply that on the first hill I would keep trying and after a little time I would look round and the rest would seem to have disappeared.

In the middle of June I hit another record, the 50-mile, in the West London Ladies C.A. held in Berkshire, finishing in a time of 2–5–16, beating my own record by twenty-nine seconds, and the second-placed rider by ten minutes or more. The Berkshire course was the Bath Road, and its fame in the annals of cycling history made it a satisfying course on which to set up a record.

I travelled over for the Isle of Man week and won my races there on both road and track, and then it was back to Cheshire for the 25-mile championship which I won with 1–0–55, beating Jo Bowers by over two minutes. In the space of less than three weeks I had won five time trials, two road races and a track race, setting new records along the way.

At this time I was riding a frame which was on loan to me from a well-known racing bike firm, and 'loan' is the operative word so far as I was concerned. It was returned in due course of time, unlike some others they had lent to other leading riders. I remember also that I was given a tracksuit by them with the company's name across the back and, in order to avoid advertising, I unpicked the fine machine stitching, leaving a lot of little holes, which I then had the tedious job of stitching up.

On the 6th July I went down to the London track at Herne Hill for the 3,000 metres pursuit championship, the title that Jo Bowers had taken from me the previous year, and I succeeded in taking it back from her. The next day there was a 50-mile road race in Buckinghamshire which I won, with Jo nearly five minutes behind in second place. By now it must be obvious to the reader what an important part Jo Bowers has played in my cycling life. Just as in the early years Millie Robinson had been the one I did battle with, Jo Bowers as she then was (she later became equally well known as Shirley Killingbeck), became the one to beat. Things have not altered – we are still battling it out with each other after more years than either of us cares to think about. She and Joan Kershaw have both had great cycling careers. With myself I think we form a triumvirate that must be unequalled in sport anywhere for the length of our parallel careers at the top.

On this same successful week-end, Nim Carline retained his 24-hour title with a distance of 475.18 miles, so there was cause for celebration in the Morley camp. Perhaps some day Nim will set about putting down on paper accounts of his tremendous long-distance cycling in different parts of the world, but particularly his six 24-hour and two 12-hour title victories.

I was still battling away at the idea that women cyclists should be allowed to race against men, because it seemed to me that that was the way to improve the standard of women's racing and, one day, a *Daily Mail* reporter turned up at my home to interview me about it. I continued hanging out the washing while he stood behind me making notes and I told him that the Russian girls had opportunities of mixing with male riders which improved them in international competition.

Many journalistic interviews I have given have highlighted the 'housewife' angle and, while I welcomed publicity for my sport, it was difficult sometimes talking to people who had no concept of bike racing in the international sporting scene. Occasionally they would turn up at awkward moments, and I could not help feeling just a tiny bit resentful sometimes, when I considered that they were being well paid for asking questions in their working time while I was answering them in my leisure and domestic work time! I felt particularly annoyed when I could not recognise what I was supposed to have said when it appeared in print. It was almost as if they had interviewed somebody else altogether.

In July I won the national road race championship in Northamptonshire by nearly four minutes and then, the following day, the Rosslyn Ladies 100-mile in a time of 4–22–52. Surprisingly, Jo Bowers was beaten into third place by the relatively unknown Marion Kelham, who was second with 4–44–10. In the middle of the month I defended my 50-mile championship on a Warwickshire course, and not only retained the title but set up a new competition record of 2–4–53 – the first time a woman had gone 'inside' 2–5.

Regrettably, it was not possible for me to defend my 100-mile championship in this year because it clashed with the world championships. The girl who won the title, June Pitchford, is another rider who has been consistently at the top for many years. As I prepare this story, June is almost certain to become the British Best All-rounder for the second successive year, an honour she richly deserves, and she is getting faster all the time!

So, it was back to the Rocourt track at Liège where I had won my first world pursuit winner's medal in 1959. I expected Reynders, in front of her own crowd, to be my most dangerous opponent, and also that some relative unknown would challenge the two of us. In June I had secured the one mile and the 3,000 metres British records at Newcastle, Staffordshire, on what is a pleasant but not very fast track. In spite of the niggle from my back and hip, I was in top form. Then, would you believe it, I contracted a heavy cold! The team travelled over to Liège, and stayed at the same hotel as in 1959, where we received a warm welcome. In spite of my cold I quickly set to training at the track, hoping to shake it off before the serious business began.

Everything went to form eventually, with me, Reynders and two Russians, Riabchenko and Dementjeva, meeting in the semi-finals. Yet again the Russians had produced two new girls in their efforts to match their sprint successes in the pursuit. I met Riabchenko on the Sunday afternoon in rather windy conditions, and for three laps there was nothing between us, but she could not hold the pace I was setting. I had a moment of panic when I felt my saddle slipping, but managed to plant myself firmly on it, and by that time I had enough in hand not to worry. My time was 4–15.35 against Riabchenko's 4–19.48. In the other semi-final Reynders had no difficulty, with 4–15.60 against 4–26.02 so, yet again, it was to be a Reynders–Burton final.

It was the third successive year that we had met in the final, with the score one each, so this match was something of a decider. Reynders had the advantage of playing 'at home' in front of her own supporters, but I had managed to ride away most of my cold, my back felt good, and I was in the mood to show the Belgians that I was still as good as back in 1959.

I was away quickly, but Reynders, perhaps inspired by the Belgian roar, set off as though jet-propelled. The track-lights showed her in the lead. I was encouraged by some English cheers in the home straight, but it was nothing to Yvonne's support when she also passed the main stand; it lifted her tremendously and she was going away from me. So, early in the race the title seemed already lost. Two laps gone and she was in the lead by three lengths! I was getting into my stride but still made no impression. The Belgians were ecstatic and I realised another lap could virtually see the end. I was riding well, but Reynders seemed phenomenal. It called for an answer. I rode probably the best pursuit lap of my life in taking back those three lengths – my eyeballs were hanging over my front wheel – and I did it! Reynders did not actually 'crack'; there was just nothing she could do in the remaining laps, and the stadium seemed almost quiet with only the contingent of British supporters, sensing victory out of seeming defeat, still cheering. Reynders finished with 4–12.4, an excellent time on Rocourt. My time was 4–7.39.

Although I am normally a fastidious person about cleanliness, I had a 'thing' about washing my legs during a world track series – or, rather, not washing them! Out training and racing on the track, you collect enough dust to need a good wash anyway, apart from the sweat, but I took showers sitting down with my legs out of the way to keep them dry. On the victory rostrum I was perturbed that my sweat-caked legs looked dirty to the photographers of the world's press!

Cold figures often conceal the real difference between performances. I suppose most people would consider my ride the year before at Milan, when I beat four minutes, as my greatest pursuit. I recall the Milan final with particular pleasure because of the record, but I remember Rocourt as the absolute pinnacle of my pursuiting and know it was an even better performance. Rocourt is comparatively slow; Vigorelli smooth and fast and worth more than the eight seconds which separated the two rides. I feel bound to say that British women's pursuiting has not advanced during the intervening years, except in the case of the outstanding Mandy Jones. A 4–7 could still win a British national title at the Leicester track, which is much faster than Rocourt.

Charlie had taken Denise along with him that year, and he carried her on his shoulders to greet me at the finish – it was all very emotional. Again, I felt very proud when our national anthem was played. A photograph of the three of us appeared on the sports page of the *Daily Mirror* but, as usual, the Yorkshire papers were cool. The *Yorkshire Post* managed all of three inches while giving twice as much space in the next column to a local athletics meeting in a Leeds park.

Great Britain had not had a very successful championships; Hugh Porter had taken the bronze medal in the amateur pursuit, laying the foundation of his great international career, but there was little else to cheer about, both Jean Dunn and Christine Rowbotham going out in the quarter-finals of the women's sprint. I must confess that I had always been a little wary about Christine following my bad crash at Fallowfield because I considered she was the cause of it, and she was aware of this. Tragically Christine died a few years ago, fighting against her illness in the same way that she had tackled the great Russian sprinter, Ermolaeva, at Rocourt, gutsy as always. I retain a precious memory of her from Belgium. While I was eating dinner at the team hotel following my victory, Christine appeared from upstairs and walked quietly across to me. Shyly she pushed into my hands a box of chocolates. 'That's for your win tonight,' she said, and slipped away, leaving me to choke over the rest of my dinner. The Fallowfield incident was forgiven for evermore. I was deeply touched by this little act of spontaneous kindness; the chocolates, of course, were only a symbol – a reaching out of a warm-hearted generous spirit whose touch will always remain with me.

The road race took place on a hilly course near the small town of Renaix, in the Flemish Ardennes. Charlie and Denise had followed us there, sleeping in the little car and living on chips and sausages bought in the village square. Denise thought it a great adventure, but it was a little less light-hearted for Charlie. We had ridden over to Renaix as part of our training and, feeling relaxed and fit following my pursuit win, I had high hopes of success. These were increased on the morning of the race which dawned very windy, and obviously the going would be hard, the way I liked it.

The Union Cycliste Internationale, the world governing body, usually manages to make a hash of something or other at world championships. It did so on this occasion, and I was the victim. A race car, which presumably needed to be in position in front of the race, had started late and tried to rectify the fault by hurrying past the field, which was still in one large group, down the left-hand side. All the girls were gradually forced over to the right, closing the small gap on that side of the road. That gap was precisely where I was making for at that moment in order to get to the head of things early in the race. There was nowhere for me to go except into the ditch. If I had merely taken an ordinary tumble, perhaps I should have been able to remount and continue and, at that early stage, would easily have regained the bunch. Alas, an unfriendly telegraph pole was also at the roadside, and I smacked into it – hard. Susan Crow stopped behind to offer help, although I was not aware she had because I was unconscious. Poor Susan also suffered a puncture, so her twentieth placing at the end, some minutes down, was not a true reflection of her efforts. I was taken to hospital where X-rays revealed that nothing was broken. They kept me in for several hours and apparently there was a constant stream of enquiries about my well-being. For myself, I was thankful that the track racing had taken place before the road races that year. Some years it is the other way round. Still feeling a little groggy I was collected by Charlie and Denise, and we set out for a planned week's holiday in the Italian Lakes which, understandably, I felt I needed.

For the record, it was another great victory for Reynders in the road race, with her compatriot Rosa Sels second and the Russian girl, Pouronen, in third place. It had been a fifteen-girl sprint at the end, with Pat Pepper fourth and Ann Illingworth fifth, only three lengths down on Reynders. And if I had been there? No one can say, but I have a feeling that that year could have seen a British victory, and I am not thinking only of myself as a possible British winner.

At Rocourt I had been approached by Cyril Geoghegan, manager of the South African team and a leading figure in South African cycling, with an invitation to undertake a series of exhibition rides and possibly an attempt on the world hour record at the Bloemfontein track. He suggested I might also be able to compete against junior male riders, and this interested me. South Africa was quite a strong cycling nation but they had no organised women's racing, and I think Mr Geoghegan thought the visit would possibly start something in that direction, and that South Africa would gain some prestige from having a world record broken there. Bill Long, famous internationally as an Australian official and promoter at the Melbourne track, also tentatively suggested a racing visit to that country. It seemed that my European successes had spread my name to other corners of the world, even if I was not as well known in Yorkshire, outside Morley.

My last big win of the season was in the Nelson Wheelers 100-mile, which I covered in 4–19–13, thereby ensuring the B.A.R. for the fifth successive year with a record average. Then it was off to London for the Meeting of Champions where I made a few record attempts on a day that was not really suitable for record breaking. I failed in the kilometre, but set up new figures for the mile and the 3,000 metres.

At the British Best All-rounder concert at the Albert Hall I was presented by the editor of *Cycling*, George Pearson, with the gold medal for being the first woman to ride an 'out and home' 25-mile in less than an hour. (I was also presented by Denise with a box of chocolates on behalf of a neighbour, Mrs Whitehead!) On three previous occasions only had *Cycling* presented a gold medal, and I was a very proud recipient of the fourth.

At the annual dinner of the Sportswriters Association on December 11th I received their third place award in the ballot for performers who have done the most for Britain's prestige in the international sporting sphere, and another Yorkshire girl, athletics star Dorothy Hyman, took the premier award.

One thing about cycling sport in this country is that you can race all over the place during the season, winning this and that race with nothing to show for it at the time but, because of the traditional, heavy social season, you can then spend the winter months attending functions all over the country picking up the various trophies and medals. One such function in 1964 was organised by the Coventry Cycling Clubs Alliance in January. I had won their 15-mile promotion during the previous season and was presented with a silver statuette of Lady Godiva – a lovely trophy.

I was still some way from racing fitness when I received another request from the East Germans to ride at the Werner Seelenbinder indoor track. I always enjoyed riding in East Germany, especially on this particular track, and I would train on it for hours before they would drag me away. It was small and eminently suitable for spectacular sprints and Madisons, but not a pursuiter's track. However, I appeared against five German girls in a 3,000 metres pursuit, with their top girl Elizabeth Eicholtz starting opposite me. Before the full distance Elizabeth had caught the two girls in front of her and I had eliminated the two in front of me, so it resolved into a straight pursuit match between the two of us. I beat her by two lengths and received a tremendous ovation from the always appreciative East German spectators.

It was about this time there appeared in *Cycling* an article by Dr C.R. Woodard, a famous athletics specialist and the author of books on the subject. The previous October Charlie and I had spent an interesting and enjoyable week-end as his guest at his lovely country home near Rugby. The article was the result of our meeting, and was in question and answer form. I don't propose to set it all down here, but I would like to repeat extracts from it as it sets out clearly my physical state following the Fallowfield crash and my attitude to cycling and life generally. These parts of it are germane, I think, to this book, as they summarise much of what I want the reader to know.

Cycling – March 21st, 1964

> *I can only describe her physique as exceptional. I examined her at a time when she was still suffering from the effects of her fall in the world championships in Belgium, and in her own opinion she was far from fit . . . Her muscles were wonderfully supple . . . .*

Let me interpose here some comments by Beryl Burton herself in answer to questions put by me.

C.R. WOODARD: To what in your background do you attribute your success as a cyclist?

BERYL BURTON: I was always very stubborn even as a child. I remember at school one day I was given new exercise books. I had got it into my head that these books would never, if I could help it, contain anything but good marks. Yet almost on the day I got them a teacher crossed something out with a red pencil. I was speechless with fury and the teacher had to give me a good dressing down. To this day I remember her chief comment was 'you stubborn little mule'. I had a stern upbringing, and when I was very young my mother was out at work. I had to return from school to help to do housework, feed the family, and do all sorts of chores. It was all a fight to survive, and I think it has made me very determined – and still stubborn!

Of her introduction to the club, Charlie Burton's comments were very much to the point:

CHARLIE BURTON: We pushed her for the first year. She rode with us for the second. And she rode away from us in the third!

BERYL BURTON: I always went out with the lads determined in the final tear-up never to be dropped. Needless to say I was, but that stage passed! What happened after that you know.

C.R. WOODARD: Did you ever pattern your own development and training on any other stars?

BERYL BURTON: No, most definitely not. I have always ridden to win, even when away down the list. I am not interested in basing my own performances on anybody else's style, or experience. I always ride to win.

C.R. WOODARD: You have said to me that you weren't as fit as you would like to be. What did you mean by that?

BERYL BURTON: Fitness to me is speed on a bicycle. I have yet to prove whether I am as fit or fitter than when I had my accident at Fallowfield in June, 1962. I personally don't think I have ever been 'right' since then. And when I crashed again in Belgium during the world championship, I know it really did set me back.

C.R. WOODARD: Let me hear more about those accidents, and to what extent they affected your performance.

BERYL BURTON: In June 1962 I had a bad crash at Fallowfield. It was 6–7 weeks before I rode to form again, and throughout this time I had aches and pains in the middle and lumbar region of my back. I tried to ignore this by telling myself it would go, but it didn't. Although in August–September I broke the competition record in the '25' and '100', and also won the world pursuit championship in Milan in the fastest time ever, I wasn't at that time getting a full night's sleep, and I couldn't turn over in bed without assistance. On rising I couldn't straighten up for some seconds, and then only with terrific effort.

The winter of 62/63 with its cold and damp didn't help matters, but I was determined not to be beaten by it, and commenced training in March. I didn't let the pain interrupt training or racing, although I found one leg only worked at half power. In the belief that 'speed is fitness', I beat the hour in May and the '50' record in June. In July my back was no better, and my leg worse, the pain striking from lower down my back through my groin, reaching down the inside of my leg. I saw my doctor, who advised 3–4 months off the bike but this was impossible. I had to ride in the world championships in August. This I did, and won the pursuit. Unfortunately I crashed in the road race by diving head first into a 3 ft ditch at speed. I came round in hospital unable to move my head or neck. X-ray examination revealed no breaks, but my back was now worse than ever, and my arms went dead and tingly. I saw a physiotherapist in September and his manipulation was the first relief I had. Although still sore, I did at least have a night's sleep, and much of the stiffness went. It wasn't until October I was able to see you.

C.R. Woodard: Obviously, Beryl, you didn't let it beat you, but did those accidents have a psychological effect?

Beryl Burton: Could there be any connection with the pain and stiffness I have had, and the fact that at the age of 12 I spent two years in hospital with rheumatic fever? Some of the pain I have had reminds me very much of that occasion.

Charlie Burton: When Beryl first started riding with the club she was always falling off, and we thought we'll never make a cyclist of her. She was always blinding along and putting the brakes on too late. The lads used to greet her with 'Haven't you fallen off yet?' Your remarks, Doc., about the psychology of it all, are interesting when one remembers the effect of the 1963 world championship crash. In her first big road race about a month later, she was trembling all over, and had completely lost her confidence, in what seemed at the time, an exaggerated way. She said afterwards that if she hadn't forced herself to ride in the bunch she would never have ridden massed start again. In any case she has never really taken to road racing. She is an individualist, and when racing doesn't like to be hemmed in or even in company.

Beryl Burton: Charlie's right. I hate people seeing me 'trying'. It embarrasses me. If anybody is about, I pretend to be completely unconcerned. I put on this air of calmness. I fancy I couldn't make the effort if I thought people were watching. I always prefer to be alone; I

always feel much more relaxed. You must be and you have to feel cool.
Actually I go out on a cycle to remove mental tension. To me it is the most
relaxing pastime possible. I often get wound up with people and
circumstances, but once on the bike I unload it all, and feel much better . . .

C.R. WOODARD: Is there any disadvantage to being a cycle star?

BERYL BURTON: Charlie and I agree that there most definitely is a grave
disadvantage. Our domestic life is nowhere near ordered or relaxed enough.
We don't get enough sleep. There's always something on. Late hours are
our chief worry. We do an immense amount of travelling, and never have
time to eat properly while doing it. It's a problem which we are constantly
trying to sort out, because sooner or later it will prove disastrous if we don't.

*Out of all that comes wonderful advice for all aspiring champions. First and
foremost it bears out so much of what we have constantly tried to put across
about the psychology of training and fitness. Not even the very fit Beryl Burton
could avoid the psychological effects of an accident. Learn from her how to
recover from it. Put first things first and realise that so much of it depends on
what we call 'mind over matter'. . .*

*I have been very impressed indeed by Beryl. She is not only an outstanding
athlete, but an outstanding personality. Beryl owes her success entirely to her
own efforts. She is a dedicated athlete . . .*

When the first 50-mile of the year came along, on the Southend Road in
May, I had not ridden a time trial longer than fifteen miles. Charlie and I were
preparing to move into a new house, but there had been some delay, so we had
splashed out on a new Cortina, which made travelling for longer distances
much more comfortable. This Eastern Counties event struck a really windy
day, with conditions coming back from the 'turn' very, very hard. However, I
must have been fitter than I realised, for I won with a time of 2–4–29, beating
my own record by twenty-four seconds. More importantly for me, I had gone
faster than any of the men in their race, the men's winner taking a time of
2–6–41. As a report at the time stated 'Beryl thus becomes the first woman
ever to beat men on their own terms, on the same course on the same day, in
what under the circumstances virtually amounted to the same event . . .'

I followed this by retaining my W.C.R.A. championship road race title in
Surrey. As usual, nobody else would come to the front and I did all the work
over the thirty-five miles. With a few hundred yards to go there were still
twelve glued to my wheel hoping to beat me in the sprint, but I wound up the
pace and won by two and a half lengths.

At the end of the month I brought my 25-mile record down again with a ride
of 59–2 on the E.3 course in Essex. The final miles to the 'turn' on this course
go up Rayleigh Cutting but a rider who can overcome this can turn out a good

time on a reasonable day. This effort should have brought a fifty-eight minute ride, but unfortunately road works had made the course some thirty yards too long.

I won another 25-mile and then, at the Nottingham track, made a world record attempt on the 3,000 metres. Shirley Killingbeck (formerly Jo Bowers) provisionally held the record with 4–29.2. It had not been on the books very long, I think, as a world record distance, so the time needed bringing down somewhat to nearer competition record, remembering what I have already written about the difference between cycling and athletics records. On a windy day and a track that, with due respect, is not really a track for world records, I achieved 4–16.6 to take a large slice off Shirley's record, with the odd result that the British record which I held was still 0.2 seconds faster.

Into June, and my attempt to win the national 25-mile title for the seventh time, on the course with the Rayleigh Cutting. Heavy rain and strong wind made the going very hard, and a greasy road at the Rayleigh roundabout caused many of the girls to fall, including me, even though, having been warned, I was crawling round it at about 5 m.p.h. Anyway, I retained my title with 1–1–37, almost three minutes ahead of Shirley Killingbeck who rode gallantly as she had been in bed for a week with bronchitis.

I was ready to make my annual trip to the Isle of Man for the cycling week when the Queen's Birthday Honours List was announced, and I had been honoured by Her Majesty with an M.B.E. At twenty-seven I was a particularly young M.B.E., more especially in those days, and besides being proud on my own account I was extremely pleased that it thrust the sport into the headlines for a day – it was given publicity by the press, and even the *Yorkshire Evening Post* had a big headline and photograph. I was to receive my award at the Palace later in the year and it was something to which I could look forward.

At the end of the month I had another outstanding success in an event promoted by my own club. It was a 25-mile held on the Boro' course north of Wetherby. There are different variants of this course for 25- and 50-mile trials, but all of them are known for fast times. The odd thing about them is that for most of the season the weather conditions there are not all that good, and many of the records on this famous stretch of road have been due as much to magnificent rides as to the course. Many cyclists 'knock' these courses as giving unfair advantage because of the traffic flow, but it is significant that checks over the past few seasons reveal that traffic on the Boro', while not slight, is far less heavy early on a Sunday morning than is generally supposed, and certainly less than what I have experienced on certain southern courses. This is particularly so for the girls' events which are usually over and done with before there is much traffic. Many have arrived on the Boro' for the first time and, although the weather has not seemed all that bad, have returned home disappointed. Until about this time nearly all my best rides had been accomplished in other parts of the country, and I had competed comparatively seldom in my own county.

Back to the Morley '25' with the first girl away at the barbarous hour of 6 a.m. While most people stay in bed at the week-end recuperating from the previous week, cyclists, who lead an active enough life anyway, are competing in all kinds of events, from local trials to national championships. This particular late June morning went really well: I was on top of my form and chopped another twenty-three seconds off my record, winning with a time of 58–39, beating Val Rushworth by nearly four minutes. I was particularly pleased with this, setting a new record not only in Yorkshire but in my own club's promotion. I was taking women's racing into a new dimension, and was determined to lower the record even more before I was finished.

I retained the 3,000 metres pursuit title at Herne Hill, beating Shirley Killingbeck in the final, and looked forward to defending the 50-mile title in Cheshire. I accomplished this with 2–7–10, Shirley again being the runner-up.

I raced in everything and anything, winning the Central District Ladies '25', the North Nottinghamshire Olympic 40-mile road race, and then it was over to Newcastle-under-Lyme to push my world record time for the 3,000 metres down to 4–14.9, still slow compared with my world competition time at Vigorelli.

Travelling south again to ride the Becontree R.C.C. '25' I knocked a bit more off my record, bringing it down to 58–2; I was now looking forward to the day I could ride a '57'. Here I have to record that I lost my road race title the same afternoon to Valerie Rushworth. Two miles after the start I punctured and it took me twenty minutes to regain the bunch. At the end I finished fourth, about three lengths down.

In the Dragon R.C. 100-mile I faced a hard day with windy conditions and beat Pat Pepper of Colchester Rovers by nearly sixteen minutes with a time of 4–14–48. It was not far away from my record time and set me on course for the Best All-rounder title again.

The middle of August brought the championship '100', held in atrocious conditions in Nottinghamshire. Unable to defend my title the previous year because of the world championships, I was anxious to regain it, and managed to do so with a time of 4–16–43. I beat the South Elmsall girl, Margaret Larkin, by over ten minutes and she took a very well-deserved silver medal, riding herself into a state of near collapse and finishing in tears. 'This is a rider to watch,' I thought, 'somebody prepared to ride themselves out to the last ounce.' I was concerned about her but she shrugged off her distress with 'I want to be like you.' Again, a tribute not shown in any record books, but something treasured in my mind always, and more important than medals.

This year the world championships were held in France with the track titles to be decided at the Parc des Princes in the south-western area of Paris. Before the championships I rode in the Viking R.C. 50-mile, winning with a time of 2–1–12, beating Pat Pepper, and my own record for the distance. I think it was a good performance to beat the record by three and a quarter minutes and at an average speed of 24.75 m.p.h. particularly as there was a stiff headwind against the riders for the second half. It notched up my fifth competition record of the year.

So, I travelled to France in good heart, in spite of the still niggling back. However the road race at Sallanches came before the track series, and while out training for it I had another accident. I don't remember a great deal about it. I was with a group of British men riders and a car came too close with the result that I bounced on the base of my spine. I continued in pain but, obviously, I was badly shaken, and my back told me that I should not even be on the bike, let alone contemplating a world championship. I can't really tell you much about the road race. I finished tenth, which in the circumstances was not too bad, and I suppose, in the back of my mind, I was hoping that I could pull myself together for the pursuit. The road race result was a Russian one-two, with Emilia Sonka and Galina Yudini, and Rosa Sels of Belgium finishing in third place.

In Paris I immediately went down to the track for training – testing out my back and getting the feel of the famous pink surface of the Parc des Princes. Paris is such a famous and romantic city that it may seem unbelievable to many when I say that I hardly saw any of it. After the championships British riders were accused of being too intent on sightseeing at the ordinary cyclist's expense, i.e., through B.C.F. funds. It is an accusation that had been levelled before and has been many times since. I am not going to point the finger at anyone, only defend my own position. I can truthfully say that on all my world championship trips cycling came first, second and third and really there was hardly any time left for anything else. The ordinary British clubman always had full value out of me. Not a sou or a mark was wasted on my expenses, no time out for joy-rides or shopping excursions – just eating, sleeping and training and trying my damnedest in my events. Yes, I have been to Paris, like thousands of my countrymen; unlike them I cannot tell you a thing about the place. It could have been Accrington or Weston-super-Mare for all I cared.

Injury-time again! Out training with some others of the team on the track, a male rider of another nation in front of us sat up, hands off the bars to adjust his tracksuit top, swerved, and we all came down. My wrist hurt terribly as I picked myself up and tried to ride, quickly realising that to grip the bars was excruciating. Outwardly I tried to show calmness, to shrug off the pain and pretend it was nothing to worry about, because I was concerned about keeping the extent of my injury away from the opposition. My wrist and hand were swollen, and I felt wretched and ached all over as I went to the line to defend my title. Qualifying round: Reynders 4–5.56; Pouronen 4–12.85; Burton 4–14.24. My wrist ached even more and I could not grip the bars: the position seemed hopeless but somehow we had managed to keep the news from others. I had a pain-killing injection which helped except that my hand was now completely numb and to all intents and purposes, I was 'one-handed'.

Before my semi-final against Pouronen my hand was strapped to the bars as discreetly as possible, and the thousands of spectators knew nothing about it. If my hand no longer ached, my back did, and this together with being unable to pull on the bars with both hands – which makes control more difficult as well as being a handicap to speed – made me feel that my hopes of a medal, let alone retaining my title, had gone. Semi-final wins never seem to be remembered no matter how meritorious, and doubtless most people have forgotten this one. I tried to block everything out of my mind and concentrate on getting through to the final. If I could win this then I was still in with a chance of the gold. Pouronen, I knew, was good; she would not be easy. Backache and a dead wrist had to be overcome. Result of the semi-final: Burton 4–11.32; Pouronen 4–12.56. I had made it to the final against Reynders, who had won her 'semi' against Smolentseva in 4–5.10. I thought that on the fast Paris track I could again have beaten four minutes, given reasonable fortune, but I knew, really, that this time it was not going to be possible and, the way Reynders was riding, she would come close to it.

Strapped to the bars again, I fought to the end against a Reynders who would not be denied, the Belgian girl taking another gold in 4–2.22 against my 4–9.53. I am not detracting from Yvonne's win when I say that I think I would have beaten her again that year but for my injuries, which I made no point of displaying afterward. I am not sure, but I think even to this day the opposition don't know of the handicap I carried.

My consolation this year was that I was the only British medal winner in all the racing, track and road, and I had to content myself with that, and hope that my right hand would heal quickly.

When I returned I began to give serious thought to my future. Losing my title in Paris could, at least in part, be put down to some misfortune, and a world silver medal was no bad thing – but I was feeling disenchanted. Trying like most young families to improve our housing and way of life, Charlie, Denise and I were about to move into our new house at Woodlesford, near Leeds; yet it had cost us over £100 for me to earn that silver medal in Paris, and I would ask readers to remember what £100 was worth in purchasing terms in 1964. Year after year I travelled the country every week-end, incurring numerous expenses, just to win a small prize when, really, we needed all the money we had. The cycling world was blasé about my continued success and event promoters were looking for records every time I rode. 'How about an event record this morning, Beryl?' they would say in all seriousness, with the trees behind them bending backward in the wind. It was becoming too much, and I felt I needed to consolidate my domestic life, and cease pushing my body year in and year out. I needed the simple luxury of being at home at week-ends with an extra hour or two in bed on a Sunday morning. Our lives seemed to be ruled by handbooks, entry forms, closing dates, planning travel from one place to another and decisions as to whether we could afford another pair of cycling shoes. The winter months brought no respite and sometimes I felt I could use a secretary to worry about the details. And all this strictly as an amateur in the old-fashioned sense of the word. O.K., so I loved cycling; I enjoyed racing on a bike and pitting myself against all and sundry; I was proud to race for Great Britain; I was human enough to enjoy success and breaking records in a manner no one had dreamed they could be broken and standing on a podium, watching the Union flag being raised as our national anthem was played. But I had drunk deeply from this particular cup, and now there was a slight bitterness in the taste.

With all this in my mind Charlie, Denise and I went to London in October for me to receive the M.B.E. from Her Majesty. I felt very proud when the Queen pinned the award on me – for myself and for the sport of cycling. The Queen seemed a little smaller than I had imagined and I was struck by her beautiful flawless complexion. She knew who I was, and I managed to carry off the curtsey and back away as required. Many of the people being honoured were extremely nervous, but I just felt very excited: when you have been on the line in the final of a world championship a few times there's not much left that can make you feel nervous.

The following month Charlie and I again went to London for the British Best All-rounder concert and presentation at the Albert Hall – it was my sixth successive year as B.A.R. with a record m.p.h. The men's B.A.R. that year was a fellow 'Yorkie', Peter Hill of the Askern C.C., the youngest ever to take the title.

Early in 1965 I had an operation at a Rugby hospital. For some time I had been troubled by a swelling in the groin which was particularly troublesome in wet weather as my racing shorts then became damp which caused some friction. I had a fear that it might be something serious, but examination revealed that it was really brought about by so much cycling – something of an 'occupational hazard'! For four months I did not touch a bike, a lay-off which had me fretting.

When the 1965 season started I was eager to start racing again although in an athletic sense I was far from fit. But at least I had been able to shake off the depression of a few months earlier. In my first race I was beaten by Joan Kershaw in the Merseyide Ladies C.A. 10-mile by one second and, although it made me realise I was not completely racing fit, there's no disgrace in anyone being beaten by Joan.

In May I won the Goole Wheelers 25-mile for the sixth time in seven years with 1–0–24, 2 minutes 19 seconds in front of Margaret Larkin, who by now had made a name for herself. Later in the month, still a few pounds over my racing weight although the national 25-mile championship was imminent, I travelled south to ride in the Easterly R.C. event at that distance, winning with 59–40 and beating Margaret and June Pitchford by over three minutes.

Then another disaster! The following morning I was riding to work when, as so often happens, a driver misjudged the speed of the approaching cyclist. He turned sharply across and, once again, I hit the ground. The result of this particular mishap was two broken fingers (they are still a little mis-shapen), lots of bruises and abrasions and a knee swollen like the proverbial balloon. The championship was a week away and I hoped that I would still be able to ride, but as the week passed by it became obvious that this was simply 'not on'. Joan Kershaw took a worthy gold medal from June Pitchford while I sat at home nursing my latest injuries.

The national road race championship later in June proved tough. A very stiff hill had been included in the 45-mile course at the last moment because of road works and, as a result, most of the girls were too highly geared, including myself. The finish was at the top of the hill, and Susan Crow of Middlesex R.C. seemed to have the title in her grasp with only a few hundred yards to go. I heaved away at the lowest gear I had, striving as hard as I could to pull Susan back. It was no use worrying about the others catching my wheel, it was now everyone for themselves as best they could. I caught and passed her, getting clear at the line by five seconds.

I pulled off another road race victory the following month, the W.C.R.A. race which contained an eight-strong East German team led by Hannelore Mattig. She and Margaret Larkin set a very fast pace in the early laps going for the lap prizes, but eventually they were pulled back and I set about attacking. The other English girls 'blocked' effectively and I won by forty-six seconds from Ann Horswell of Plymouth. By now I seemed to have shaken off the recent accident, and looked forward to the forthcoming 50-mile championship. It was held in South Yorkshire in heavy rain, but the conditions did not affect me and I won in a time of 2–2–41, beating Margaret Larkin by over six minutes with Joan Kershaw in third place. It was my twentieth national title, and I felt I had it in me to win many more.

Later that month I won the Sipelia road race at Sheffield by nearly two lengths from Susan Crow, who was one of the best road racing girls we have produced in Britain. I think that had she been a 'continental' more would have been heard of her on the international scene. The same week-end I recorded 59–38 on the new 'Boro' course. I was, however, more delighted by Nim Carline's third 24-hour championship win in which he clocked up a magnificent 485.9 miles.

Everything was now going well, my wrist and fingers were giving no trouble and, even if I still 'felt' my back occasionally, it did not seem to interfere with my form. I retained my national pursuit title, and then rode in the Newark Castle 100-mile where I knocked 1 minute 25 seconds off my record with a time of 4–13–4. I had to fight hard to retain my 100-mile title in August, winning with 4–24–24 from June Pitchford who was a little over five minutes behind. On this course near Peterborough June matched me over most of the second half, and any weakening on my part would probably have given her the title.

On Sunday, 29th August, the British team flew to San Sebastian for the world championships. We had been kitted out with new outfits, and we girls looked very smart in our pleated skirts and jackets – if there had been a medal for elegance we would probably have won it! The newly-built track at Anoeta, a suburb of San Sebastian, measured 287 metres with 48° bankings and straights at 13°, and was reputed to be fast. Such was the newness of everything that workmen were still building the track cabins and putting finishing touches to other parts when we arrived for training. I was feeling good and thought I could adapt to the track and had no reason to discount the forecasts of another Reynders–Burton pursuit final after we had crossed swords in the road race.

Two days later I became ill, my stomach churned and I felt terrible as my strength drained from me. Gastro-enteritis was diagnosed so, almost before I could put the finishing touches to my training, my chances were slipping away in the clutches of a 'bug'. When we lined up a few days later for the 30-mile road race I was feeling only slightly better, and thought I would be lucky to finish. In other circumstances I don't think I would have raced but I felt I had a duty to try, at least. Early in the race I tried a break, more in despair than anticipation that it would succeed, and it was an old adversary, Naessens, who brought me back. After that it was merely a question of staying with the bunch, from which a small group broke just clear to sprint for the line. Elizabeth Eicholtz of East Germany was the winner from Reynders and Pouronen, Ceiren of Belgium and Herse of France, with the rest of us a little behind. Elizabeth was a well-liked girl with the British riders and, failing success on our part, her win was a popular one with us. Incidentally, it has always seemed to me that women's road titles were won over too short a course and that they should have been longer and, in certain years, on a hillier terrain. For me this year, however, the distance of thirty miles was quite long enough!

Looking back, I realise I would have been wiser not to have ridden the road and conserved my depleted strength for the track, and at least saved myself the ignominy of being eliminated in the qualifying round of the 3,000 metres, for that is what happened. I cannot even remember my time in that ride and certainly made no note of it. I simply wanted to get home and away from Spain as quickly as possible.

The amazing thing about all this is that apparently the reason for my spectacular failure was hardly known. *Cycling* magazine merely reported the fact of my early dismissal from the pursuit and a week later, summarising the championships, said that I was as astonished as everybody else. Not a bit of it! I was ill and that is all there is to it. That stomach complaint dogged me for about eighteen months afterwards. I had all kinds of tests, including one by the Liverpool School of Tropical Medicine, but nobody could come up with a diagnosis, and gradually it disappeared. But over that period I lost weight and have been slimmer ever since. With this and constant back trouble I sometimes despaired, although I managed successfully to conceal my worries from the cycling public. If the reader is beginning to feel a little weary of these medical problems, I can only plead that they happened, they affected me, and they must be part of this story.

I cannot leave my recollections of the 1965 world championships without reference to dear old Tom Simpson – he did us all proud with his victory in the professional road race. Nobody expected a British rider to win this one, until Tom came on the scene and fulfilled our wildest dreams. His tragic death two years later on the cruel slopes of Mont Ventoux while riding in the Tour de France almost cut out the heart of the sport in this country. I'll make further reference to it later.

I finished the season's racing in style, with a competition record in the Worcestershire C.A. 10-mile. This short distance has never been my favourite, particularly in later years, but I held the record and took another four seconds off it that rainy morning. For the seventh successive year I was the British Best All-rounder and with Morley winning the team B.A.R. and Nim the 24-hour title it had been a good year for the club, which was very important to me.

Before the presentation of the year's awards in December I went on my long-projected South African trip, which lasted six weeks. It was a great adventure for me to travel so far, particularly as I had been invited as an individual, and was something that I could never have dreamed about as a young girl.

Making such a trip today would involve me in all kinds of problems and, indeed, would not be possible unless I was prepared to sacrifice competition for goodness knows how long, as I expect I would be hauled before the Racing Committee of the British Cycling Federation and given a hefty suspension! But, in those days, although there was a growing opposition to South Africa competing against other nations in all kinds of sport, it was some years before that country was banned from international events. Although cycling has filled my life it has not been to the exclusion of everything else: my home and domestic affairs, such as baking and knitting, absorb a great deal of my time, together with my love of opera, to which Eileen Gray introduced me in East Germany years ago. I would not say I was a political person but I was aware of the problems in South Africa and the views taken by many people of that country. However, given the political and sporting climate of the time, I had no compunction about making the trip. I flew out with high anticipation, but before I left a few people took the opportunity to point out what I could expect to see vis-à-vis the black and coloured inhabitants of the country, and that I should 'keep my eyes open and observe'.

I was met at Johannesburg airport by Mr and Mrs Geoghegan who drove me down to their home in Durban: it was a fascinating journey. My hosts were kindness itself, and with the wonderful climate there was a twelve-month calendar of outdoor social events. I seemed to be attending a barbecue almost every night and I envied them being able to plan ahead in the near-certainty that the weather would not let them down. I made sightseeing trips to Cape Town and other places but, while I was enjoying myself tremendously, I had a nagging feeling that I was losing my racing fitness which I had hoped to carry forward from the end of the English season. I was able to go out on my bike during the day, usually alone, but sometimes in the company of John McDonald or Mike Payne, both leading South African track riders. For once in my life I was free of all domestic cares and in a wonderfully warm climate, and I felt that I should be turning this to good use in a cycling sense. Diffidently I suggested that perhaps I should actually appear somewhere on a track and get down to some serious riding, but that move was always being put off while the lavish hospitality continued.

Meanwhile, I was looking about me and one day I saw a group of black men being rounded up and searched in the street by the police. I asked whoever was with me at the time what was going on and was told that there had probably been a theft and that the police always searched the blacks in the immediate vicinity. I thought it repugnant that they should be under suspicion simply because of their proximity to the alleged offence, but was even more appalled by their public humiliation.

I took the opportunity to discuss with people their life-styles and told them of my life in England – they could hardly believe that I was so successful as a sportswoman while doing all my own washing and housework and having a full-time job. Many of the women did go out to work, but it seemed that they did so in order to get out of the house and mix with other people during the day – certainly it was not from any economic necessity. And, of course, they had black servants to take care of the domestic chores.

Eventually I did manage a few five-mile races on the track, riding against juniors in which I acquitted myself well without causing any sensations. As the time approached for me to return to England I managed to convince everybody that it really was time to have a go at the hour record. I travelled to Bloemfontein and spent a day or two trying to put my body in shape for the attempt. The track is situated at several thousand feet above sea level, quite fast and, yes, I think I could have taken the record there if I had been better prepared mentally and was at the peak of fitness. The hour record is a tremendously difficult test of a rider, calling for supreme fitness and the correct approach and preparation. Choosing the correct gear and time of day to 'go' and getting a host of smaller details right is also crucial for a rider. The South Africans were inexperienced when it came to judging the needs for such a record, and I had to rely mainly on my own judgement and past experience. The reason why I failed again at the 'magic' hour is mostly due to the fact that I was not psychologically prepared. Throughout my racing life my mind has worked almost like a computer, preparing my body in advance to make supreme efforts; and the uncertainties of a world championship programme have more than once upset me for that reason. My finely tuned 'clockwork' can cope with being given only a few hours' notice when the overall mechanism is prepared for a championship series spread over several days, but my body protests when there is a late change of timing even of a thirty minutes in the running of a pursuit match. In England I could think several weeks ahead to a road race or time trial, mentally approaching it even while dealing with other races in the meantime and, of course, in a time trial, you have at least a few days' notice of the precise time of day at which you will be calling on your body to make an effort. If I had had the confidence and the will to push my hosts into letting me take the attempt earlier when I was fitter, then everything could have been different, but for whatever reason they chose to run my visit the 'wrong way round' as far as tackling the record was concerned. It was a disappointment, both for myself and the South Africans, but the round of parties continued to the end.

I came home with a set of Zulu ceremonial attire, including a shield, spear and drum, which Mike Payne had generously given to me when I had admired it at his home. It looked incongruous passing through customs alongside racing bikes and wheels! Unfortunately, Charlie was late in meeting me,

My first race. A mid-week '10', summer 1954

1959. My first world championship medal. The pursuit gold at Liège. Ready to start the lap of honour held by my old friend and rival, Milly Robinson

1960. Out on my own and on the way to victory in the world road championship on the Sachsenring

(facing) Congratulations from the late Tom Simpson after winning the world road title in East Germany, 1960

The lap of honour on the Sachsenring

With Charlie after I had signed the 'Golden Book of Cycling'

At the Seelenbinder track, East Berlin, 1960. On my right Jean Dunn and
Karl Barton. On my left Lloyd Binch and Mick Gambrill. Back row: Arthur
Maxfield (Manager), Brian Laughton, Peter Carter, Barry Hoban, Charlie
McCoy and Alan Killick

Early cycling for Denise. After the sidecar I carried her like this for a few years

October, 1960. Attempt on the world hour record at the Vigorelli, Milan

A hot day at the Herne Hill track in 1961

1961. World road race championship in the Isle of Man. Jo Bowers and I leading the field

Deciding the 1961 world road title. I lead Reynders, who won, and Jacobs who came third

World track championships in Milan, 1962. Winning my quarter-final on the way to the title

Leading the field with Lilian Herse of France during the 1962 world championships at Salo, Italy

With Charlie and Denise after winning the world pursuit gold at the Rocourt track, Liège, in 1963. Also in the picture is Tommy Godwin

On the podium at Rocourt with Yvonne Reynders (2nd) and Riabchenko (3rd)

Working in Nim Carline's
rhubarb fields in the mid-sixties

Heerlen, Netherlands. At the
front in the early stages of the
1967 world road race

Crossing the line to win the world title at Heerlen

With the Russian girls Zadorozhnaya and Konkina after the Heerlen victory.
Behind is the British team manager, Charles Messenger

With the *Daily Express*
Sportswoman of the Year
Trophy, 1967

(*above*) World road
championship at Gap, France, in
1972. On the line with Denise

(*facing*) Twenty-four hours
national championship, 1969.
On my way again at dawn after a
brief stop to shed my lights

(*right*) Winning the R.T.T.C.
10-mile national title in 1980

Pursuiting at the Leicester track during a national championship

Nim Carline, Morley C.C. Twenty-four hours champion in 1962-3-5-6-7, 1973; twelve-hour champion 1964, 1968

which was not his fault, as he eventually convinced me but was due to a mix-up in the time the plane was supposed to arrive. But I was feeling a little tetchy anyway with the effects of the journey and also because I had realised that somewhere, somehow, I had lost my money. In my terms the amount was fairly considerable as, apart from spending a little on a few presents, I was bringing back most of what I had taken with me. But, a few days later, my cash was returned from South Africa – Mr and Mrs Geoghegan's maid had found it in my bedroom.

The 1966 season had hardly begun when the British Cycling Federation announced that anyone taking part in an event of more than fifty miles during the month before the world championships in West Germany would not be considered for selection for the road race. As the 100-mile time-trial championship fell within that category, they were saying in effect that I could not defend my 100-mile title if I wanted to ride for Great Britain. It seemed to me that this decision was a result of some more 'in-fighting' between the B.C.F. and the Road Time Trials Council who controlled that side of the sport, and that I was to be sacrificed along the way. It could be argued that the B.C.F. would not want to select me for the road race anyway but, frankly, there did not seem to be anyone better around. I decided that I would defend my 100-mile title when the time came, and the B.C.F. could please itself what it did.

My first ride of note came in May, in the Notts. and Derby Clarion '30'. I broke Jo Bowers' record by 2 minutes 49 seconds, with a time of 1–13–12, although still some way below my peak form. Into June and I took the W.C.R.A. road championship over thirty-five miles, nine seconds clear of Ann Horswell, and later in the month successfully defended the Association's pursuit title at Salford Park, in the Midlands. The same weekend also I retained my 25-mile championship in a record for the event of 59–54 on a stiff course in Worcestershire.

A few weeks later I retained both my 50-mile and road championships on the same weekend, the first in Lincolnshire in a time of 2–4–49, beating Ann Horswell by 5 minutes 13 seconds, and the second in Leicestershire, covering the thirty-four miles 4 minutes 25 seconds faster than the late Chris Goodfellow of the Beacon R.C.C. A week later Nim Carline won his fourth national 24-hour title with a staggering distance of 496.43 miles, while I retained my national 3,000 metres title at Liverpool, so there was cause for celebration in the Morley camp. By August the question of whether I could defend my 100-mile title *and* ride in the world road race championship had been resolved – I could ride in both.

The 100-mile championship was held on the famous Bath Road course, and once again I served up one of my outstanding performances on southern roads. I won with a time of 4–8–22 to beat my own competition record by 4 minutes 32 seconds, and June Pitchford by nearly twenty minutes. Incredibly,

I had also bettered the time of Keith Stacey, the reigning Best All-rounder who had won the men's title two weeks earlier, by thirty-eight seconds. This feat had the usual amount of modest space in the sports pages but I don't think the press really grasped its significance. To ride a hundred miles on a bike isn't exactly easy; to go 'eyeballs out' for the distance is even harder; for a man to ride it in less than 4 hours 10 minutes was remarkable, particularly back in 1966; for me to have accomplished it in the time I did was phenomenal. I wonder what the scribes would have made of an athletics or swimming girl winning a national title, at any distance, in a time better than the men's championship time. The reader can ponder that for himself.

Now every spare moment was devoted to training, and I had my mind focussed on the forthcoming world championships in Germany – I had to show the rest of the world that my international career was not yet finished after the debacle of Spain the previous year. Before travelling to Frankfurt I captured the 15-mile record in Worcestershire in 34–56, so that I now held all the competition records except the very specialist long-distance 24-hour.

The road race came before the track series in West Germany, a situation which I was never happy about, much preferring to ride the pursuit first and, again, it was a victory for Yvonne Reynders with me in fifth place. The distance was a ridiculously short forty-six kilometres although, to be fair, it was a tough circuit on the Nurburgring. I thought I would try to break the field wide open from the start. Only Elsy Jacobs of Luxembourg, Pouronen of Russia and Keetie Hage of Holland came with me and after a lap we were still together, with me making the pace and the other three glued to my wheel. Back in the bunch Reynders, sensing danger because we were apparently going to stay away, performed one of her famous 'chases'. Yvonne really could ride, and she left the field to join our leading group. I think that she and I together would have been capable of dropping the others, leaving the destination of the gold to be decided between us at the finish. Instead, she merely dropped in behind and I continued to tow them. Several times I turned round and urged Reynders and the others to come to the front and 'do a turn'. There were no takers, seemingly they were quite content to sit on my wheel and let me set the pace. My desperate attempts to shake them came to nothing, they were stuck to my wheel like leeches. At all costs they were not going to let me escape, preferring a sprint finish with nearly the whole field if necessary. I knew then that I was not going to win a road medal that year, for in a massed sprint I would only finish in the middle of the bunch and, in a sprint with my four 'leeches', I was likely to finish fifth. I decided it was better to finish fifth and and carried on towing the others. Even on the two-mile hill which we climbed five times, there they were, locked on – and I thought it a shame that riders of the class of Reynders and Pouronen should act in this way. I had a minor disaster when my chain unshipped, but I was quickly underway again, the unadventurous others still hanging on. I finished fifth in the same time as the winner, Reynders. For the record Hage was second and Pouronen third and Jacobs fourth. The record books show in their usual cold fashion where the road medals went that year, but if I was Reynders or Pouronen I would not feel particularly proud of my medal, though I suppose they were paying me a compliment, riding that way. I was surrounded by journalists of all nationalities after the race, all of them sympathetic – even the Belgians – and I had to take what comfort I could in being the 'moral winner'.

That is why I like the pursuit: you can suffer from bad luck of one sort or another but so far as the actual racing is concerned you have to be good to win, and better than your opponents. So, I put the road race to the back of my mind and concentrated on the pursuiting at the Frankfurt track.

Again the moguls of the Union Cycliste Internationale seemed determined to spike things in their usual clod-hopping fashion when they paired Reynders and me in the qualifying time-trial round. There was little doubt that we would both qualify on time for the next, match-racing, round but it was unsettling for both of us and unfair to the spectators to see two possible finalists riding against each other on the track at this stage. The next infuriating upset was to discover that I had to ride twice on the first evening at seven o'clock and again at nine. I have previously explained how I set my mind to a time when I am going to call on my body to make an all-out effort and now, with this bombshell, all my mental rhythm was destroyed. Two things made me even madder. One was that all the teams except the British knew about this arrangement beforehand, and the other was that it was six o'clock when I was told that I would be racing in less than an hour and I had been about to start on a steak and salad in the belief that I had at least three hours to digest it. This kind of thing never happened when Eileen Gray managed the women's team. She would sometimes sit around half the night while U.C.I. brass made up their minds about programme timing, and even then insist that they put it in writing before she went off to catch a few hours' sleep.

I went on the track showing nothing of how I felt, but seething inside – Charlie had meanwhile scooped my dinner into a plastic bag for me to have a bite during the evening – and the sight of Reynders on her bike across the track did nothing to assuage me! I had a score to settle with dear Yvonne, and meant to show her who was boss right at the start. The track-lights which flash as the riders cross their finishing line winked simultaneously for a few half-laps, then I drew ahead and did not let her off the hook. My time was 4–8.03 to Reynders' 4–9.24, and I retired to the trackside in a better frame of mind and with some appetite for cold steak. Aino Pouronen was the third-fastest qualifier with 4–12.08 and June Pitchford just scraped into the next round with 4–18.29. Later in the evening I came against Audrey McElmury of the U.S.A. and eliminated her with a 4–7.15, leaving me with high hopes that this year I was again going to win a medal of some sort.

The air was cool after rain earlier in the day by the time I came against Pouronen in a late-afternoon semi-final. I did not feel comfortable against the Russian girl and, although I beat her easily enough with 4–14.36 against her 4–22.37, it was a ride without rhythm and I had to work hard to accomplish it. The final was due later in the evening. It is a great physical strain to ride two pursuits within a few hours of each other, the pursuit being an event in which even one ride seems to drain you. Hence, supreme fitness and a body with a fast recovery rate are essential. Can you imagine an Olympic runner going at peak effort in the semi-final and then running the final about four hours later? It is even worse for cycling pursuiters and sprinters. There's no easing-off, to finish comfortably in the first five to qualify. You have to ride your heart out to win and with a time that will give you an 'easier' draw in the next round.

In the other 'semi' Reynders beat Hannelore Mattig of East Germany, 4–11.64 against 4–17.91, so while I was certain of at least the silver I knew that yet again it was Reynders who stood between me and victory. Even at this late stage our management did not seem certain when the final would take place, 'thinking' it would be at eight o'clock. But I had started to think for myself and had decided that, since a German television sports programme which would presumably want to screen the finals was coming on at nine, I would be racing shortly after that time, following on the third place ride-off between Mattig and Pouronen. I was correct.

The viewers of Europe had a feast of pursuiting that night for, in a great match, Mattig scraped home against the Russian, 4–14.76 against 4–14.9, and there was a feeling of expectancy among the crowd as Reynders and I took our places. The tension was almost unbearable, but I think I managed to hide my feelings despite shivering in the cold night air. Charlie, who as usual had made the journey to the championships, gave me a word of encouragement. He was there, unofficially as always, having tuned up my bike and wearing the 'lucky' jacket which, by now, was beginning to look a bit decrepit. Without Charlie being close at hand I could rarely bring out my best on these occasions.

Having already seen one exciting contest, the spectators at the track and the millions watching television could hardly have hoped to see another one as close, but that is the way it went – a final to end all finals. My only regret is that it did not appear on British television, but of course I was not swimming, running, jumping, playing with a ball or riding a horse, so I could hardly expect it.

'*Mesdames, les coureurs – attention!*' The start, the lunge of the first pedal thrust, out of the saddle round the first banking, settling down once the revs were optimum, and we were matching each other with the track-lights flashing together at each half-lap. I came round each banking of the track anxiously watching the lights, pounding away to the half-lap position as though my life depended on it, desperate to reach the point before Reynders' light flashed. I had started faster than usual. With the Belgian I knew there would be no coming back at her. I had to match this formidable opponent pedal stroke for pedal stroke. We had been adversaries for so long, reigning the world of women's cycling, and now we were like two old pugilists who would fight until one dropped of exhaustion. She had beaten me in the road race but now there were just the two of us, and there was no wheel for her to follow. I was going to impose my will as the best unpaced rider in the world. The cold night air caught at my lungs as I summoned all my strength to the combat. 'Don't lose your rhythm,' I anxiously told myself. 'Keep pedalling, hold it straight, follow the line, it's just as hard for her.'

The British supporters were cheering, urging me on and, remembering that the final was on television, national pride helped me to keep up the pace. It was relentless, Reynders was not giving an inch, but neither was I as we zipped round, the lights flashing together, together, together. How many more laps? I had lost count. I felt that I was wobbling, yet my eyes told me the front wheel was holding its line. My eyes were misting, I felt my strength was ebbing, yet my legs were still pumping rhythmically as though they belonged to somebody else. The bell signalling the last lap sounded harsh, like an alarm clock waking me from a dream, and I forced the last gramme of effort from my body. Round the banking into the straight and a sideways glance across the track showed me Reynders was going to equal me at the last half-lap. But I sensed she was 'cracking' – in the brief glimpse I had, her shoulders were heaving. I could do it – I could win! I hurled myself over the final metres, clipping the inside of the track as much as I dared; to fall now would be tragic. There was one loud explosion as the line officials fired their pistols seemingly in the same instant, and I was hanging over the bars, letting the bike 'run down', carrying me of its own volition on a winding-down lap. As I came into the trackside Charlie was running toward me. 'Have I won, have I won?' I shrieked hoarsely, and then he was at my side grabbing me and the bike. The naked eye could not separate us at the end, only electronics could split the blink of an eye into minute fractions of a second. The times: Burton 4–10.47 – Reynders 4–10.79. I was again the world champion by 0.32 of a second! The British contingent was ecstatic, Charlie had tears in his eyes. I could hardly stand for a few minutes and the cold air seemed to have vanished as the sweat poured from my body, the applause round the velodrome gradually dying to an excited buzz. Then came the podium, the flowers, 'God Save the Queen,' –

and I had notched up another victory for Morley and Great Britain.

I returned from West Germany and it was straight back into domestic competition. Again, the contrast of the crowds and the excitement with the lonely pounding on an English road making the tubulars hum on a Sunday morning when others are still abed. Came the Tees-side R.C. 50-mile and I rode my best of the year at the distance in 2-1-14, beating June Pitchford by over nine minutes. More importantly, only Ian White of the Clifton had done a better time in the corresponding men's race, and he was one of the country's leading men at the distance. Then I made an attempt on my W.R.R.A. 25-mile record, and on a Saturday morning clipped sixty-two seconds from it in recording 59-32. Next it was the Northampton and District '25' where I won the ladies' event with 58-56, my second fastest time of the year, and also bettered the time of the winner of the men's race by thirty-six seconds. The season drew to a close with my being the British Best All-rounder champion again with an average of 24.812 m.p.h., but it was not to be quite the end of *my* season for, a few weeks later, I was again invited to Ghent to ride on the indoor track against Reynders, and I feverishly resumed training.

The match was an omnium, which is a series of different races in which the best overall performance determines the winner. Usually omniums are contested by a number of riders, but this was to be a match between Reynders and me, the events consisting of a sprint, a pursuit and a flying 500 metres. I expected Reynders to win the first and third events, with the odds also slightly in her favour in the pursuit where I thought the small indoor track would suit her better than me. As I thought, Yvonne won the sprint, but I made her try – I was not giving anything away. In the pursuit she made the fast start that I anticipated, being three lengths to the good after five of the eighteen laps while I was still settling. I had to honour my rainbow jersey in front of this Belgian crowd and show them that I was a better pursuiter than Reynders, I buckled down to my work and it seemed as if I was rejuvenated with the Frankfurt form coming back into my legs. In no time at all I had drawn level and was moving into an increasing lead when Reynders punctured. Each of us should have restarted at the point where we had been when the puncture occurred but, instead of the twenty lengths or so lead I had, the officials had somehow reduced it to about half that. There were only five laps remaining, and I knew there would be a Reynders onslaught to pull back her deficit, which she was capable of with her fast start. Within two laps she was almost back on level terms, the crowd was shrieking, but I was getting back into my stride and put on the pressure and that was the end of Yvonne. Score 1-1, with the decider to come – a 500 metre flying-start time trial. Reynders went first with a time of 35.9 seconds, a very good time and one I did not expect to beat. I gave it everything – the crowd were roaring wildly and the atmosphere was inspiring, with even British supporters managing to make themselves heard. My time was 35.8, and I rode my lap of honour wearing my world's champion jersey with pride as the band played our national anthem. Reynders was a great rider, but I had beaten her on her 'own midden' on terms which favoured her, and left no doubt in Belgium who was the 'queen'.

At this time Britain was not showing very well in the sporting arena generally, and one would expect that any success abroad would have merited attention but, as usual, my exploits and those of other cyclists were played down. Our own magazine reported: 'To beat the world is already great, to beat a deadly rival in such convincing fashion on her own ground in the middle of winter gives us cause for rejoicing, and frankly, we are glad that *Cycling* was there to see it.'

The Best All-rounder dinner and prize presentation was held at the Rainbow Room in London and it was a great night for West Yorkshire for, apart from what I had achieved, Arthur Metcalfe of the Leeds St Christopher club had won the men's B.A.R. and, of course, there was Nim's title at the 24-hour distance.

At the beginning of 1967 I was presented with a gold medal by the B.C.F. Originally it had been intended to have it presented at our club dinner, but there was a feeling that the occasion should be brought to a wider public, and so it came about that I had the medal presented to me on the 'Look North' television programme from Manchester.

In April I rode in the W.C.R.A. road race handicap over twenty-three miles at Chobham in Surrey, giving eight minutes start to some and four minutes to the rest and winning with a margin of forty-seven seconds over the second-placed rider. At this time I was busy working for Nim, humping rhubarb roots weighing up to a quarter-hundredweight for eight hours a day, but had not yet moved into full training. I rode in the Norlond Combine 10-mile and smashed my record with a time of 23–5, beating Margaret Allen (née Larkin) by 1 minute 57 seconds. It was a cool but sunny morning, and I was delighted with my performance, still being short of training miles. Margaret by this time was riding for the Morley club, so we won the team award as well. The frame I was using then was handbuilt and supplied by Ron Kitching, famous as a supplier of cyclists' needs from his Harrogate establishment.

I was 'flying' again and at the end of the month captured the course and event record in the Huddersfield Star Wheelers 15-mile held near York: I won with 36–1, Margaret Allen was second and Pauline Dobson (née Hunter) was fifth. Between us we set a new team record for the distance of 1–58–1, bringing it under two hours for the first time. Again I was caught up in the full swing of riding every week-end, often in two events, and usually in the south or the Midlands. I tried a new course at Basildon in the Havering C.C. 25-mile, winning by over a minute. If I had been riding in the men's race I would have been equal seventh in a very 'hot' field of top men at this distance. The effect of the Spanish illness seemed at last to have worn off, and my back trouble was not too bad; by this time I had learned to live with it.

Two days after my thirtieth birthday I knocked twenty-nine seconds from my own 30-mile record, winning the *Notts and Derby Clarion* promotion with 1–12–43, but the chance of a new team record went when Margaret fell heavily at a roundabout. I stopped when I came across her to see if there was anything I could do to help, but Margaret sent me on my way, although she was hurt badly enough to require hospital treatment. It was a foul day, windy and wet, so my ride was worth something.

After winning the Rutland C.C. '25' and the Newark Castle '25' I was looking forward to the national championship, hoping for a good morning with the weather. It was held in North Nottinghamshire, and I won it for the ninth time with 58–15, a new championship record.

I won a road race in Wales, and then set an event record in winning my own club's 25-mile in 58–35 with Margaret and Pauline completing the winning team.

Next it was off to the Isle of Man for my annual trip where I won the '25' and the '10' with an event record, and I looked forward eagerly to the Nunbrook Wheelers 50-mile in Yorkshire feeling confident that given a decent morning I could break my own record. Starting shortly after 6 a.m. I won with exactly 1–56–0, the first ride by a woman inside two hours and an improvement by more than five minutes. I was over the moon with this effort; to be inside the two hours even by a few seconds would have been something – but a full four-minute margin seemed colossal. It was a good day for racing and I took full advantage of it, as did Ann Horswell, who made the long journey from Plymouth to record 2–1–59. To round off the day Margaret and Pauline helped me to a new team record, an improvement of more than ten minutes. It was a great week-end for Morley because Nim Carline had retained his 24-hour title in the south of England with a distance of 480.27 miles.

I knew now that I had it in me to lower my other records before the season was finished. The following week I travelled to the Midlands to ride the Beacon Roads C.C. 10-mile which had a strong team of Dutch girls entered, winning with a time that knocked twenty-two seconds from my previous record. Next it was the '50' championship with 1–59–27, a new championship record in my ninth title win over the distance.

Everything was going well on the bike, but coping with the planning was still a headache. I was also receiving an increasing number of letters which I tried to answer, while fitting in my training, work and domestic chores.

At the Newcastle-under-Lyme track I defended my 3,000 metres pursuit title, winning the final against ʼJune Pitchford with 4-10.4, the fastest in competition in this country at the time and a good ride on a not very fast track. For good measure, the same afternoon I won the handicap sprint from Barbara Mapplebeck, the international sprinter, who gave me twenty-eight yards start, and was second to her in the scratch sprint.

It was at this time that Tom Simpson met his death while riding in the Tour de France and, like all club cyclists in this country, I mourned. Tom had been at the track at Ghent during the previous winter when I rode against Reynders, taking part in the six-day race. It was the way he tackled his cycling and indeed life itself – 'give everything you've got all the time and every time' – which endeared him to me because that is the way I have approached my life and, by extension, my sport. He had kissed me jubilantly after my success, as pleased, I think, as I was myself. Tom never forgot that he was British, even though he was domiciled in Belgium and was so popular there that they regarded him as one of their own. There was even a thriving Tom Simpson fan club. I doubt if there has ever been a more popular 'Anglo' in that country.

Following his death, writers who had paid scant attention in the past to the sport and to Tom's prowess became instant experts and dragged cycling through the mud. The sport had more media coverage than ever before in this country. I do not seek to re-open old wounds, but the circumstances of Tom's death were, on the whole, glossed over: the altitude of 6,000 ft (remember the fuss about the Olympic Games being held in Mexico?), the temperature of 100° in the shade (only there was no shade on the extinct volcano that is Mont Ventoux) and Tom's reckless courage which led him past the point of endurance.

An article by the then editor of *Cycling*, Alan Gayfer, headed *What shall we do without him?* stated:

. . . One is drawn to compare him with men like Lawrence of Arabia, who became more Arabian than the Arabs, the better to dominate them and understand them, yet remembered all the time his English upbringing . . . Because in a sense this is what Tom Simpson had done for us; he had opened a whole new world of cycling to the insular British. He had done this by forcing the Continent to accept his attacking view of cycling, by forcing us here at home to recognise that his views were right and we were wrong.

Tom's last known words were 'put me back on my bike'. He could have no finer epitaph than that.

By this time I was as fit as I had ever been and was, somehow, putting in 400

miles a week in training, and I vowed that more of my records would come
down with a bump. The first opportunity came in July on the Southend Road
in the Becontree Wheelers ladies '25'. I knocked 1 minute 55 seconds off my
previous best with a time of 56–7 on a calm but humid morning which made
the going seem hard all the way. I began to look forward to a fifty-five minute
ride. Staying in Essex I rode the British Road Race championship the
following day and won by nearly six minutes over Barbara Mapplebeck.

I next had my sights on the 100-mile championship in August. I thought it
was possible to ride the distance in less than four hours, and the
championship, held on the Fosse Way course, seemed a good time to do it
considering the way I was riding. Unfortunately it was not the best of days, a
strong headwind in the earlier part of the course putting me behind schedule,
although I picked up in the latter stages. The ride of less than four hours
which most people considered impossible for a woman was not to be – not this
time, anyway. But my time was not very far from it: 4–4–50. It was about
three and a half minutes faster than my previous best and beat the winner of
the men's race by nearly four minutes – only three men had gone faster at that
point in the season. Margaret Allen, Pauline Dobson and I won the team race
for Morley.

I began to think of the forthcoming world championships, this year to be
held in Holland. I knew my form was good, but at thirty years of age I
wondered if the distance of 3,000 metres on the track was the type of event
where I could begin to slip back. The great stamina and strength I had built
up over the years was admirably suited to time trialling, particularly over the
longer distances, but did I have the zip to take on the world at something
around four minutes?

From among its 10,000 racing girls, the mighty U.S.S.R., which had
already stated 'Beryl can't go on forever', produced two marvellous pursuiters
from the top of their tree of specialised training with a view to breaking the
Burton/Reynders monopoly. Russia had searched far and wide to find girls
who could put a stop to Yvonne and me, and they came up this year with Raisa
Obodowskaya and Tamara Garkushina. Raisa, aged nineteen, came from
Kharkov in the Ukraine, and Tamara, twenty-one, from Tula. The latter was
described as being a builder's labourer, and from the look of her it did not
surprise me, for she had a thick body with massive shoulders and muscles that
any man would have been proud of. Like most of the Russian girls I have met,
she could smile occasionally when she thought she had to. Raisa, though, was
different from all the others. She was a beautiful and naturally happy girl,
always smiling and bubbling over and radiating a wonderful charm.

From the outset, when the qualifying round was ridden, everybody knew
what they were up against. Obodowskaya recorded 4–5.10 and Garkushina

4–5.86, superb times on the slowish Amsterdam track. I was third at this stage with 4–10.83 and Hannelore Mattig of East Germany fourth with 4–14.8 and Reynders, seemingly lacking the fire of old, fifth with 4–17.21. June Pitchford just made it to the next round with 4–20.68.

When the quarter-finals arrived Obodowskaya rode a 4–9.86 and Garkushina 4–6.45, so they were obviously retaining their form. I knocked out Jacky Barbadette of France, 4–10.59 to 4–19.42, and the other quarter went to Reynders in a thrilling match against Mattig, 4–14.42 to 4–14.52. In the 'semis' I was against Obodowskaya, seeded on our times in the previous round and, somehow, I could not rise to the occasion, the Russian girl beating me by 4–7.68 to 4–14.34. I was disappointed with the result but was more upset at my losing margin. Garkushina had the expected victory in the other 'semi' against Reynders, 4–7.11 against 4–20.24, so the final was between the two Russian wonder girls, while I was left to fight against my old adversary Reynders for the bronze medal. It was the beginning of a new era in world pursuiting, which Garkushina and Obodowskaya dominated for several years.

There is a twinge of sadness in recalling my match against Reynders for third place because, although the thousands watching may well have thought our international careers were at an end and that it was fitting we should ride against each other to take a minor placing, I was not thinking along those lines myself. However, maybe Yvonne was, for this ride proved to be her swansong as a world 3,000-metre rider. For the record I took the bronze with a time of 4–8.93, ironically my fastest of the competition, which underlined the fact that I had suffered a reversal of form in the ride against Obodowskaya. Raisa was only fractionally faster in going down to her compatriot in the final, a 4–8.19 against another scorching time by Garkushina of 4–5.25.

My sights were now set on the road race to be held over thirty-three miles at Heerlen, taking in the Ubachsberg Hill and with twelve nations represented in the field of forty-three. I tried to pick myself up psychologically after 'only' taking the bronze in the pursuit and in this I was aided by our masseur Eddie Soens and the British team manager, Charles Messenger. Charles and I have disagreed with each other about some things over the years, but he was a good manager who knew his job, and he had worked tremendously hard throughout the year. For his pains he was sacked without explanation by the B.C.F. after the world championships, much to the dismay of all the riders who had represented our country in Holland.

Looking at the entry I noticed Russian names that were new to world cycling, and I wondered if they had produced some more 'secret weapons' like Obodowskaya and Garkushina. Determined to find out their strength I decided to make an attack fairly early if nobody else had already tried, in which case I would go with them. After five miles the field was still together, the pace fairly comfortable, and I thought it time to 'test the water' and sound out the opposition. I was near the front and I turned on the power, shot away and was quickly clear. The Russian, Zadorozhnaya, was the only other rider to latch on to me. Steadily we pulled away, the Russian desperately hanging on to my wheel. On to the Ubachsberg for the second time. I did not lower my gear but hammered away, letting the disappointment of the track find its way out through my legs. Zadorozhnaya had a despairing look as I glanced back at her and went on my way, over the brow of the hill and into 104-inch top gear, keeping up the revs and swooping down; the Russian was fighting hard, and the time I gained on her was fractional each mile. She was good, because she, too, was alone yet drawing away from the rest of the field, and if there had been any weakening on my part she would have been onto me. It was reminiscent of Leipzig seven years earlier, alone against the rest of the world. Could I, the oldest in the race, really solo away from the rest? Was there a counter-attack coming from behind? Just how far ahead was I now? Each lap was a challenge, with a fight to have the Ubachsberg unroll under my wheels one more time, and the comforting thought that the others still had it to come. Into the last lap, and a glance over my shoulder. No-one in sight. I felt fine. More effort – I could do it, keep going. A few miles from the finish and a feeling of cramp. Spare me that! It was O.K., everything was smooth, the finish . . . and I was again the world road champion after 1 hour 26 minutes 30 seconds, most of it riding alone with the cream of the world trailing behind. Zadorozhnaya proved her worth in taking a meritorious silver medal. She was 1 minute 47 seconds behind me so I had not dropped her by too much, but the third-placed girl, Konkina, was 5 minutes 47 seconds behind that. Of the five riders behind me four were Russian, only Smits of Belgium getting among them for fifth place. The red jerseys had hoped for a one-two-three, but Yorkshire had put a blight on their plan and I stood proudly on the podium, wearing my new black tracksuit with a large white rose on the front. 'This was like one of Fausto Coppi's greatest victories' was the opinion of the foreign journalists, and there could have been no higher praise for the oldest-ever world champion. My tally of world medals was now seven gold, three silver and one bronze – not a bad haul, I thought, from my beginnings as a sickly schoolgirl. The rose on my track suit should really have wilted. The *Yorkshire Post* gave two inches of space to my victory and the *Yorkshire Evening Post* one inch, but to be fair to the latter they managed a photograph as well.

It was a great week-end for Britain at Heerlen because Graham Webb also won the men's amateur road race, making a sensational double. So, with Hugh Porter taking a silver at Amsterdam in the professional pursuit it was a good 'worlds' for us.

At Nottingham I successfully defended my W.C.R.A. pursuit title, beating

June Pitchford in the final. For the fun of it I had entered the national sprint championship as well, and took the silver medal, which could hardly have been expected. I made it through to the final against Barbara Mapplebeck, another West Yorkshire girl and the best sprinter we had at that time.

At this time Alan Gayfer, editor of *Cycling*, summed up my feelings exactly in an article reviewing the recently completed world championships. He wrote:

> The techniques of training came in for much discussion, with Beryl Burton getting very annoyed over criticism of her training techniques for having 'only' got a bronze medal, when she was going to be required to go on to win if possible – and thank Heaven it was – a gold medal on the road. The least one can say is that if those responsible, whether managers or selectors or committeemen, are going to expect Mrs Burton to carry on taking the whole weight of women's racing on her shoulders, literally one against 10,000 in this case, then they could have the grace to let her get on with the job in her own way. She has, after all, been at international racing longer than most.

I was criticised for riding too many time trials when I should have been 'training' for the world pursuit. Where and against whom? There wasn't (and still isn't) a track in West Yorkshire where I could train. As it was I rode when I could at Fallowfield, Herne Hill, Welwyn, Nottingham and other places. If the 'knockers' themselves had been willing to provide funds I would have been quite happy to spend some time abroad each season having more international competition. As it was, my cycling was costing our family much, much more than an ordinary household would normally allocate to sport and recreation. It was like having two jobs, really. My paid employment had to finance the unpaid cycling, while the domestic routine, travelling and training had to be fitted in somehow as well. It could be said, of course, that I did not *have* to do it; I could have curtailed my competitive cycling to local events, or even given it up altogether. That's quite true, and I can plead only that the love of racing on a bike was deeply ingrained, and that I was prepared, along with Charlie, to make personal sacrifices to that end, particularly if along the way I could win medals for my country. All I expected in return was that people within the sport should have a little understanding of the problems. I was not then, and never have been, one of those fortunate 'amateurs' who could devote all their time and energy to sport and, in the case of some sports, make a not inconsiderable amount of money along the way.

I managed all the usual household chores, occasionally while listening to opera on the record player, or 'talk' programmes on the radio, but more usually planning in my mind the route I would take when I went out training and thinking ahead to the week-end race. Sometimes I would come home from work and after a meal do some housework before going out training, while Charlie would perhaps also manage some jobs about the house, though more probably he would be fixing the bikes for the week-end, or helping a clubmate put something right on theirs. Television played no part in our lives. We just did not have the time to sit passively watching a screen, and I am one of those people who have always to be engaged in some activity. I just cannot sit still, unless it's for interesting conversation or something that requires sitting down. On journeys to races I fill in the time knitting. Just sitting in the car for several hours doing nothing would be a complete waste of time for me, and anyway knitting always helped me to relax.

We remain to this day one of the minority of households without a television. Nothing has changed. I still work most of the year outdoors, and fit in the training and housework, and it leaves me no time for the small screen. I keep abreast of what is happening in the world from the radio while I am engaged with something else. This outlook has probably helped me when I have been immobilised with injuries. I had a driving need to be back on my feet as quickly as possible!

Feeling a little tired after the racing in Holland I rode the following week-end in the Yorkshire Century 100-mile. The men's race that morning was of great interest because of the state of the table in the Best All-rounder competition. York's Clifton C.C. were in the unprecedented position of having three men in the lead – Pete Smith, John Watson and Roy Cromack – with Mike McNamara of the South Yorkshire club, Rockingham C.C., in fourth place. Only Watson of the Clifton boys was riding that morning, and McNamara had a good chance of improving his position if he could better his previous '100' time. Mike won in 3–58–45, a splendid performance and a three-minute improvement approximately, with Watson in third place with 4–3–26. John also improved which gave us the prospect of an exciting finish to the season-long competition. Mike was still in with a chance if he could improve his 12-hour distance, but it would have to be a big improvement to somewhere about the record of 271.8 miles which had stood for nine years. He would get his last chance the following week-end in the Otley C.C. 12-hour.

I recount this situation among the men because it has a strong bearing on what I shall be describing in my next chapter, but meanwhile I can recall that I won the women's race that morning with a time of 4–10–56, beating Ann Horswell by 7 minutes 8 seconds. It was a difficult day with a headwind over part of the course, more particularly in the last twenty-five miles, but I was described as having an 'off day'. If I had been riding among the men whose entry contained many of the best in the country, I would have finished equal seventh! I had become a victim of my own success, and the fact that I had just returned from a gruelling world championships counted for nothing.

7-42 a.m. on Sunday, 17th September, 1967. The beginning for me of the Otley C.C. 12-hour on course V181. It was a gloomy morning with a fine drizzle which was to last another four hours. A very strong men's field of ninety-nine had already been despatched, all hoping to improve their standing in the British Best All-rounder competition, and one of them, Mike McNamara, seeking not only victory, but a record mileage which could place him on top of that competition. A few girls were to follow in their own race, and I led them off, two minutes after Mike had started. I had set my sights on beating my eight-year-old women's record of 250.37 miles, a distance which had staggered the cyling world at the time, and one which I doubt anyone thought could be bettered.

However, I was feeling very fit, with a successful world championships behind me, and was already certain of the Women's B.A.R. title, so I had nothing to lose in making an all-out effort. As the morning progressed I was riding easily, keeping up a good speed, and was well over my target of a few miles over 250. The drizzle continued but it was not cold and, fortunately, there was little wind. I began to slide through the field, catching first one man then another, each one in my sights acting as a spur to greater endeavour. Through to the outskirts of York, on to Tadcaster, back to York, the relentless quest went on. I began to be puzzled by the cries from knots of clubmen gathered round the course. They were shouting something which seemed to include the name of 'Mac'. 'They must mean Mike McNamara,' I thought, 'but what does that mean? He must be well in front of me.' I knew I was on to a 'ride' and that if I could keep going I stood a chance of setting new figures for the 12-hour by a woman. I redoubled my efforts. My wheels hummed, eventually the drizzle stopped and a pale watery sun struggled through the clouds. Over to Wetherby and then north to Northallerton. It was well into the afternoon and the weather was holding. I passed the 200-mile point in a time of 8–33–37 to learn that, incredibly, I was a few seconds 'up' on Mike. 'It can't last,' I thought. 'I know I'm moving well, but surely he'll pull away in the last few hours.'

A long-distance event such as this is a tremendous strain on the body. You are not only putting a great deal of physical effort into riding, but the body is eating up energy so, fairly frequently, you need to 'take aboard' food and drink handed up to you by your helpers, in my case Charlie and Eddie Whiteley. It has to be sustenance which can be easily digested, of high calorific value, and which is tempting to the rider and easily consumed. In short, it proves to be quite an expensive day's eating!

On to the finishing circuit which was reached after 206 miles, and I realised that I was doing a 'dream ride', and that barring accidents I could smash my own record and set a new standard in women's long-distance racing. My back was holding, my legs felt good and only a slight churning in my stomach caused, no doubt, by the high intake of mixed foods caused me any concern.

For nearly nine hours 'Mac' and I had been slogging away. I had passed all the other men. Somewhere, out on the road in front of me, he was there, just out of sight, doing the ride of his life, bent on achieving a colossal mileage. Crowds of club-folk were gathered around the finishing circuit, cheering and shouting encouragement. Two minutes had separated us at the start, and for all these hours I had been nibbling away at that 120 seconds. Could the impossible happen, that a woman would beat all the men in a 12-hour? I redoubled my efforts knowing that 'Mac' was riding as he never had before, chasing the competition record and willing himself to that B.A.R. title. I could hardly believe that I was matching him; an impossible dream could come true. The finishing circuit was over 15.87 miles and I was forty-two seconds faster than Mike the first time round. Finally I had to nip over a hedge to answer a natural call and, in case the reader is wondering about such things, that is the way it has to be. Back on the bike, and hammering away again. "Mac' must beat me,' I thought, but to finish second was going to be something amongst all those men in such a contest, and I knew that a new women's record was 'on'. I sucked a Rennie to help my stomach, the legs and breathing fine, back and shoulders also.

On to the second circuit, the miles adding up and time slipping by when, twang! I heard a spoke break in my rear wheel. Anxiously I rode on, praying that the finely tuned wheel would not become sufficiently 'out of true' to start rubbing on the brake blocks before I picked Charlie up somewhere ahead at the roadside. The wheel held. Out with a spare. It slipped into the frame and the gear meshed into place with the minimum of delay and I was on my way again. For all those hours 'Mac' and I had battled across Yorkshire and slowly I had brought him back to me – a duel if ever there was one. I knew now that I had a chance of beating him and, according to my mileage at that point, it would be the record to break all records. Every second became vital. Somewhere ahead the Rockingham rider, realising the situation, must be striving to pull away, even if only by a few precious yards.

Unbelievably, or so it would have seemed more than eleven hours earlier, the Rockingham colours were in sight on the road ahead. I redoubled my effort yet again, surprised at how good I was still feeling. In theory, I should have been at least ten miles behind him, but there he was, giving his last ounce of effort to the final miles. He knew that he required something over 270 miles, and he was succeeding, only there I was coming up on him! I drew inexorably closer, the wheels humming along the country lane, just two riders bent on great athletic endeavour. No cheering crowds at this point, no excited television reporters, the occupants of the odd car that passed unaware of the drama. I came to within a few yards of him and then I froze, the urge in my legs to go faster and faster vanished as though with the click of a switch. Goose pimples broke out all over me, and for some seconds I just stared at his heaving shoulders, the sweat-stained racing jersey. I could hardly accept that after all those hours and miles I had finally caught up with one of the country's great riders, who himself was pulling out a record ride. 'I'll have to pass him,' I thought. 'Poor 'Mac', it doesn't seem fair.' I drew alongside, both of us still striving, every yard of ground being greedily covered as the minutes ticked by to the end of the twelve hours. Then came the moment which has now passed into cycling legend.

'Mac' raised his head slightly and looked at me. Goodness knows what was going on in his mind, but I thought some gesture was required on my part. I was carrying a bag of liquorice allsorts in the pocket of my jersey, and on impulse I groped into the bag and pulled one out. I can still remember that it was one of those swiss-roll shaped ones, white with a coating of black liquorice. 'Liquorice allsort, 'Mac'?' I shouted, and held it toward him. He gave a wan smile. 'Ta, love', he said, popping the sweet into his mouth. I put my head down and drew away. There I was, first on the road, ninety-nine men behind me, not knowing whether to feel elated or sorrowful. 'Mac' was doing a sensational ride but his glory, richly deserved, was going to be overshadowed by a woman! Into lap three of the finishing circuit, and the records show that I pulled away by another fifty-seven seconds, and then into the fourth, where 'Mac' pulled back a few. The seconds ticked away. I passed one timekeeper with some minutes left and then the next came into view and beyond him a hill which I did not want to climb yet again. I climbed off the bike with forty-five seconds still in hand, but I felt that I had done enough.

I sat in the back of the car and sucked another Rennie while Charlie drove me home. My mileage was 277.25 and I had beaten Mike McNamara by 0.73 of a mile. He had set a new record in achieving a total mileage of 276.52, beating the previous best by 4.72 miles, a record which had stood for nine years. It seemed a pity that a fine rider and popular sportsman should have what would have been his finest hour somewhat blighted but he still had the satisfaction of being the competition record holder at twelve hours among the men. It was two years before John Watson of the Clifton C.C. improved on my figures and brought some equilibrium to the record tables.

Some people have suggested that women's performances get closer to men's the longer the distance involved, and this seems to be happening in marathon running now. Certainly I seemed to have supported the theory with my 12-hour ride. Unfortunately, I can't see it being put to the test again in cycling, because the best girls are losing interest in the longer distances, which is a pity.

I certainly think married women might be better suited to longer distances because they are used to keeping up the pressure in their daily domestic life, which consists of one job after another. I find that in the middle of one job I'm already thinking about the next. You develop more of a drive than men, because so much more has to be fitted into the day.

If anyone thinks that I went home to a long rest, they are wrong. The Cycle Show and also the London six-day race were taking place at Earls Court, and I had promised to be there on the Monday morning. I went to bed at 9.30 that night and was up again four hours later, not having slept much, cleaning all the debris from the car after the previous day. After that came the drive down to London where I spent most of the day and night on my feet until the early hours of the next day and the six-day race. The crowd gave me a wonderful reception for my world championship win and the '12' record, and it would have been nice to have been a professional and collected a fee for my attendance round the show stands but, apart from expenses, all it meant for me as an amateur was that I gave up two days of my holidays.

My ride gained a few inches of space in the daily papers, and the *Yorkshire Evening Post* managed a short piece tucked away at the bottom of page seven. Again I must emphasise that I was not too troubled on my own account by the rather dismissive attitude of the press, but it made me mad that cycling itself was down-graded in this country. Can you imagine the headlines if a woman had accomplished a similar performance in athletics, swimming or any other sport? Our own sport's magazine commented: 'The saddest part of Beryl Burton's phenomenal ride over the week-end will be that she will never get, in the general press of this country, the credit she deserves for the rides she has done and continues to do . . .'

There was a happy conclusion to the season for Mike McNamara when a week later he finished third in the Harrogate C.C. 50-mile with a time of 1–52–25. This, with his 12-hour and '100' rides gave him the British Best All-rounder title, and I was very pleased and happy for him.

The Olympic Games were to be held in Mexico in 1968 and, as usual, there were to be no women's cycling events although, goodness knows, they had just about everything else. It would have been nice if some of the 'worlds' medals I have won had been Olympic ones – not that they would have been any harder to win since I would have been riding mostly against the same girls. However, for some reason, the general public in Britain take more notice of Olympic medals. Aware of my disappointment that there would be no opportunity for me to ride in Mexico, *Cycling* magazine had struck a medal made of Mexican gold especially for me. It had been fashioned by a craftsman from an old Mexican coin, and special permission had had to be obtained from the Bank of England for the gold to be used. It is a beautiful medal which I treasure, and wear on appropriate occasions. On one side it says simply 'Cycling' and on the other 'BERYL BURTON, first woman to break a men's athletic record, Otley C.C. '12' 17.9.67, 277.2 miles'. Alan Gayfer made the presentation at the W.C.R.A. dinner in London toward the end of October.

In November I had some wonderful news. The clubs of the British Cycling Federation had overwhelmingly elected me 'Best Cycling Personality of the Year' and then came the result of the *Daily Express* readers' poll naming me as the top girl sports star. And, at last, the one that really counted – the verdict from the sportswriters themselves that I had done most for British sporting prestige abroad. This was wonderful recognition and I was tremendously pleased for the sport, and I hoped it would result in increased coverage during the following year. For the third time I was also awarded the F.T. Bidlake Memorial Award for my 12-hour ride, the first to win it more than twice. All this was providing a tremendous climax to the year, and all the years of endeavour seemed at last to have brought me some recognition in the eyes of the general public of my own country.

A slightly sour note was struck, however, near the end of the year by the B.B.C. Sportsview Review of 1967, a TV programme watched by millions. I had not, as far as I was aware, been seen in any of their sports programmes, as they seemed to have a policy of ignoring cycling, so an award was not something to which I had given much thought. In the viewers' poll I was placed second to Henry Cooper the boxer, rather to the relief of the B.B.C. I was to learn later. Henry graced his sport for a number of years, bringing honour to the country by his sporting demeanour, and was a most worthy recipient of the award. I was on the screen for about two seconds and then, following due honour to Henry, the programme was filled up with English cricket and football teams, while Graham Webb and I who had won world championships were ignored. You would think that finishing second in the poll would rate a little more of the time available, wouldn't you?

But to return to the Sportswriters Association dinner where I was presented with their award. I really enjoyed myself that evening, even though the major speech which was made by the Earl of Harewood, President of the Football Association, was peppered with allusions to football in Greek mythology and hardly made any references to me or the other award winners.

I started my speech to the assembly as follows: 'Mr Chairman, fellow Yorkshire landowner the Right Honourable Earl of Harewood – we pronounce that Hairwood in Yorkshire, like the village near Harrogate . . .'

I concluded: 'In the Morley Cycling Club we have a saying that we try to live up to – "smile when you lose, and laugh like hell when you win." I've found it a good maxim to try for, even when I've stood on the rostrum with tears streaming down my cheeks, grinning at Charlie in the crowd in a similar condition – they've been tears of joy. Tonight, ladies and gentlemen, I'm laughing, and thanking all of you for your reception, and for considering me and the sport of cycling worthy of the honour of voting me your Sportswoman of the Year.'

At these gatherings I was conscious that I was representing my sport, and I was glad to be able to demonstrate that the so-called 'minority sports' of this country were not to be regarded lightly. Cycling is not a minority sport world-wide; it is also not a minority sport in this country in the terms of the numbers who participate. It is a minority sport only in that it is not fashionable in certain circles. There is still too much talk of the 'humble pushbike'. If the cars on our roads were made with as much expertise and care as even the cheapest bikes, the average motorist would be amazed at the quality of his vehicle.

A final word about these functions. The professionals were able to claim a fee for their time, whereas we amateurs were entitled to expenses only. I always tried to play fair in that Charlie and I would, with Yorkshire thrift, take the tube and not a taxi, and keep other expenses to a minimum. I never inflated my expenses – the money I claimed was for genuinely 'out of pocket' expenses and nothing else. This meant that Charlie and I incurred some personal expenses which we did not mind doing in view of the occasions and the honour of being present. However, I learned from experience that few, if any, acted as frugally as we. If this seems to add a mercenary note to what should be joyous recollections I mention it because I know some people wonder about these things. There are those who give the proverbial 'nod and a wink' and think that I probably don't 'do too badly' out of my amateur cycling. If only it were true!

As the social season drew to a close with a luncheon held in Sunderland where I received the Vaux Tankard from the brewery of that name as the North Sportswoman of the year for 1967, I began to think about the coming competitive year, increasing my mileage and gradually easing myself into serious training. Apart from my international successes I had broken six records the previous season, and wondered if I could keep wheeling down the same road. I still had it in the back of my mind that I would like to lower the 100-mile record and, if at all possible, bring it inside four hours.

My first outing of note was a hilly 30-mile in Staffordshire, which I won with a time of 1–19–10 despite a puncture which meant riding the last two miles with a wobbly rear wheel. Early in May I won the Havering C.C. '25' with 59–29 on a cold windy day, so I knew that my best form was returning. The same week-end I won the Norlond Combine '10' in twenty-four minutes and finished fifth in the handicap 28-mile road race also promoted by the Combine. I was on scratch in a handicap where I gave my opponents five and ten minutes start, an impossible task, and I was 1 minute 11 seconds down at the end. It was my thirty-first birthday, and perhaps I should have been feeling my sporting age because Denise, now twelve years old, had just competed in a boys' and girls' race over five miles and recorded 16–58. It was the beginning of her racing career.

Early in June the Queen's Birthday Honours List was made public. I had been elevated to the rank of an Officer of the Order of the British Empire and I was deeply honoured since to move from M.B.E. to O.B.E. does not, I believe, happen to all that many.

The first major race of the year was the national championship '25' in Lancashire on a good course and I retained the trophy with a time of 59–4, with June Pitchford second and Ann Horswell third, leading the Gordano Valley team to a new competition record. I had had a go at a few records at Herne Hill during the week before the '25' but conditions were far from ideal. I missed the world 3,000 metres record by 0.3 of a second, but I succeeded with the flying-start mile record which had stood for ten years, taking 0.2 of a second from it.

Our own Morley '25' a week later was a success for our girls, as I won the ladies' event with 59–13, Margaret Allen and Margaret McCarthy taking second and third places. Brian Scarisbrick won the men's race for the third successive year with 57–54, and I was heartened that I was over two and a half minutes closer to him than I had been the previous year. My time, in fact, would have given me fourth place. A week later I won the Nunbrook '50', getting inside two hours by one second. The men's event was won by Hugh

Smith of West Suffolk Wheelers over a powerful entry, and if I had been riding among them I would have finished second, beating Brian Scarisbrick by nineteen seconds.

The following week-end it was down to the Southend Road again for the Southend and District '25' where I was close to my record with a ride of 56–25. Our contest had followed that of the men and the conditions were, if anything, slightly worse, yet my time would have placed me second if I had been racing among them. Only the great Alf Engers went faster that morning with a wonderful 54–24. Alf Engers had held the '25' competition record in 1959 and was now returning to the sport after a few years devoted to his other love, fishing, with the avowed intention of re-taking the record. Alf is arguably the greatest 25-miler we have ever had in the sport, and the record currently (1984) stands in his name with a staggering 49–24, a time he accomplished in 1978. He did not take the record in that 1968 season, but managed to do so the following year when he broke it again, won the championship and then held the title again for five successive years between 1972 and 76, a feat I do not think we shall see repeated. Alf was not only a great competitor but one of racing's outstanding characters, with his flamboyant gypsy appearance and studded ear-lobe. A master-baker, he thought nothing of turning out bread until the early hours of the morning, and then hurrying away to perform outstandingly on the bike: another 'hard' man, not unlike Nim Carline.

My sights were now on the 50-mile national championship in Nottinghamshire. I took the title for the tenth time with 1–58–20, a new championship record. The Gordano Valley girls set a new team record to beat Morley in the team race, a broken spoke in my front wheel upsetting my concentration but in the end probably making little difference. The following week was the road championship in Berkshire over thirty-five miles, a flattish course with one hill on the nine-mile circuit. Attacking on this hill in the first lap I shook off the rest of the field to win by 2 minutes 35 seconds from Barbara Mapplebeck.

Later in the month I rode on the Southend Road, again in the Becontree Wheelers 25-mile, winning with 56–44. This event was notable in that Ann Horswell became the second-fastest woman rider when she also 'beat the hour' with 59–8. Ann was not the first girl apart from me to achieve this; Jo Bowers had done so in 1963 and the previous day Carol Barton of Long Eaton Paragon had won the Colchester Rovers trial with 59–57 – more and more girls were achieving average speeds of more than 25 m.p.h.

At the end of July, with the four-hours '100' in mind, I rode the Newark Castle promotion and on a day of crosswinds managed 4–1–41, beating June Pitchford by over twenty-nine minutes. If it had been only slightly calmer I think I would have reached my target, but I was satisfied with my performance as in the men's race held at the same time my ride would have rated second place to Ant Taylor of Solihull, and beaten their second-placed rider by nearly eight minutes.

The next goal was a week later in the national championship '100' in Essex. My ambition was to take my ninth title at this distance and beat the four-hour barrier. The enthusiasm of the club-folk there is probably greater than anywhere else and I have always been wonderfully received. It was a wet day and quite windy and I was concerned about the many traffic islands to be negotiated in the damp conditions. Before the start I had thought that the record would be beyond me, and I set out with only the aim of winning the title. However, everything went well, and as the miles slipped by in the plumes of spray I slowly began to realise that I was on target. I covered the first quarter of the distance in less than an hour, likewise the second and, with the rain dripping off my nose and the occasional sweep of my hand across the glass of the stop-watch clipped to my bars, I pounded along realising that the third quarter could be even faster. Charlie and Nim Carline were out on the course, and one of them shouted something about Greatwood as I went by, puzzling me until I remembered that John was the course record holder with a 4–2 and that he was riding in the men's race which preceded the girls'. I thought that they were reminding me that I stood a chance of beating his course record.

Over the final miles my wheels were zipping through the wet and I was still feeling good, keeping an eye on the time, forcing myself to urge my legs round but keeping a rhythm against the top gear. The last ten miles, five miles, and the record was on. Another glance at the watch and I had to blink hard in the rain – there was still a chunk of the four hours remaining in which I could pulverise my own record! Straining every muscle, hammering away – and the finish comes into sight. Then I am sitting up, the rain in my hair collecting now around my ears and neck, the bike eases down and I shiver in spite of a little coil of steam which traces along my arms.

My time in retaining the title was 3–55–5 and I felt slightly annoyed at myself for not making it a 3–54 and at the weather-gods for not giving us a better day. But there it was, the first ride in less than four hours by a woman, and not by a slender margin at that. John Greatwood had won the men's race and I had bettered his time by 3 minutes 23 seconds while he himself was joining the select band of men who had beaten four hours. Only three men in the country had ever covered a hundred miles faster than me, and I wasn't sure whether to rate this or my 12-hour of the previous year as my best performance. *Cycling* reported . . . 'It must be hard for lay-folk, non-cyclists or others to appreciate what this performance means. It is comparable with the stupefaction that would result from a (woman) athlete beating the four minute mile by a sizeable margin.' On the same day Martyn Roach set a new men's record for the 12-hour, still 140 yards short of my distance, but to be fair to Martyn, he had a rough day.

Margaret Allen and Margaret McCarthy had supported me splendidly with their performances in the '100' and as a result Morley won the team award with a new record. There was a great spirit within the club, and we were all anxious for Nim to win the 24-hour championship for the sixth time a week later. In a great battle Nim, now forty-years-old, went down to Eric Matthews who clocked 489.628 miles to Nim's 480.904. While he was battling round the roads north of London I was doing the same to the west of the capital on the Bath Road racing in the Camberley Wheelers 50-mile in atrocious conditions. It surprised me that my winning time of 1–56–40, achieved in thick mist, was only forty seconds away from my record.

This year the national pursuit titles were fought out at the Salford Park track in Birmingham with the weather still miserable. I had only just finished retaining my title against June Pitchford with the second-best time I had recorded in Britain (4–14.7) when, to the accompaniment of rolling thunder, the rains came down. In the same programme Barbara Mapplebeck lost her sprint crown to seventeen-year-old Bernadette Swinnerton, the first of an amazing line from the family of Roy and Doris Swinnerton in Staffordshire.

It was about this time that I was approached by the Automobile Association to help with a promotion that their magazine, *Drive*, intended to publicise. I cannot remember now exactly what it concerned except that it must have had some kind of 'past and present' theme. Charlie and I made more than one visit to Hertfordshire in connection with it and generally put ourselves out, which we were always prepared to do if it helped the image of our sport, particularly in the eyes of the 'four-wheeled' brigade. At one point I met Lilian Dredge, a noted pre-war rider who had taken the Lands End-John o'Groats record in 1939, and we were photographed riding along together. At the end of it all, nothing came of it. Charlie and I received no payment for the expenses we had incurred, to say nothing of the time given to the A.A.

It was world championship time, and off I went to represent my country for the tenth successive year with the feeling that I was becoming a permanent fixture. The championships were in Rome, the city of history and romantic dreams. For me, it was simply a venue with a velodrome in which the world's finest cyclists would strive for the all-important medals. I would love to wander around Rome, following the tourist trails, and see its treasures and sights, but that will have to wait for some other time.

I knew that I would be at a disadvantage against the best of Russia and many other countries. They could choose girls whose entire training had been concentrated on the medal requirements, girls who had come from the 'top of the heap' and been schooled amid keen rivalry to bring success. I had been time trialling on English roads and my pursuiting was comparatively negligible, while on the road I had raced in handicaps, attempting to catch up the others using my time-trialling skills or, if the field started together, time trialling away and riding alone. I was not really versed in road-race tactics, so all I could offer was individual effort which, at world level, was hardly enough any more. I knew the others would glue themselves to my wheel and the likelihood was that I would be beaten in the sprint among the leading group. If only there had been a time trial over any distance! I knew that in a straight race I could still beat anyone in the world on the road. I could still probably beat them on the track, too, in a pursuit if I had devoted a lot of my time to it.

Despite the lack of emphasis in Britain on tactical skills we do have something the essence of which is difficult to put into words: we have a unique club life where cyclists enjoy themselves and share a way of life which is acknowledged and envied by the rest of the cycling nations. If we produce a few world-class riders along the way it really is a bonus. And we have done just that, namely Harris, Webb, Porter, Simpson, Mandy Jones and a few others. Most of us are individualists who rose to the top by our own efforts and in our own way and it is intriguing to consider whether we are the sort of people who would have 'made it' if we had been born in one of the top cycling countries.

In Rome the track racing was on the fast timber-surfaced Olympic velodrome, and I was feeling pretty good, apart from my doubts about whether I could overcome the Russians. The first surprise was that Garkushina had not arrived with the Russian team because she had been badly injured racing in her own country. In her place was a girl who was new to me, Nina Korotaeva, but nobody doubted that she, too, would be a world-class rider.

In the first round I came up against Jacky Barbadette of France, and managed a satisfying time of 4–6.19 to her 4–23.63. Obodowskaya showed a 4–6.04 and Korotaeva 4–7.52. The weather was so hot that the air expanded in one of my silk racing tyres and caused an explosion like a cannon. Fortunately the wheel was stacked in a trackside cabin at the time and, unlike at Rocourt nine years earlier, I had a spare. We had to ride three times from ten in the morning until late in the evening.

I was drawn against Audrey McElmury of the U.S.A. in the morning quarter-final, and after she had taken an early lead I disposed of her with 4–5.83 to 4–8.17. Korotaeva went faster with 4–5.74 in beating the Italian Tartagni, and Keetie Hage of the Netherlands put in the ominous time of 4–3.64 to beat Mattig of East Germany by nearly seven seconds. Earlier Obodowskaya had easily disposed of Elizabetta Maffeis, the other Italian, with 4–8.73.

In the afternoon I had to face my semi-final against Korotaeva, and there was a feeling that the Russians had instructed Obodowskaya to do just enough to win against Maffeis without setting a 'hot' time so that she would draw Hage in her 'semi' while I had a hard ride against her compatriot. As it happened, the favourite did not have matters all her own way against Hage, who was proving to be the revelation of the championships, but she came through with 4–6.59 against 4–7.65. The afternoon had clouded over a little and there was some breeze as I went to the line against Korotaeva knowing I had to win this to be certain of another world medal. Could I make it a gold? I expected the Russian to be something special since she must have been rated number three in her own country, which would rank her as one of the world's best, and I felt that we had not yet seen the best of her. It was close for a long way; I held her, then matched her, expecting at any moment that the pressure would come. Finally, I took the initiative and, with a few laps remaining, put on a spurt leaving it to my opponent to parry the challenge. I was not going to leave matters to a last-lap 'scrap' if I could avoid it. Nina could not respond and joyfully I zoomed to a time of 4–7.81, beating the Russian by over two seconds. For the eighth time in ten years, I was in the final of the world championships.

The final came at 11.30 that night after Hage had disposed of Korotaeva for the bronze. We had been at the track since ten that morning and had already ridden twice in the 'quarters' and 'semis'. What demands the clowns of the U.C.I. were placing upon us! The idiocy of these characters was further revealed when there was a shower just before the start of the final. The track was too wet to ride and I told them so, and so did Eileen Gray. 'You must ride,' I was told, 'or you will forfeit a medal.' 'You can keep your medal,' I replied. 'I'm not riding until the track is safe.'

Meanwhile Obodowskaya had mounted her bike on the other side of the track. If her team bosses had told her to ride I suppose she did not have much choice but I did. Nobody was going to tell me I must race, if I thought the conditions weren't right. Seeing my determination, the officials threw sawdust down and then swept the track. Still I refused. They used hot blowers on the track, which improved matters a little, but there was a misty dampness in the air which kept a glitter on the boards. I should point out that a banked velodrome, particularly a board track ridden with silk tyres blown to a pressure of about nine atmospheres, is a far cry from a flat road. And there was a world championship at stake.

The U.C.I. heirarchy again insisted. Eileen Gray argued strongly on my behalf, while I made a tentative, slow circuit with the bike slithering up and down. Shaking, I insisted that the track could not be ridden at racing speed. I had the impression that the Russians were leaving all the arguments to us, making us out to be the 'awkward squad' in the eyes of the crowd, while Raisa waved to them, probably privately hoping that our protests would succeed.

The professional sprinting had been put back because of the conditions and the U.C.I. officials had brought our final forward thinking, in their usual crass way, that the state of the track would be good enough for the women pursuiters. Ron Baensch, an Australian who is as tough and fearless as they come, declared that if he was not prepared to sprint on the track I was correct in not wanting to pursuit. Eileen Gray continued to protest and finally challenged Chadelle, one of the chief officials, to a ride round the track. Seizing a bike Eileen hoisted her skirt and straddled it, saying that if he would ride the track, so would she. Perhaps Chadelle thought this was an undignified procedure, but more probably he doubted his chances of making a circuit without a tumble and he declined the invitation. Whatever anyone may think of all this it is a measure of the lengths Eileen was always prepared to go to on behalf of the British girls. Following further argument Eileen persuaded me to start, telling me not to race but just to proceed round the track.

Shaking, I did so. The countdown was given and I wobbled away, turning the pedals just sufficiently to give me some forward traction, frighteningly aware that my tyres were not adhering fully. There was a clatter from the other side of the track as Obodowskaya came down and the starter's pistol exploded into the night to signify a halt to the proceedings.

Eventually the track dried out enough for safe racing, and the final was under way. I went into a slight lead from the start, and had held it for two laps when the Russian girl came hard at me and shot into the lead. After four laps she was in the lead by nearly three seconds, a good margin. I knew what I was up against but, as always, Morley was uppermost in my mind and I gritted my teeth and drew on all my resources. Painfully slowly, I began to pull her back. Could I reverse our positions before the finish? I was trying my damnedest, but I could make no further impression on that flying red jersey, and Raisa was the world champion by 0.76 of a second. Another disappointment, another occasion for smiling and leaving the laughs to another day – but I was quietly pleased with my time of 4–2.66 and the slender margin of my defeat. I thought it was a good amateur performance, in the best sense of the word, against the 'state professional' from the U.S.S.R.

The following road race at Imola indicated yet again that I was the strongest woman rider in the world on the road. It was quite hot with a strong wind, and a few girls succumbed to the heat. I towed them round the thirty-four miles in a pretty fast time, and those of us who were left at the front at the finish sprinted for the line. Fifteen of us finished in the same time as the winner, Keetie Hage of the Netherlands and, in this company, my sprint was not good enough, particularly after I had done nearly all the work, and I was placed thirteenth. With the exception of the *Daily Telegraph* there was, disappointingly, no report in the British press by anybody who knew what they were writing about. Instead there were the usual brief reports like the one in the *Yorkshire Evening Post* sports edition which was headed 'Beryl Burton beaten again', and was followed by two inches of copy which gave quite the wrong impression. I had taken second place in the 3,000 metres, and again I was the 'moral' winner in the road race. 'Moral' wins don't count for anything, I know, but abroad I was still carrying the flag of women's racing on my shoulders. I was still the one other riders dare not let out of their sight, and I had notched up my twelfth 'worlds' medal.

For the record, Bayba Tzaune of the Soviet Union took the silver and Morena Tartagni of Italy the bronze. A shining beacon from the championships was Hugh Porter who won the first of his four rainbow jerseys as professional pursuit champion to go with the silver medal which he had won a year earlier.

Another season was coming to an end but I had one more big challenge. The previous winter the well-known cycling journalist, the late Jock Wadley, had put to me the possibility of riding the classic Grand Prix des Nations time trial in France. (The 'Nations' is the premier time-trial contest of the world, dating back to 1932, with many famous names of continental cycling among the winners, none more so than the greatest time triallist of them all, Jacques Anquetil, who was the winner nine times between 1953 and 1966, in addition to achieving his five Tour de France victories.) I knew that I could not actually take part in the 'Nations' as a competitor – since all the contestants had to be professionals – and men! – but I was certainly eager to ride the course and see how I would compare.

Through the respected French cycling journalist, René de Latour, an approach was made to the organiser, Felix Levitan, who, incidentally, is one of the co-organisers of the Tour de France. He had the power to say yes or no – and the answer was yes. I asked Jock if he could let me have some details of the course, including gradients and recommended gears. Unfortunately, a completely new course was to be used and Jock could not offer any help in that direction. Charlie and I also had to consider the expense; although the 'Nations' organisation was prepared to allow me to ride the course in front of the professionals I was, of course, not part of the actual race and I would have to be privately funded. Through the kindness of Ron Kitching of Harrogate financial help was forthcoming but, as usual, we had to find the balance ourselves.

The classic, promoted jointly by *L'Equipe*, the famous sports paper, and two other leading French newspapers, *Parisien Libéré* and *France-Soir*, was over a course of 73.5 kilometres, starting at the town of Auffargis to the south-west of Paris, traversing a south-easterly direction for nearly a third of the distance before turning north-west and entering Paris to finish at the Municipale velodrome at Charénton on the edge of the Bois de Vincennes. The French papers showed great interest in my appearance, and when it was suggested that I would cover the course at a speed faster than 40 k.p.h. there was some shaking of heads and, no doubt, gallic shrugs at the temerity of '*l'Anglaise Burton*' thinking she could cover this tough course at such a speed.

The day before the race I set out on the bike to reconnoitre the course, with Jock and Charlie leading by car. I had travelled only a few miles when I came across some road works, where lorries were buzzing about and the road was covered with mud. I had to negotiate this carefully and press on, the route taking me into a small town and a market square thronged with shoppers. In the built-up area on the final stretch to Paris, the course covered several back streets, many of them cobbled, went through a building site, past Orly airport with its busy traffic, and then on to another section where a water pipe was lying next to a deep trench and looking as though it was going to be there for quite some time. I climbed back into the car as it began to rain, feeling very worried. Jock was also perturbed. It was he, in his enthusiasm, who had arranged all this and confidently put about among his French journalist colleagues that I would cover the course faster than 25 m.p.h., and he immediately became anxious about my morale.

Jock had arranged accommodation in a small comfortable *pension*, and we returned there in pensive mood. After dinner I gave some press and radio interviews, voicing my concern about the course. 'It can be as hilly as the organisers want to make it,' I told them, 'but it should have a passably good surface.' I was assured that it would be different by the following day.

I could have done with a good night's sleep, but my back was troubling me again and I only managed a fitful rest. The next morning I unwound gradually, hobbling about the bedroom, and Charlie had to massage my back before we went down to breakfast. Fortunately, when I mounted the bike the pain and stiffness eased.

The night before, Graham Webb had arrived at the hotel. Now a professional, he was riding the 'Nations' also, and we rode the ten miles to the start together to loosen our legs. I had had a late breakfast of steak and rice while Charlie tuned up the bike, fitting a second chain-ring to give me a wider choice of gears to cope with the hills and deciding to take a chance on the lightest wheels and tyres. It was accepted that he left all the decisions about riding, training, what to eat and when to eat it entirely to me, while I always left decisions about the bike to him, except that I insisted on a particular size chainwheel for training.

The morning was grey and overcast, but the rain had stopped and the roads had dried out. It was Sunday, 22nd September, 1968, and I was to ride in the company of some of the top professionals of the world. Men like the great Felice Gimondi of Italy, Herman Van Springel of Belgium, Louis Ocana of Spain and Rini Wagtmans of Holland. I felt that the eyes of France were upon me, and I went to the line in Auffargis wearing my Morley club colours feeling nervous, but managing to hide it as usual.

The countdown – I came off the saddle and lunged away, down on the drops, into top gear and finding a rhythm as quickly as possible. I would give it all I had from the start – if Jock was not to eat his words I had to be in Paris, forty-six miles away on the route I was taking, in no more than 1 hour 50 minutes. The first of the 'pros' was to start twelve minutes after me, and I think the general consensus was that somebody would catch me before Paris. On the road somewhere in front was a gendarme on a motor-bike, his siren screeching and giving warning of my approach; fifty metres behind him was a police car, lights flashing; another fifty metres behind that there was another police motor-bike and then, at a suitable distance behind, came me. Following, there was a car with my name on a big board across the front carrying the spares and, further behind that, a press car and Jock Wadley anxiously checking his watch (so he told me afterwards). Never had the Morley colours been carried with such an escort – a real *'son et lumière'*. Crowds of people collected in the villages, cheering and clapping and shouting encouragement, the roads being closed to all other traffic so that I could concentrate on my ride. At every intersection along the route police were blowing their whistles as only the gendarmerie can, warning others of my approach. Some of them looked surprised, as though they had not expected me so soon. The assurances about the road works, the mud and the pipe-laying had been justified. They had all mysteriously disappeared overnight as though they had never been, and I zipped on, my legs feeling fluent, the rain holding off. I could not engage the big sprocket and used the second chain-ring once or twice on some of the hills.

In the press car Jock was feeling pleased. He had a Belgian press photographer with him who had made the journey from Brussels just to follow me, and he was delighted with the coverage he was getting. The countryside gave way to built-up areas, a lot of sharp turns, some cobbles and tough little hills. I swung the bike about, picking my line at each corner, using as much road as I needed – what luxury, no cares about traffic or hazards. The streets were packed on both sides, mile after mile of cheering crowds who lifted me along, a surge of sound in front and behind – *'Allez, la Britannique!'* What a complete contrast to the reaction to our almost surreptitious events early on Sunday mornings in Britain.

I crossed the Seine at the Pont de Conflans. Into the district of Charenton, and I had only a few hundred metres to go. Jock had swung away to arrive at the velodrome before me but, to his consternation, he found the track racing still in progress there. Agitatedly he told the officials that I would be arriving at any moment. 'Nonsense,' they replied, 'even if she's doing a 40 k.p.h. ride she won't be here just yet. There's time to finish this race.' 'She's doing 42 k.p.h.,' Jock insisted. 'Nonsense,' they repeated.

Thus it was that I swung on to the track to find myself caught up with three riders in the final laps of an elimination race. Amid much hullabaloo and scurrying officials I circled the track. Riders in the 'Nations' had to complete two laps to finish their ride, and I set about giving it all I had before the cheering crowds – fortunately the track riders had swung up the banking out of my way. I crossed the line for the second time and sat up and stopped pedalling, but excited officials waved me round for another circuit because the timekeepers were not ready. Thus it was that 'my' Grand Prix des Nations was longer, by an extra circuit of the large Municipale, than that of all the other professionals on the road behind me. I discovered later that I had also been riding the last few miles with a ½-inch nail embedded in one of my tyres!

My time was 1–45–22, an average speed of 41.853 kilometres per hour, not far behind the slowest of the 'pros', with Felice Gimondi the winner in a new record speed of 47.518 k.p.h. To round things off properly I insisted on taking the same dope test as the men as I wanted no mutterings about artificial aids, something I have never resorted to throughout my career. Gimondi, the great Italian ace, had beaten me by only twelve and a half minutes in setting up his record, and my only regret was that the distance was not longer because I think my showing would have then stood even more comparison. The following day the French papers were generous in their praise of my performance and added little biographical notes about my working on a farm, about Charlie and Denise, and my English records. The French public knew, of course, about my pursuit and road race medals in world championships, but I think they were taken aback with my riding in their great time trial. The prestigious newspaper, *Le Monde*, carried an article about the 'Nations' the following Wednesday written by Jean Bobet, brother of Louison, one of the greatest French cyclists and four times a winner of the Tour de France. It was headed 'La Dame à Bicyclette', and I reproduce the first part of it with some pleasure:

Last Sunday a 31 year-old British woman, Mrs Beryl Burton, covered the 73.5 kilometres of the Grand Prix des Nations course at an average speed of 41.853 k.ph. Mrs Burton's performance is all the more interesting because she did the job with a smile and a dignity that we had believed incompatible with women's cycle racing. The British cycling star had managed to persuade the organisers to let her ride over the route of the Grand Prix des Nations which, in Great Britain, is considered the supreme competition. In fact races against the watch, which are called by the very appropriate name of 'Time Trials' are the most widely practised in Britain because they cause the least disturbance to traffic. They are organised with great care. Competitors are obliged to cover the course 'out and home' in order to balance the effect of wind. Mrs Burton has won all the national titles at this type of competition. She even beat the men in the Twelve Hour Championship time trial – twelve hours during which she pedalled at the average 36 k.p.h.

At the finish of the Grand Prix des Nations last Sunday Mrs Burton was satisfied. She felt that she had justified the faith of those few friends who had clubbed together to make the trip possible; for Mrs Burton is an amateur. She had refused to ride for a French firm which offered her an interesting contract. She rides for her own pleasure, and for a medal which will be displayed at home in the middle of her countless other trophies.

Asked if I would like to return the following year to ride again, I gave a resounding 'Yes, please!' but alas, twelve months later other matters had intervened and it was not to be. I shall always be grateful to Jock Wadley, whose death a few years ago left a large gap in cycling journalism, to Felix Levitan, and to everyone else who helped to make that ride possible. Whenever the going in life seems a little hard I close my eyes and savour again the thousands of bike-mad French fans shouting *'Allez, la Britannique!'*

A few weeks later I went to Buckingham Palace to receive my O.B.E., this time taking Denise and her club-mate Ann Pallister with us. The year finished with the Best All-rounder prize presentation where I received the trophy for the tenth time with a record average of 25.942 m.p.h. I was beginning to wonder just how long it could go on.

The year 1969 opened with several wins in 10-mile events, in one of which Denise was fastest schoolgirl with an excellent 31–50, pretty good for a thirteen-year-old. We were not pushing her into racing, or even cycling, but it seemed to come naturally. Her interest was genuine and Charlie and I were delighted.

Although still not quite at peak fitness I knew my form of the previous year was just waiting to be polished when I won the Long Eaton Paragon '25' in mid-April in 59–53, with Maureen Wroe in second place just over five minutes behind. By early May I was in full flight when on a windy Fenland course I broke the 30-mile record with 1–12–20. Only four men were faster that day, and I knew that I could bring this particular record down much further. It was only the third time I had ridden the 30-mile, one of the less popular time-trialling distances, and it provided my thirty-fifth competition record.

By the time of the national championship '25' in June I was very much 'on song' and looking forward to taking the title for the eleventh time in twelve years. Seven Morley girls travelled down to Wiltshire for a real onslaught on the team prize, among them Denise. I retained the title with 58–30, Maureen Wroe was seventh and Margaret McCarthy twenty-fourth, and the club achieved its objective of taking the team shield. Denise finished with 1–16–4, beating her friend, Ann Pallister, by a few seconds. They all set off back to Yorkshire in a happy frame of mind while I rode back, nearly two hundred miles, with Nim Carline, intent on some long-distance training. There was no better man to train with when the chance occurred than Nim. I was beginning to pack in the miles because I had decided I would like a crack at the 24-hour distance, hoping that perhaps I could achieve a ride comparable with my 12-hour record. Accordingly, my other races, always ridden hard to win with the largest possible margin, were becoming secondary to what I hoped would be a great 24-hour adventure. I felt sure I had it in me to record a mileage that would make the sport 'buzz' even more than the half-day rides I had accomplished.

Following my customary annual trip to the Isle of Man, where I won the '10' and the '25', I rode in Morley's two-day promotion of six races at York, winning the '10' and the '25' there also. At the end of June I won the Rutland C.C. '25' in 56–58, and the following week at South Shields I won a kilometre on the track in 1–17.6 and the pursuit in 4–17.4. There was no national kilometre championship in those days, so I have ridden only a few in my career, but if the present-day Leicester track had been in existence then or, alternatively, I could turn the clock back fifteen or twenty years just for a week-end, I would love to see what time I could turn out, particularly if I trained specifically for it. Remember, at that time I was training with a 24-hour in mind!

In July came the national championship '50' promoted by the Viking R.C. in Essex, and on a day of slight crosswind I retained the title and increased my tally of title wins to thirty-one. The time was 1–56–15, a championship record which still stands. It was surprising, really, that I had such speed in my legs for in the previous two weeks I had covered nearly 1,200 miles in training. Maureen Wroe rode splendidly for sixth place and, backed by Margaret McCarthy, Morley won the team award.

For the first time in my life I stopped work for a few weeks to pack in the miles, and I trained relentlessly day after day. High summer was a slack period at Nim's farm which gave him also the opportunity to put in plenty of training miles for the 24-hour. Nim held the record distance for the whole day race with 496.37 miles, and my aim was to beat that and top 500 miles, which I hoped would set a new record and win. When I say 'win' what I really hoped was that my distance would be greater than that of any of the seventy-four men. There was a separate ladies' trial with four entries including, beside myself, Christine Moody of Birdwell Wheelers who held the women's record with 420.05 miles; Joyce Blow of South Lancs. R.C. who was riding a trike and held the record for the three-wheeler, and the late Wyn Maddock of Notts and Derby Clarion who was by then very much a veteran, but continued in competition for many years. I have made a point of specifically mentioning these ladies because, in an age when some physical endeavours far less demanding than racing for twenty-four hours on a bike seem to warrant so much press attention, they go quietly about their demanding sport without fuss, and simply for the possible chance of a medal or certificate. The media these days seem obsessed with marathons and so on, so it surprises me they have not paid any attention to 12- and 24-hour time trialling.

Such was my concentration on this one event in the 1969 season I did not enter for either the pursuit or road championships, and although I had already been selected to ride in the world championships in Czechoslovakia I had intimated that I might not be available.

In the few weeks before the '24', which was promoted by the Mersey Roads Club and the Merseyside Ladies Cycling Association, I had felt some pain in my knees which had not stopped me winning races but gave cause for concern as the big day approached. Looking back now, I think I never gave my legs a rest. I was doing housework in the early part of the day, and then going out training for about five hours as hard as I could, after which I would then come home and, instead of putting my feet up, I would stand in the kitchen cooking a meal and continue being active about the house until I went to bed. I took some heat treatment and massage but the condition grew worse, and I wondered if I should ride. My instinct and outlook told me that I should when common sense and medical advice insisted that I should not. I continued training. In myself I was very fit, clocking up great mileages in spite of the knees, feeling that if I was to ride I could not miss a day's training and knowing that each day would end almost in tears. I was determined that nobody should know about the trouble I was having except Charlie and Denise and the people immediately concerned. I was not going either to withdraw from the race or make excuses in advance for possible failure.

At 6.23 p.m. on July 26th, 1969 I left the timekeeper as fit as I had ever been in my life for a long-distance ride. Only Charlie among the onlookers knew that my knees had started to ache before I had turned a pedal. It was, perhaps, foolhardy and doomed before the start, but I had set my heart on victory and a record which would top 500 miles. I still feel quite sure today, without a shadow of a doubt, that but for the knee trouble I would have succeeded.

The course started near Chester and took in Cheshire and North Wales, and it was raining steadily as I went on my way. From the beginning I slogged away at top gear, following the principle of Nim to give it everything from the 'off'. No taking it comparatively easy for the first few hours, no worrying about 'blowing up' later. I went for the target as though I was riding a 10-mile. At the first time-check after thirty-two miles I was already leading and over two minutes faster than Nim, and I continued this way, pumping the high gear relentlessly, knowing that I was taking a calculated risk. At 61.3 miles I had taken another half-minute out of Nim, the 107-inch gear rolling nicely, knees protesting a little but answering all the pressure I was giving them. The rain had stopped by now. Into the fading light and I halted briefly to don extra clothing for the night and to have my lights fixed. At 100.4 miles I clocked 4–11, a time good enough to win a men's 100-mile event. Into the night and I pulled back man after man including Roy Cromack of the Clifton, one of the favourites, spotting rear lights ahead and then my own light picking up the reflectors. A brief merging of our front lights and then they were behind me in the darkness and I was alone again with my thoughts – and my aching knees!

On the North Wales coast road, breathing steadily, feeling great, only the niggling knees giving me cause for concern. Eventually I caught Nim, the man who attacked from the start, and as I passed him I knew that up to that point I was really 'on a ride'. The 150.9 check at Queensferry, and I was through and into the night in a time of 6–22. At 200 miles and 8–42 I was way ahead of everyone, passing the checks and knots of club-folk to whistles of amazement. If only my knees would hold! Into the dawn, rather chilly, some mist swirling, no longer was there an ache in those damned knees but a definite pain which seemed to come from inside the joints.

Nim had now been passed by Roy Cromack and it seemed that although strictly speaking we were riding different races, it was really a tussle between him and me. Eventually I had to stop while Charlie massaged my knees, complaining that I had been going too fast all night to take a 'proper' feed. There had been no bad patch, and I had made the halt only to relieve my knees a little. My thighs and calves were O.K., it was just the bit in the middle! At 345 miles I had been twenty-three minutes faster than Cromack, but my stop of a few minutes had reduced his deficit. I plugged on through the morning and then the middle of the day, when the pain overcame me and I had to stop again. Sitting at the roadside I saw Roy sweeping by, obviously very fit and pulling out a tremendous ride. If I had been able to continue at that point I would still have been in the lead on time, but I knew it was no use. From a riding point of view I was in good shape and no way distressed; my leg muscles could still answer the call and I had the strength to push the big gear – even my back was behaving. But the pain from my knees was just too much.

I had remained silent about this before the start, and I kept my silence when I retired from the race, so much so that the *Cycling* report stated that I had 'blown completely', which was rather galling to read in the following week, but I suppose they were not to blame for having that impression. It was the greatest disappointment of my cycling life, even more than missing gold medals at world championships. This was an occasion for trying to raise a smile – not laughing.

Roy Cromack, then a school-teacher who later became an officer in the Royal Air Force, set a record of 507 miles which still stands, and it was a great performance by a fine rider. Would I have beaten 500 miles? Would I have beaten Cromack? Call me big-headed if you like, but I think the answer to the first question is yes; to the second question – possibly. I climbed into the car with the veins behind my knees looking like plastic tubes and I could not bear to touch them myself, let alone allow anyone else to do so. That, simply, is why I had to retire. I could perhaps have faced the pain; I could have ridden all-out in an exceedingly tough long-distance race – to do both was just a little too much.

I trust these latter comments have not detracted from Roy Cromack's ride. His was a new record and a wonderful achievement for him in a field that contained many notable 24-hour riders, such as Eric Matthews who was second with 492.8 miles, and Nim himself, who retired before reaching 300 miles. And Christine Moody also quietly plugged away to finish with a distance of 429.2 miles, a new competition record. Her athletic prowess on the bike has never received the popular recognition it deserves.

The general consensus was that I had been 'pushing' too high a gear, and that it was inevitable that I would pay the price. I can understand how this reasoning came about, but it is a wrong conclusion. I had been riding high gears most of my racing life and not only did I require that 107-inch top gear, I needed it most of the time because that is what I felt comfortable with. If I had tried rolling along on lower gears, I would simply have been making more revolutions and, with the knee condition I had, it would not have helped.

While I was sitting disconsolately in the back of the car near the race H.Q., a tall, slim man came along and introduced himself. It was Dr Tim Stahl, an expert on sports medicine who has officiated as the race doctor at many Milk Races. He came to visit me a couple of days later and arranged for me to be examined to assess the trouble. Fundamentally the joints were sound but I had been overworking them in not taking any rest periods other than when I was actually asleep. I had simply been on my feet or cycling just too much during the preceding weeks and the joints had dried out.

My next hurdle was the 100-mile championship two weeks later, and in the week before the title race I saw two specialists who told me that my knees had taken such punishment that they needed complete rest. My morale was low, and really I should have forgotten all about the '100'. However, I had entered, along with team-mates Maureen Wroe and Margaret McCarthy, and for their sake I thought I should ride. I realise now that I should have taken it more easy on this Cheshire course and then at least I probably would have been able to finish and given the club a chance of the team title. But this is so foreign to my nature that I had to ride flat out from the start. For over forty miles my knees held and I was well in the lead, then the trouble started again and there was nothing else to do but 'pack'. I was in tears. The horrible thought came to me that this could be my last race, my competitive cycling having reached an ignoble end with me sitting on the grass verge by a Cheshire road.

When Margaret McCarthy heard that I had retired she felt unable to continue. Our only joy at the end of the day was that Maureen Wroe won the race for Morley in a time of 4–36–8, taking a richly deserved gold medal, so that the individual title stayed 'home' after all. I telephoned Eileen Gray, who had been hoping that I would be fit to ride in the world championships, but it was quite obvious that I had to withdraw.

It so happened that as a result of all this I missed an extraordinary world championship series in Czechoslovakia. Russian troops had just invaded the country but the championships carried on in front of a packed stadium – albeit in an unreal atmosphere. The Russian riders were mercilessly booed at every opportunity, except during the final of the women's 3,000 metres between Garkushina and Obodowskaya, which was ridden in complete silence!

I started treatment at St James Hospital in Leeds – two hours a day under the direction of Dr Stahl. Incredibly, four weeks after the 24-hour debacle Dr Stahl saw me win the Clifton 50-mile comfortably in 1–59–22. My form was holding, and I only wished that the 24-hour had been still to come.

I then received a £3 fine for riding on the motorway! Earlier in the year I had attended a London function and had ridden down to the home of Fred Fisher of the North Road Club, near London, where I changed for the evening and took the tube into town. I had arrived back at Fred's about 2 a.m., snatched some three hours' sleep and set off to ride back to Yorkshire at six in the morning. The roads were very quiet and I was following the route of what is now the old A.1., when at some point it turned into a motorway, prohibited traffic apparently having to turn off on to a 'B' road. After a few miles on this road a police car pulled alongside and the man in uniform told me I was about to get myself killed. As the police car was only the third vehicle I had seen all morning, I doubted it. I had to drag my bike up the steep banking onto the nearby 'B' road. I was duly summoned, and pleaded 'guilty' by letter. This episode caused some merriment in the club, despite my pleas that there was no obvious sign that you had to turn off to avoid the motorway, but I took my revenge some time later when Nim and I were travelling the same route. I deliberately rode on his inside as we approached the crucial spot and, out of the corner of my eye, watched to see which direction he would take. Sure enough, he was about to make the same mistake until I warned him.

I was now as fit as I had ever been, but the knees still gave me some pain during all-out effort and were a cause for concern for the rest of the season. There was also the additional problem that I still required a 100-mile time if I was to retain my Best All-rounder title, so accordingly I entered the Yorkshire Century event. Fortunately it was a good morning and I covered the distance without any problems, winning with a time of 3–59–9, a performance that had not seemed possible a few weeks earlier. I was 'flying' again and by mid-September I had put the disappointment of the 24-hour behind me, determined to put some mark on the season apart from the Best All-rounder title. The opportunity came in the Tees-side R.C. 50-mile on the Catterick course, where I won in a time of 1–55–4, slicing fifty-six seconds from my 1967 competition record.

A week later I won the Worcestershire C.A. 10-mile and called a halt to the season. But there was to be one more competitive ride when I received an invitation from the famous Scottish club, Heatherbell Ladies, to attend their dinner-dance and, they hoped, ride in a 25-mile they were promoting on the following morning. It would give me the opportunity of racing actually among the men, something which was permissible in Scotland but not in England and Wales. The festivities, where I had the honour of being piped to the platform, went on until the early hours – not exactly the best preparation for racing a few hours later!

The following day was dank and misty, and I started last in a field of thirty-two, with the Scottish B.A.R. champion, Jock Ritchie, off one minute before me. He had missed out on the previous night's enjoyment to be sure of being in good form, and he looked very nervous as he went on his way. At halfway I was second to Jock by about twenty seconds and, despite heavy rain in the second half, I was enjoying myself as I began to reel in some of the men. Jock won the race in 58–31 and I was second, only nineteen seconds behind. Andy Kirk, the Scottish 100-mile champion, was third, exactly one minute behind me.

Ironically, even as Charlie and I were driving up to Scotland, a joint party of delegates from the British Cycle Federation and the Road Time Trials Council had held a special meeting and altered the rules so that the following season women would be allowed to compete against men in England. While being generally welcomed – I was certainly all for it – there was some head-shaking about the decision, mainly concerning the effect it would have on the women's associations and races promoted only for women. On the whole I think it has worked out all right over the years so far as time trialling is concerned, and has had a negligible effect in road racing and on the track.

For the eleventh successive year I had won the Best All-rounder award. Maureen Wroe, Lynn Harris and I had won the B.A.R. team award and Maureen had taken third individual place in addition to her 100-mile title. Mentally, I was preparing for the coming year, the opening of a new decade which would see the world championships held in England, and I wondered if I could make a return to the international scene.

I started 1970 far from well, with what I thought at first was a dose of flu, but which turned out to be a virus infection which affected my sense of balance and seemed to bring a recurrence of my back and knee problems. I was now riding races among the men, one of which was a 'two-up' ridden with Nim in the Clifton '25', where we finished eighth in 59–4. I worked hard at getting fit again, and it began to show when I finished eighth amongst the men in the Sheffield Phoenix 25-mile at the end of April. At that time it was the highest placing by a woman in a truly mixed event. At last things 'clicked' and in the middle of May I won the Concorde women's '25' with 58–14, beating Ann Horswell by nearly four minutes, and a week later won the W.C.R.A. road title, riding clear and winning with over five minutes in hand.

I now had my eye on the championship 25-mile near Bicester, and was successful in my attempt to take my thirteenth title win in a time of 59–48, with Ann Horswell nearly four minutes behind. Morley also won the team title, with Maureen Wroe sixth and Lynn Harris eighteenth. I was very pleased with Denise and Ann Pallister who finished in 1–11–6 and 1–11–3 respectively.

Later in the month the national track championships were held at Leicester, which already had a new surface and was being prepared for the forth-coming world title battles. In the national pursuit I beat Bernadette Swinnerton in the final with 4–14.6 while Maureen Wroe, whom I had beaten in the 'semi', went on to take the bronze.

In July I rode in a W.C.R.A. road race over forty miles in Staffordshire. The field contained a strong Dutch team, including Keetie Hage, and not only they but also some of the others 'marked' me all the way, hanging on to my wheel. If I tried to sprint away, fair enough – they were there. But when I slowed to a ludicrous pace they were still there. In the end I lost interest and finished fifth in the bunch. There were some recriminations afterwards about the riding by our girls which allowed Hage to win. It was the beginning of an attitude of mind and approach to road racing which has bedevilled British women's teams ever since. Only the exceptional Mandy Jones has come through in recent years to show an aggressive approach to road racing in this country. I am convinced that the main reason I was able to beat the other girls in pure tests of speed was that, then as now, they simply weren't doing enough. I don't mean just in training, but in everyday life. They are carried too much and too many things are done for them. Many parents of racing girls think that if they do a lot for their girls they will make them better riders, but I don't think that's so. I think girls have to do some grafting if they are to get the best out of themselves.

I then defended my 50-mile title on the Boro' course. The previous day I had ridden at the Nottingham track, where I had had a crash and arrived home late not feeling too good. I had had only a few hours of disturbed sleep before turning out with my elbow plastered and other bumps on my hands, hip and head. To make matters worse it was a foul day, wet with a powerful crosswind which made the going hard all the way. I retained the title with a time of 2–1–58, beating Ann Horswell by nearly seven minutes, with Maureen in third place, and I was glad when it was all over.

Two weeks later I managed a good '50' on the Catterick course (which I think is even better than the Boro') in the Cleveland Wheelers promotion. I was only sixteen seconds away from my record with 1–55–20. A motorist baulked me at one of the roundabouts and I had no choice but to turn along the wrong road before getting back on course, otherwise I think I may have broken my record that morning.

The teams for the world championships at Leicester were announced and I was nominated for the pursuit and the road. After the W.C.R.A. race in Staffordshire I had threatened not to ride if I was selected for the road team. The course, based on Mallory Park, just wasn't for me and I could see no chance of breaking away on its nearly flat contours, particularly if, as I suspected, I was likely to have British as well as foreign riders hanging on to my wheel. Out of the whole British Isles I think the technical people could have found a more testing and sporting course, on which I would have been happy to take my chances.

I was still feeling a little unwell from the virus earlier in the year and the crash at Nottingham, but I pushed this to one side when I knocked seventy-two seconds from my '25' record at the beginning of August in the Hartlepool trial, clocking 54–55. It was a staggering improvement and only five of the top men at the distance had a faster time that day.

I dearly wanted to succeed at Leicester, and wished that the championships had been held in this country some years earlier when I was at my peak as a pursuiter. I made my way through the earlier rounds and came up against Geneviève Gambillon the French champion in the quarter-finals, beating her by 3.01 seconds. As I came to the line for my ride against Gambillon all the V.I.P.s in their special stand decided it was time to lunch with H.R.H. Prince Philip who was visiting the championships, and left in a body. I thought that the British among them could have stayed a few minutes longer to give support by their presence. I was very annoyed. A British rider was about to try her best for the country, and what they did could have been demoralising to some. His Royal Highness could have spared them for five minutes I am sure!

In the 'semi' I came up against the great Garkushina, and I made her fight all the way. Down by nearly a second after the first lap I held a slight lead by the end of the third. Lap four and the Russian was down by a fraction, and I held her for another lap. At the end of lap six Garkushina had reversed our positions but, fighting desperately, I managed to hold her for another two until the bell, but she drew away over the final lap. Result: Garkushina 4–7.89; Burton 4–10.83.

Obodowskaya had the better of Hage in the other 'semi' and in an all-Russian final Garkushina took the gold with anothe 4–7 ride. Before that I had ridden against Hage to decide the destination of the bronze medal. Hage set a hot pace from the start and took the lead, but with great effort I managed to restrict it to about a second after three laps. Striving to win a medal – albeit the bronze – in my own country, I reduced the deficit until, at about halfway, we were level. I held the Dutch girl for a time and slowly began to edge ahead. I was feeling better than at any time in the series and resisted Hage's late challenge to win with 4–10.55 to 4–11.64. It was satisfying to stand on the podium in England and receive a medal, and I only wished it could have been the gold, but I had to accept that the Russian girls were faster and I could not turn back the clock. After all, I had dished it out to them in the past!

One amusing recollection I have from Leicester is of an event which occurred in the University Halls of Residence where the teams were billeted. Eileen Gray, anxious as ever to see to the welfare of the Great Britain team, asked Carol Barton what she would like to eat at a particular meal. Carol replied that she would like an omelette and Eileen placed a tick against 'omelette' on her list before asking how many eggs she wanted, to which Carol replied 'two'. Eileen put another tick next to the one she had already made, to indicate two eggs to the chef. When the omelette arrived it was on a huge oblong plate, and was of massive proportions – the chef had deciphered the two ticks as indicating an 11-egg omelette!

Before the championships *Cycling* had published letters which criticised me for my decision not to ride the road race with phrases such as 'Is she afraid of getting beaten?' and 'Has she reached the stage where she is not big enough to accept defeat?' These writers seemed to have missed the point. On that particular course I felt reasonably certain that I would not win no matter how I tried, especially with some members of our own team riding against me. I knew I could show well and probably finish in the first six or so, but I considered that the finish would be a bunch sprint and that we had sufficient racing girls who had a better chance of a medal in such a finish. It was also suggested in some quarters that I should take part in the road race with a view to riding a race which would help any of our girls with a 'lead-out' if such a one and myself were in contention at the end. Well, I already had experience of that from previous years when there was likely to be a bunch finish. 'Give me a lead out in the sprint, Beryl, and we have a good chance of a medal' they would say. I had always obliged but, as we crossed the line and I looked around me, I would discover that the 'sprinter' was never any better placed than I was. I thought this was one year when they would be better off without me. In fact one-tenth of a second covered the first twenty-five riders at the end of the race, and I don't doubt that I would have been among them – but not in the first three. I expect that if that had been the case some would have said that I should have stood down to allow the selection of a girl with a better chance in a sprint!

Later in the month I took my eleventh 100-mile title in Warwickshire with a time of 4–19–56 and, with Maureen Wroe and Lynn Harris backing me, Morley took the team medals. I won a few more races to wind up the season, notably the Yorkshire Century R.C. '100' where I clocked 4–11–27 to seal my twelfth win in the B.A.R., with an average of 25.729 m.p.h. When I had started out on my racing career in the evening '10s' on the Morley–Bradford road I did not visualise such a long run at the top.

The 1971 season started late for me; the first race I can recall was our own club's 'three-up' over a 25-mile course on the York–Hull road, when I rode with Nim, now a 42-year-old veteran, and Roy Caspell. The three of us enjoyed ourselves in finishing second to the Hull Thursday team with a time of 54–48. Denise and Ann Pallister teamed with Paul Gill, and they finished just outside the hour.

My next venture was not a competitive event, but a sponsored ride round Britain which covered over 2,000 miles in aid of the Samaritans. The ride was organised by the Lancashire Club, Clayton Velo, and I was one of fifteen well-known cyclists who rode in relays of four at a time, supported by a double-decker bus serving as back-up vehicle and dormitory, and living mostly on sandwiches and soup as we made our way up to the north of Scotland and back down the country into Cornwall.

Feeling relaxed and fit I won a '25' in Nottinghamshire in 58–39 the week before my bid for a thirteenth national championship. On a windswept course in Cambridgeshire I succeeded with a championship record of 57–48, with Ann Horswell second, but I was more pleased with the Morley team victory, however, because the two backing me were none other than Denise and Ann. With remarkable consistency they again finished next to each other in the placings, Ann with 1–7–54 and Denise twenty-three seconds behind. Denise and I became the first mother and daughter to win national medals in the same event in cycling, and probably the first in any other athletic sport. Denise had also become the youngest ever senior medal winner at fifteen.

The next outing was the Morley '25' on the 'Boro' course and in the women's race I finished in 57–16. The men's race had been won by Bas Breedon of the Rockingham C.C. in a time of 57–43, twenty-seven seconds slower than mine. As Bas was one of the fastest riders in the country and a former British champion and record holder at the distance you can imagine how pleased I was.

The next major objective was the 50-mile championship which, like the '25', I was hoping to win for the thirteenth time. On a course near Kidderminster, I was successful with 2–0–33, Maureen and Ann helping me to win the team title. After that it was the road race title over a 40-mile course in Derbyshire. I broke away shortly after the start and left the others, winning by nearly eight minutes. Following this was the 3,000 metres title on the track. I won through to the final at the Kirkby track before rain intervened and we had to return the following Wednesday evening when I beat Bernadette Swinnerton with a 4–16 ride.

In the Essex C.R.A. 100-mile I returned 4–5–24, a time which would have placed me third in the men's race on the same course – in a very strong field.

This put me in good form for the championship over this distance, which I won for the twelfth time on a day of strong winds in a time of 4–9–16. Maureen and Ann again helped me to win the team title which meant that the club had made a clean sweep of all the individual and team titles that season. The day was not without drama because Denise was struck by a car when she stepped out into the road to get a photo of me crossing the line. At first it was feared that she had a serious head injury and she was rushed to hospital in Peterborough while I was left standing at the roadside in tears. As it turned out her injuries were no worse than concussion and shock with cuts and bruises, but she had to stay in hospital overnight. When she came out of hospital the following day a local clubman kept her at his home for a few days until she was fit to travel back to Leeds.

Denise's little box camera had been wrecked in the accident and out of the blue a complete stranger, a lady who had read about the accident in the paper, sent her the money for a new one. Such unexpected acts of kindness are very heart-warming in this often hard and cruel world.

The British team travelled to northern Italy by boat and train for the world championships at Varese – twenty-three hours of stuffy boredom – and we arrived feeling tired and hungry. Our tempers were not improved when we discovered that along the way our bikes had temporarily gone missing. We then faced a coach journey of fifteen miles from Varese into the mountains, which may sound an idyllic place for the team H.Q., but in fact the hotel attracted people from the towns because of its noted 'night-life' and was extremely noisy which I did not like one little bit, quite apart from the fact that it was so far from the track.

On the second day of competition rain interfered with the programme, and the schedules unbeknown to our team were altered, causing sprinter Ernie Crutchlow to miss a ride and the chance of further progress. The same thing almost happened to me, but through the manager of another team I discovered in time that I was supposed to be at the track. It would be easy to blame our Team Manager, Tommy Godwin, but he had to cope with the situation that the B.C.F. had handed him, and it was difficult for him to look after the team's welfare fifteen miles from the track and also be on hand to guide and oversee the team in competition.

However, I was in good form and ready to challenge the Russians, this year represented by Garkushina and Lyubov Zadorozhnaya. Garkushina cracked out a superb qualifying round of 3–54.71; my time was second best at 3–59.79 and the other Russian was just outside four minutes. I knew that Tamara was going to be the one to beat for the gold and if our form held we should meet in the final. In the quarter-finals Garkushina beat Bernadette Swinnerton, I beat Tartagni of Italy and Zadorozhnaya beat the American, McElmury. In the final 'quarter' Keetie Hage of Holland, with about a kilometre to go and in a comfortable lead, punctured and was awarded the round against Polanska of Czechoslovakia. Garkushina and I had been the fastest over the full distance and should have been kept apart in the 'semis', instead of which we were paired together. The judges ruling was that, based on her time at two-thirds distance, Hage would have ridden a faster quarter-final than me but, even if this reasoning is accepted, their calculations were based on faulty facts. Hage had been given a time of 2–23.17 when she punctured at two-thirds distance, and a moment's thought will show that this time must have been incorrect, even allowing for the standing start. The timing had obviously been stopped earlier than two kilometres, probably at the moment Hage showed signs of difficulty and before the race was actually halted. In any case, if the officials wanted to theorise they could have taken into account my known fast finish. There seemed to be no way that Garkushina and I should meet in the semi-final except in the muddled thinking of the U.C.I. officials.

However, I returned to the hotel not knowing about the pairings and prepared myself mentally for a meeting against Zadorozhnaya, the 'easier' of the two Russians, or Hage. Any Russian in a semi-final stage would be a tough proposition, as would the Dutch girl, but I felt confident I could beat Zadorozhnaya or Hage, a victory over either of them giving me the chance of another gold. It would be nice, I thought, after all these years at world championships, to lift the title again, and I knew that I was going as well as ever. Perhaps Garkushina would not be quite as good this year. I knew that I was in with a great chance, whatever happened, but I would give her a tough race and, if I did go down, at least I would have the silver. Thus I mused, blissfully unaware of the way the pairings had been worked out.

Even while I was asleep the President of the B.C.F., Arthur Campbell, was putting in his protests to the stone-faced and immovable U.C.I. officials. I travelled to the track the next day keyed up for my two races, still unaware of what had taken place the previous night. Incredible as it may seem, nobody had told me about it! I prepared for my ride against Zadorozhnaya when, five minutes before the start, the blow was struck. The Russian preparing to ride against me was Garkushina! I was furious and near to tears and although I managed to keep my temper under control I was inwardly devastated. The fact that the decision had been kept from me until the last possible moment made matters so much worse. Had I been told first thing in the day it would have been a blow, but I would at least have had the opportunity of making a mental re-adjustment. Another example of bad judgement on the part of our officials, who should know their riders and consider how they react to given situations.

Choked and miserable, I was never in with a chance. Had I met her in the final as I had hoped things might have been so different. I know the result would have been closer and in the event of my defeat I would at least have won the silver. For the record Tamara's ride was 3–57.81 and I was well beaten by eight seconds. To be fair, perhaps, to the view that the U.C.I. officials had taken, Hage had the measure of Zadorozhnaya in the other 'semi' with a very fast ride of 3–56.31 before going down in the final to Garkushina. I had pulled myself together for the ride-off for the bronze medal, and it turned out to be very close. I almost decided not to ride for the bronze until I reminded myself that, if I was physically able to, I had a duty to do so. I'm glad I did now, for it gave me another 'worlds' medal. Result: Burton 3–58.56; Zadorozhnaya

3–58.72. Even after all the years that have passed since then I still feel a twinge of annoyance when I think about that occasion.

There is another little story about this particular medal which is worth telling. It was my fourteenth medal at world championships, and I was to win another before my international career came to an end – a grand total of fifteen. For years, whenever the matter has been discussed or mentioned in print, I have always been credited with fourteen. I never questioned the number as I never sat down and added up the score. As I stated very early in this story, I push medals from my mind once they are won and, indeed, I never used to know their whereabouts in the house at any given moment. That may say something about my housekeeping, but they tended to get put into the bottom of drawers and other odd corners or not put back together after they had been loaned out for display. But when we were sorting things out in our new house in 1984, Charlie picked up a canvas bag and, hearing a rattle, tipped out the contents onto the floor. It was my championship medals which he had finally collected together before our move and, for want of somewhere better, he had put them into the bag. Casually he began to count them and was surprised that there were fifteen. Like me, he had never consciously looked back over my career to keep a 'score', but did expect to find fourteen medals. Thumbing through the record books, both English and foreign, and counting the number of times my name appeared in the championship lists, the total was, indeed, fourteen. We were perplexed by this until we went through the years, carefully recalling each 'world' win and comparing this with what the records stated, arriving at a total of fifteen. The medal which has, somehow, not been credited to me, is the bronze ride at Varese, the story of which I have just recounted. On that occasion the bronze medal in the women's sprint was taken by the Czech girl Zajickova. For some reason her name is printed again in the record of the women's pursuit. Somebody made an error at the time and it has been repeated ever since without question.

The road race at these world championships was on a course which I would have preferred to be tougher or longer – there was only one decent hill to be negotiated. The story can best be summed up by the headline in *Cycling*, 'Beryl does all the work for Konkina'. I finished ninth in a massed sprint of the twenty-five riders who contested the finish, and the report began 'Beryl Burton did everything except win in this women's world road race. She attacked, she chased, and even sprinted, and if in the end she was 'only' ninth then she can take comfort in knowing that she had made the race.'

It was the old story, all the field hanging on to me for a sprint finish, nobody prepared to come up and work with me and perhaps form a 'break'. For the record, behind the Russian, Konkina, came Morena Tartagni of Italy and Keetie Hage of Holland. The American girl Audrey McElmury was fourth in the field of forty-two, inches away from a medal spot, and paid me a nice compliment afterwards. Describing the race she said 'She (Burton) doesn't have enough snap on the hills. If she'd only get away from them just a little they'd never be able to catch her. But as it is she goes up steadily in a big gear and it's easy to sit on her. But whichever way you look at it, she's still the best woman rider in the world.'

In the Birmingham St Christopher's '25' I improved my season's best with 56–29, while Denise did her best time with 1–5–8, a very pleasing improvement. My win brought my British Best All-rounder average for the season to 25.463 m.p.h. and gave me my thirteenth win in the competition.

Chapter 12
*Mother and daughter ride the world championships – San Sebastian and
Barcelona – W.C.R.A. and the B.C.F. – Another 'bug' – Montreal*

I rode well in a number of early season events in 1972 but the first big win
came in the Glade C.C. 50-mile on Spring Bank Holiday, where I beat all the
men to win with a time of 2–0–30. Second was Andy Bell of Letchworth Velo,
over a minute and a half behind. The following day I rode the W.C.R.A. road
race championship at Basildon over a 25.3-mile course, winning by 2–29 from
Pat Pepper of Colchester Rovers. Denise, now sixteen, finished in third place.
I retained my '25' title in the Manchester Ladies promotion on a course in
Cheshire with 58–55, Maureen and Ann backing me for the team title. It was
my thirty-ninth R.T.T.C. championship win and my fourteenth '25', with a
near five-minute margin over Gill Clapton of the Hounslow club. Denise
finished fifteenth on that day, a good performance as she had an injured elbow
following a crash when racing in Holland. She had broken away from the field
of sixty in the 75-kilometre race and had unluckily skidded in the gravel on a
corner when it seemed she might win. Already she was making her mark in
the higher echelons of bike racing.

At the end of June I collected another national record when I won the
Barnet 10-mile in 22–6, following this the next day with the road
championship over thirty-four miles in Essex. I had a margin of 6 minutes 10
seconds and had time to rub down and then watch the sprint for second place.
Denise was sixth, and I was a little angry with her and some of the other girls
for hanging back for the sprint in a slow race. The mental attitude to road
racing was all wrong, and girls who could time trial quite fast were cruising
around instead of making a race. It was all so negative.

At the beginning of July near Newark I won the 50-mile title for the
fourteenth time with a ride of 1–58–59, nearly ten minutes clear of the second
girl. Maureen Wroe had now become Maureen Pearson on her marriage, and
she and Denise helped me to another team title.

Two weeks later I rode among the men in the Middleton R.C. '25' on the
York–Hull road and, in a pretty strong field, I was on the scratch mark in the
handicap section. I justified that position by winning with 56–49, forty-nine
seconds clear of Brian Richards of the Kirkby C.C. I worked hard and trained
hard and made my mind dominate my body, refusing to accept that the
passing years could make any difference to my ability to win.

In the Meanwood Wheelers 25-mile in Yorkshire I was again in a men's race
in a very 'hot' field, which included the great Alf Engers, who won with a

dazzling 52–35. But he was the only man who managed to beat me, for I was second with 54–44, a new women's record. I had beaten my previous best by eleven seconds, and the next man by twenty-one seconds! Maureen Pearson and Margaret Allen backed me for a new women's team record, lowering the time to an aggregate of 3–24–0.

I had again been selected for the road and pursuit in the world championships to be held in the south of France, for the track series at Marseilles and for the road race at Gap, and it meant sacrificing my chance of retaining the 100-mile title which was to be held at the same time and which June Pitchford subsequently took.

In the pursuit at Marseilles it was the same four girls as the previous year who battled through to the semi-finals but, so far as I was concerned, there were no upsets of any kind. I was beaten by Garkushina in the semi-final, and went down to Zadorozhnaya in the ride-off for the bronze.

The road race at Gap was held over sixty kilometres with some climbing, and I looked forward to showing well, in spite of my seniority by some years over all the field bar that stalwart, Elsy Jacobs of Luxembourg. There was an extra interest for me as Denise had also been selected; I think it was another 'mother and daughter' first. At the end of five kilometres came the first hill, a twisting climb, with the field all together, and I made a move to the front. Forcing the pace, I kept the tempo going over the top. Already some riders were dropped from the bunch as I increased the pace, and a nice break of eight was formed including, I was happy to see, one of the British girls, Carol Barton. It also included two other former world road champions, Konkina and McElmury. At the end of the first lap we had a lead of sixteen seconds over the chasing group, which I learned later included Denise, with the remainder some way behind. On the main climb for the second time, and I again made them groan with the effort of staying with me, and one of the Russians dropped behind. After two laps we had increased our lead by over two minutes on the chasers. Another strenuous lap, trying to set the hardest pace possible, with the others sitting in behind until at last Zadorozhnaya made a move, out of the saddle and over the hill. It was a good effort by a class rider, but on the descent I hammered away with the others leeched on to my wheel and gradually brought her back. The next climb and the going was still hard with me doing all the work, and Barton was dropped after a spell of sharing the pace with me. It was a great effort by Carol, who rode alone to the finish, staying clear of the rest of the field for a meritorious seventh. As our little group climbed the last hill I was feeling good in spite of my efforts, but the others stuck where they were, waiting for the sprint. Top gear for the descent at goodness knows how many miles per hour and then on to the last two kilometres, slightly uphill, where Chapron of France finally came to the front. I matched her, and then for the first time in the race had other riders around me. Konkina went, and faded; as Zadorozhnaya took up the running, from somewhere at the back of the group of six, Geneviève Gambillon of France shot past everybody. Zadorozhnaya was second and Konkina third and I was fifth in this leading group, over three minutes ahead of Carol who, in turn, was nearly forty seconds clear of the next rider, with the remainder of the field spread way back. Denise finished twenty-third, understandably fading a little near the end and dropping from the chasing group.

It was another failure of mine to take a medal against class riders who were afraid of me. (Gambillon had been stuck at the back of the group all day taking an 'arm-chair' ride and making no effort to keep our break clear from the rest of the field.) How I would have loved it if the distance had been a hundred kilometres instead of sixty.

After France it was straight into our own national championships at the Kirkby track, near Liverpool, where I won the pursuit for the eleventh time, beating Carol in the final. During the season my club-mate Roy Caspell had been fulfilling the potential that we had earlier recognised and, following a great 12-hour ride which was fractionally longer than my record (and made him club champion at the distance!), he was leading the men's B.A.R. In the Yorkshire Cycling Federation 100-mile he pulled out a wonderful 3–55–36. The club was hoping that this would clinch the B.A.R. title for him, and if I succeeded in the women's B.A.R. it would give the club a unique 'double'. On the same day that Roy rode the Y.C.F. '100' I rode in the Yorkshire Ladies C.A. promotion at the same distance and managed another performance inside four hours with 3–57–49. If I had been riding in the men's event, which was held over the same course, I would have finished third, just behind the second-placed man. This ride put me at the top of the B.A.R. table.

Two weeks later I improved my season's 25-mile time in the Colchester Rover promotion with 54–56, faster than all the men in their event on the same course. Their winner was Roger Queen of Luton Wheelers, four seconds slower, heading many of the fastest men in the country.

During September I rode the Boro' in one of the Campagnolo Trophy Competition events. This was a series of races throughout the country during the season, points being awarded for placings in each event to decide the Trophy winner, and competition was fierce among all the specialists over twenty-five miles. The winner of the Huddersfield Star Wheelers promotion was one of the great 25-milers, Dave Holliday of the Gordano club, with a personal best of 53 minutes exactly. Frank Taylor of Notts and Derby was second with 53–56 and I was third with 54–56. A lot of good men finished behind me that day so I was delighted.

There was a dramatic finish to the men's B.A.R. Roy Caspell had won the

12-hour championship and then later succeeded with an even greater distance, as I have related. With his 50-mile and 100-mile times it appeared that he would win the title when Bob Porter of the Hounslow club, who had faster '50' and '100' times than Roy, rode in the West Suffolk 12-hour and his mileage gave him a fractionally better average. In a last-gasp effort Roy raced in the Harrogate Nova C.C. 50-mile hoping for an improvement but, although he raced to a personal best time of 1–55–37 to finish third, the improvement was too slight to dislodge Porter from the top. I was also in the Nova race, finishing sixth with 1–56–44 which improved my B.A.R. average a little.

I ended the season with a visit to Sussex where I attended a dinner and stayed up late, snatching a few hours' sleep and then winning the Brighton Mitre '25' with 58–56. I had retained my form to the end, and it had been another successful year, rounded off by the night of the year at the Rainbow Room in London where I received my awards and, more importantly, was able to relax in the company of so many of the people I had met up and down the country during the season. It was my fourteenth successive Best All-rounder title, with a record 26.112 m.p.h.

The following season started where the previous one had finished. Shortly after my thirty-sixth birthday I rode in the Nunbrook Wheelers '25' on the Boro' course and finished fifth behind Alf Engers with 57–53, and in the afternoon I was among the 150-strong entry in the Don Valley Wheelers 10-mile. I finished second, only four seconds behind Malcolm Johnson of Rotherham C.C. with a time of 21–25. I not only established a new women's competition record, but smashed my own record by the colossal margin, for the '10s', of forty-one seconds.

An interesting race at this period was the Yorkshire Ladies 10-mile which I won, with Denise taking second place and Morley the team prize. I received a special prize of a racing jersey in the Yorkshire Ladies colours in the memory of Christine Rowbotham, and I was very touched because, as I have previously recounted, I have my own little memory of Christine. There were more wins at the 25-mile distance, including a '58' ride in the Spartan Wheelers, and then Denise and I filled the first two places in the Yorkshire Ladies '15', taking the team award as we had done earlier in the '10'. Eleven years later, when the idea of this book was beginning to formulate, we again carried off the team award in the same event.

The '25' championship again, this year held on the Boro', and I won for the fifteenth time with 57–26. Denise was fourth, only a few seconds away from a third-place medal, but she had the consolation of sharing in the team award. I was looking forward to defending my 50-mile crown, the chance to do so coming shortly after. Before that, however, I won the national road-race title, the fourth in a row, by nearly five minutes from Denise, and then cracked my

50-mile record with 1–54–7 in the Sharrow event, winning from a strong men's field.

You might find it difficult to appreciate that my motivation was as high as ever, even though the novelty of winning national titles and breaking records was behind me. But this is what time trialling is all about: the ability to beat the targets you set yourself. Your motivation is that you want to prove you can do better than you did last time, assuming similar conditions. In fact I wasn't so much riding for the titles themselves, as trying to beat my own competition records at the distance. I only really started thinking about going for the twenty-fifth B.A.R. title, for instance, when someone pointed out that I had already won twenty-two.

About this time I was experimenting with a 62-teeth chain-ring, I think now it was because I had it in mind to try some road records. The question of gearing is something which always interests keen cyclists, and the large gears I have used during my career are often the subject of some discussion. The thing which I think will surprise most people is that in training I use low gears – nothing above a 70-inch. I could always tell immediately if Charlie had altered a chain-ring without telling me, because the pedals would not go 'over the top' as I felt they should and would berate him when I returned from a training ride. It may be that training on low gears and racing on high gears works for other riders, too. I don't know. I do know it works for me. Riding a gear of 89-inch on the track eventually caused me some difficulty, and I tried gearing up to 92 which, in view of the big gears I used on the road, should have worked. Somehow it didn't, but 87 never felt right either.

There was another good win at the end of July when I won the Rockingham '25' in less than fifty-five minutes. Behind me was Billy Hudson, the speedy Irishman who came across to the mainland to ride with the Morley club, Vic Smith of Hull Thursday, Dave Shorrock and many other top male riders. With Malcolm Cowgill, Morley carried off the team award as well. At this time, also, Nim won the 24-hour title again with a mileage of 490.31, his sixth success, so our little Morley club was still going well.

The national pursuit title was the next objective, which I won with 4–13.9, the first time I had been on a track all season. Plans had just been published for the building of an international track in Leeds and I said then that I would 'believe it when I see it'. All the plans must now be gathering dust in the Council archives – but what a difference it would have made for West Yorkshire cyclists if they had had a velodrome to race and train on. At the time I simply could not find either the time or the money to travel to Leicester during the week for pursuit training unless I was to curtail my other racing activities, so I had to represent my country without track preparation against girls who had trained and raced on decent tracks. It was rather like asking a good runner to take on a hurdle race at international level without any hurdles training, and only one event of its kind under his belt previously during the season.

I then hurried down to Essex for the 100-mile title race, again going from one extreme to the other of bike racing. The previous year I had not been able to defend the title, and now I wanted it back again. I managed it in 4–6–27, eighteen minutes ahead of June Pitchford, and Denise took fourth place with a very good performance at this distance for someone of her age. The same day and over the same course Ian White of Clifton won the men's title, making it a Yorkshire 'double'. My winning time would have placed me fifth in their championship.

I travelled with the British team – a team which included Denise – to Spain for the world series toward the end of August, and frankly, I was not expecting too much: for the reasons I have already stated I thought the pursuit was now beyond me, although I did expect to be concerned in the later rounds, and the road race would not be long enough for me to weaken the rest, so they would simply travel at whatever speed I cared to set.

The track events were held at San Sebastian, not a place with good memories for me, and in the pursuit qualifying rounds I was third fastest with 4–11.8. Garkushina left nobody in any doubt that she was again to be the winner this year with a marvellous 3–59.28, and second spot was taken by Keetie van Oosten-Hage with 4–2.97. Van Oosten-Hage was the same Keetie Hage with whom I had battled previously, now riding under her new married name. This year another British rider, Carol Barton, was going well, getting through the qualifying round and later pulling out a great ride of 4–10.27 to beat the American Miji Reoch by almost two seconds. I came up against the Czech, Polanska, whom I beat easily enough by about five seconds, but Garkushina and van Oosten-Hage were turning out marvellous rides too. And so to the semi-finals, where at long last I had another British rider with me, Carol having battled her way through. Unfortunately, the day before her ride she crashed on the road in training and was considerably bruised down her right leg. She was hardly in the best condition for her 'semi' against the mighty Garkushina but battled bravely to record 4–10.91 against the Russian's 4–3.89. In the other 'semi' I raced against the Dutch girl who took an early lead and never seemed in danger of losing it. I was now no longer really comfortable on the track and realised that determination and fitness were not enough. I managed another 4–7 but van Oosten-Hage was about five seconds better. So, uniquely for the British team, we had two girls riding against each other for the bronze, with the satisfaction that Britain was at least certain of a medal. Carol had been ill earlier in the year, which had reduced her cycling – in later years also she suffered ill-health – and, consequently, we never saw the best of one of the classiest riders our country has produced. For the record I beat her with 4–8.8 to 4–12.31, but she made me battle all the way, leading for the first four laps until I began to flow. In the final it was a Russian victory over the Netherlands – 4–1.6 to 4–4.48. The first two places had gone as expected but many were surprised that I was still good enough to gain the bronze – my fifteenth world championship medal. Hugh Porter won the fourth of his gold medals in the professional pursuit – a wonderful performance.

We travelled across to the other coast for the road race at Barcelona on the Montjuich circuit, which was fairly hilly but, again, too short for my liking at thirty-four miles. At the end it was a sprint of eighteen riders in which I took eighth place, with Denise finishing twentieth a couple of minutes behind. Van den Broek of Belgium was the winner, van Oosten-Hage taking another silver and Rebrovskaya of Russia the bronze, and yet again I had done nearly all the work, only Laenen of Belgium and van Oosten-Hage making a tentative effort at one point. The race can best be summed up by quoting Geoffrey Nicholson's report in *The Observer*: 'The Russians were not prepared to risk anything by joining Mrs Burton in an attack, while she was unable to open anything on her own account. Even at 36 she is still clearly the strongest competitor in women's cycling. But devotion to time trialling has developed only her ability to set and keep an unyielding pace. She could have towed the other riders like a line of trucks for another hour if need be. But she hadn't the sudden change of speed which would enable her to break away from the hangers-on. And in the end the course was neither long enough nor severe enough to allow her simply to burn them off.'

At this time a certain acrimony was creeping into the relationship between the W.C.R.A. and the B.C.F., which surfaced at the Association dinner when Eileen Gray criticised the treatment the girls were receiving from the governing body in comparison with male riders, particularly as far as finances were concerned, and pointing out the difference in performance between the men's and women's teams at the recent world championships. As we learned from mixing with the other teams at the 'worlds', various invitations were sent to B.C.F. headquarters for women's teams to race abroad, but these sank without trace in the B.C.F. offices. In particular I was constantly asked by the Russians why we (the British) never accepted any of the invitations they had made, and I could only reply that these had never come to our attention. Any team would, of course, have had to meet its own travelling expenses and, no doubt, the B.C.F. felt unwilling to meet such expenditure. As it was one of the poor relations of the sporting life of this country, this was understandable but, as the W.C.R.A. would probably have been willing to go a long way to finding the cash, it would have been nice if we had been given the chance, at least, to do something about it.

Charlie and I had struck up a particular rapport over the years with the Russian officials, especially their team doctor Robert Guralnik who was constantly asking when he would see me racing in his country. I would dearly have loved to race over there, and it is one of the disappointments of my long career that I never made it.

It was plain that the B.C.F. were not going to spend much money on the girls in international racing except at world championships, since already the strength of the team had been reduced, and the two trips abroad that year (to France and Holland) that some girls had made had been financed by the W.C.R.A. But no matter what the W.C.R.A. wished to do, they could only move internationally under the aegis of cycling's governing body – the B.C.F.

I started 1974 in hospital. The doctors were trying to find out whether my 'bug' was the old one from nine years previously or another I had picked up from Spain in the last season. I had so many tests carried out on me that when they wanted to do the final test I refused. I had just had enough. This test involved a tube with a light on the end being lowered down the throat into the stomach, and though I finally relented it made no difference. I am probably still carrying the 'bug' around to this day.

At the end of May I raced in the W.C.R.A. week-end against a strong Dutch team and a team from France. I won the 10-mile time trial with Denise third and this was followed by a '25' which I won with 56–57. The next stage was a 27-mile road race which I won from the Dutch girl van den Plaat and this made me the overall winner from Cahard of France.

The summer sped by. I retained my '25' and '50' titles, and then travelled to France with an English team to ride in the six-stage Four Days at Le Havre. Having won the time-trial stage, I was second in four of the other road stages and then won the last stage, running out the overall winner by fourteen seconds from world champion, van den Broek. Denise also rode and finished eighth, the British team finishing third in the team placings.

I won the national road-race championship on a hard course which suited me almost on my own doorstep at Wakefield, with Denise finishing eighth, and the next 'big one' was the pursuit title at Leicester where I reached the final against the other logical contender, Carol Barton, winning with a time of 4–13.6 against Carol's 4–19.97.

The 100-mile championship took place on a course near Stamford, the day after my pursuit win at Leicester, so I was not feeling in top form! Nevertheless, I won with 4–19–11 and June Pitchford ran me fairly close with a time some three minutes slower. But at least my form was holding for the world titles at Montreal. I had been to so many by now that I almost wished I did not have to go. I travelled to Canada, though, conscious of the honour of wearing a Great Britain jersey and prepared to try my hardest.

Garkushina was unstoppable that year, starting out in the qualifying rides with a 3–58.46 ride. I managed 4–8.6, and Carol was faster with 4–7.25. We both departed from the scene in the 'quarters', Carol going down to Mary-Jane Reoch of the U.S.A. and that old adversary, van Oosten-Hage, proving too good for me. In this same round Garkushina turned out a fantastic 3–52.5 in beating Rambouts of Belgium before going on to win the gold against her compatriot, Smirnova. This was Tamara's sixth pursuit gold, one more than I had won at the same discipline, a wonderful achievement by a great rider. I would dearly have loved to have ridden against her at my pursuiting peak and fully trained for it.

So, I was left with the road race, and I expected the tactics would be the same as in previous years. I had not settled very well in Montreal, and from where our team was staying there was an interminable ride through heavy traffic to the outskirts before you could put in any serious training. I could no longer 'switch on' to world competition like I used to. I had ridden about six road races that season, and that was more than usual, and I would be racing against girls who rode them every week and would have sixty or seventy under their belts by this time. But I knew that I was still stronger than any of them. Barring accidents nobody would drop me, but I just lacked the 'zip' to make the necessary break.

The race was over five laps of a 12-kilometre course, with a good hill to climb – the one and a half mile Mount Royal. Carol Barton had crashed while training and was not in very good shape, and the day before the race Denise had also taken a tumble, her second in Montreal, requiring three stitches. On the first lap she took another fall after touching a wheel and retired after being among the leaders on Mount Royal the first time round. Carol, feeling her injuries, struggled gamely before retiring on the second lap.

At the end of two laps I was with a leading group of twelve and, although we were not moving very quickly, the rest seemed already out of it. During lap three our pace quickened a little and three of our group were dropped, followed a little later by van den Broek, the defending champion, Rebrovskaya and Kuznetsova of Russia and Kwantes of Holland. Our remaining group of five crawled round the last two laps, nobody willing to put on much pressure. This time I declined to make the pace for the others: Gambillon of France, the winner two years before; Tzaune of Russia; van Oosten-Hage of Holland and Laenen of Belgium.

Once or twice I would try a bit of 'kidology', shaping as if to try for a break, which galvanised them all into action, seeking the Burton wheel. Then I would sit up. Mount Royal for the last time and I was feeling fresh, for it had been easier than my own training stints in the Yorkshire Dales. Nearing the top, the others seemed to be struggling a little, Gambillon especially, and it had to be a split-second decision 'to go' or 'not to go'. Well, I chose not to go and, though I was first into the half-mile finishing straight, Tzaune hit the front and Gambillon shot by her at the line to take her second victory in three years, with the Russian second and van Oosten-Hage third, Laenen fourth and me fifth – all in the same time.

One can only reflect on whether I should have tried for a break over the last climb, and it can be argued that at worst I would still have taken fifth place, but it is all in the realm of conjecture. I made an instant decision at a particular moment, and without consciously realising it then I think it was a decision brought about by my lack of aggression at that time. The adrenalin just did not flow in Montreal.

It was my last world championships, a total of fifteen medals of one sort and another, and it could and should have been more. I had to be left with the satisfaction of knowing that despite my seniority in years no other woman in the world could shake me off and that, given enough miles, I could beat them all. But they don't plan the distance of road courses to suit one rider, which is fair enough, and I have to leave it to the cycling historians to note my record of consistency over sixteen years. Certainly I don't think any other rider has ridden more world championship races than I have.

I didn't miss the world championships in the years that followed. There would have been no point in my going, because in the last series I just froze, certainly on the track and probably on the road too – I don't know why. I knew I was capable of achieving something, which was the upsetting thing about it. I still get nervous for big events even now.

Back in England and I rode in the Yorkshire Century '100', clocking 4–20–27 to finish fifth behind Mike McNamara, with Denise and John Baines helping me to a team win. At the end of September in the Harrogate Nova 50-mile I improved my year's best with 1–55–50, bringing my British B.A.R. average for the season to 25.302 m.p.h.

My final memory of 1974 is when Charlie beat me in a ride to Blackpool! We were to attend the B.C.F. dinner and prize presentation and decided to ride over, with Charlie setting out first, the idea being that I would catch him and we would arrive together. It was a tough headwind and I never did catch him. My excuse that I had 'gone off course' met chortles of mock disbelief, and I think anyway that Charlie was quite proud of himself.

Chapter 13
*Personal problems – the 50-mile record – 1976 R.R. championship – Pursuit
finals at Leicester*

I was racing again by March 1975, and in mid-April was inside the hour at Cambridge and my first '50' in early May brought me a time of 2–0–48 in the Warwickshire R.C. event, only two men going faster.

June brought the W.C.R.A. international week-end which opened with a 10-mile time trial which I won with Denise second. In the following '25' I clocked 57–33 for another victory, and this was followed by the road race when I was unplaced behind the Dutch girl, Ann Riemersma. Overall I won with a total of 104 points to Riemersma's 96, Denise third with 95.

Two French teams had been hosted by the W.C.R.A. for this international in anticipation of a British team being invited to the Le Havre stage race which I had won the previous year. The invitation was duly received by the B.C.F., who felt that they could not fund the travelling expenses of the girls, and the invitation was declined. On discovering this, the W.C.R.A. pressed for the invitation to be renewed and the expenses were found for a manager and four girls. It was typical of the worsening relationship between the B.C.F. and the W.C.R.A. at that time, with the governing body declining overseas invitations for our girls.

However, while all this was in the air, I had my 25-mile title to defend in the East Midlands, where I was successful with a time of 58–45. It was my forty-seventh R.T.T.C championship and I began to look forward to the time when I could make it a half-century. Denise finished third that day.

In the W.C.R.A. road championship I was only narrowly beaten at the line by Faith Murray, who won many national sprint titles in her career. Denise was fourth, by this time firmly established at the top of the sport. The Harrogate International Festival of Cycling came at the end of June, and in the women's '50' on a day of bitter north winds I managed a win in the slow time, for me, of 2–6–51. In the '25' I hit top form with a time of 55–46 and Denise finished second. I decided to give the national road race championship a miss, the winner being Jayne Westbury, with Denise collecting another medal in second place.

Denise was now beginning to realise her potential. She travelled with the team to the Le Havre stage race and made it a Burton double by winning, as I had the previous year. This must be another record – mother and daughter winning an international stage race in successive years.

After retaining the 50-mile title in Warwickshire I raced two 100-miles on successive week-ends, first the Goodmayes in Essex where I pulled out another ride inside four hours with 3–59–51 and then the national championship, which I won for the fifteenth time in 4–11–40.

While I was concerning myself with this Denise was riding in the national pursuit championship at Leicester. I had decided to give this a miss, feeling that if I performed well I would be asked to ride the world championships again, something that I now preferred to avoid. Denise kept the Burton flag flying once more by winning the title, and she certainly seemed to be following my wheel marks, just getting the better of Margaret Gordon-Smith in the last lap, 4–19.17 to 4–19.66.

As I wished I was not selected for the world championships in Belgium but Denise was. I was thrilled when, on the same Rocourt track where I had won my first world medal back in 1959, she gained the bronze medal behind van Oosten-Hage and Reoch and, again, I suppose it was something of a mother-daughter record. In the following road race Denise finished twelfth.

My year was proceeding almost placidly; I was retaining my form and apart from a stiff back on occasions I was having a trouble-free season. In the Yorkshire R.C. 50-mile I recorded 1–58–27, finishing in sixth place among the men, and was part of the winning Morley team. I had already ridden a '1–55' in the Pennine race in August, so I was set fair to retain the B.A.R., and I had another fast time before the season ended with 57–9 in the Huddersfield Star '25'.

My B.A.R. in this year was the seventeenth in a row with an average of 26.047 m.p.h., nearly 2 m.p.h. in front of June Pitchford, and Denise had taken third spot; but Morley now lacked a fast third girl and we were unable to take the team title, which went to Prescot Eagle.

Starting competition again in March, 1976, in the Featherstone R.C. Hilly '30' I rode regularly in races with a largely male entry until I reached peak form on the 9th May in the Otley '25' winning with 56–31, my 100th ride under the hour. At the end of the month Denise and I raced in the W.C.R.A. international week-end, where I won the 10- and 25-mile time trials in fast times, but in the road race where six of us were sprinting for the line one of the English girls slammed into me and we both hit the deck. I was fuming afterwards, but picked myself off the ground to take sixth place, being second overall on points in the three stages, with Denise third behind Riemersma. A week later it was the W.C.R.A. road championship and, in another sprint finish, Denise and I were equal sixth.

The discord between the W.C.R.A. and the B.C.F. rumbled on, and now that the latter were taking a greater interest in the women's side of the sport the W.C.R.A, which had fostered it for so many years, were beginning to lose their grip. It was right and proper for the governing body to interest itself but it could have handled matters more diplomatically and worked with, rather than against, the W.C.R.A. I know that a number of invitations were sent to the latter for me to race abroad, and as a matter of protocol these were forwarded to the B.C.F., where they seemed to disappear. Even when Denise and I had been named personally in an invitation from the Dutch Federation to ride over there, a team was sent that did not include either of us, to the chagrin of the Dutch. I would have been happy to take up some of the invitations and ride in a Morley jersey if need be for expenses only, but as usual the B.C.F. played its cards close to its chest and we never heard of the opportunities.

That my form was as good as ever showed in the Richmond and Darlington '25' on the Catterick course where only two of the country's fastest men could beat me – Mike Gadd and Arthur Caygill. The race was on a Thursday evening, a much more civilised time to ride than early Sunday morning, but even so there was not a great amount of traffic about; the conditions were perfect. My time was 53–21, a new competition record by 1 minute 23 seconds, and Denise recorded 58–56. I had long hoped to ride a '53' but had never expected to take such a large slice from the record. The 25-mile championship was won for the eighteenth time with 58–44 and two weeks later the 50-mile also with 2–1–24 on a Shropshire course.

It was about this time that I became unhappy in my personal life. The problem was basically between Denise and me. She was now a world-class rider, and I was honestly pleased about that, although there were wagging tongues who claimed I was jealous. Our trouble had a domestic basis which I suppose is not uncommon between mother and daughter when the latter is still living at home, but we were not an ordinary household and the tension was heightened by our cycling activities. I had worked very hard all my life, and fitted in my racing and training with a job as well as the household work. Rightly or wrongly I felt there were times when Denise could do more, and that Charlie did not support my point of view. Perhaps the constant strain of competition clouded my judgement – I don't know. I have tried to set this down objectively so the reader will realise my state of mind at this particular time. Denise and I are happy with each other now and goodness knows much has happened to her since that time, enough to make any mother concerned and worried for her daughter.

Matters came to a head during the Harrogate International Festival of Cycling. I rode in the 50-mile promoted by the Nunbrook Wheelers, who also promoted events at the same distance for amateur men and the professional roadmen. It was rather windy, but still a day on which some decent times could be expected from the high-class fields riding on the Boro'. The fastest of the 'pros' was Les West, a rider who had taken fourth place in a world title race, but his 1–48–46 was beaten on the day by Vic Smith, one of the great amateur 50-milers, by twelve seconds. I had already retained my 50-mile title and was expected to beat the rest of the girls, but I don't think anyone anticipated the time I turned out that morning. It was one of my greatest rides in all forms of competition and I smashed my own competition record by almost three minutes in recording a time of 1–51–30. Observers considered that under calmer conditions I would have beaten 1–50. As it was, if I had been riding in the professional field I would have been placed fourth!

Denise finished second with a very good time, but I had beaten her by about twelve minutes and I knew I was in for a hard tussle when we lined up the following Saturday for the national road race championship held over a testing course based on Rudding Park, near Harrogate. We were both wearing the Morley colours, but it was to be a no-holds-barred teeth-baring fight.

It was ferocious from the start and after the first lap all the main contenders were out in front. A stiff climb and a long drag on the four and a half mile course 'made the selection' as our French friends say. Denise and Carol Barton were with me together with four others, all internationals, and the nearest chasers were already ten seconds behind. Another lap and Lynn Armitage and Faith Murray had been dropped as the relentless pace continued, and on the fourth lap I made a number of attacks, trying to split up the group and pull away. They stayed with me, but none made a move on their own. I kept up a furious pace, stringing them out on the hill, and it told when Cathie Swinnerton and Terrie Riley tangled and crashed; the former had to retire but Riley remounted and gamely continued some distance behind Denise, Carol and me. It had been a battle of attrition that had seen the rest of the field dropping behind, but I could not shake either Denise or Carol and it was going to be a three-up sprint to sort out the medals. We foxed a little down the finishing straight and then simultaneously erupted into a savage sprint – three hundred metres, two hundred – the line approached – I seemed to be blowing myself apart as Carol, on the left, began to weaken, and mother and daughter lunged across the line. It was probably the best road championship ever, made more piquant because Denise and I had given and asked no quarter in those last desperate metres. The verdict went to Denise by the proverbial whisker, and it would be nice to record that I felt pleased for her as I heard the judges' decision announced. But this is not a story for some romantic magazine, it is a real life narrative about basically ordinary people with jangled nerves and emotions, our bitter conflict played out in almost gladiatorial fashion. Looking at it in purely race terms I thought Denise had not done her whack in keeping the break away and that once again I had 'made the race'. It is easy to see how this resentment became an extension of the personal problems we had at the time. Cycling was the one thing which should have bound us together but I couldn't help my attitude toward her.

I was surrounded after the finish but Charlie was not with me, and it was the final straw. Feeling choked and miserable I stood on the podium and refused to shake hands with my own daughter. It was not a sporting thing to do. I did our sport a disservice in allowing personal acrimony to intervene, and I can only plead that I was not myself at the time. It is the only occasion in my life that I have reacted in such a way when victory had gone to somebody else. Denise had ridden the race in the way she thought best and it had produced the spoils of victory. It would perhaps have been better if Carol had beaten both of us in that sprint for the line, but life is not like that. I left the house and went to my mother's to try and sort myself out.

The newspapers, including the Sunday press, enjoyed themselves. 'Bike ace Beryl snubs daughter', was the huge headline in *The People*. No sound report of the race, of course. If only so much attention had been paid to me when I won my world championships!

I tried to pull myself together. I had been selected to ride with a four-girl British team in a three-day race in France and I hoped the change of air might do some good. Denise was also in the team which hardly helped, but I tried to concentrate on cycling and a British victory. It was a hard trip with an overnight channel crossing and only one day to acclimatise, but we performed well until the last day. I was leading and should have been the overall winner, but we made tactical errors during that final stage, and let victory slip to a Swedish girl. On the whole, though, it was not a bad result as I won the points section and Britain also won the team prize.

Denise won another national title when she lifted the pursuit crown at Leicester, and it was no surprise that she was named for the world championships in Italy. This was the occasion when Yvonne Reynders made her amazing come-back to the international scene, taking third place in the road race in which Denise finished nineteenth. In a hard-fought pursuit series she went out in the quarter-finals, the championships that year being a triumph for that amazing girl Keetie van Oosten-Hage who emulated me by taking both a road and pursuit gold in the same year.

Following my return from France I rode in the Yorkshire Cycling Federation '100' and nearly made it inside four hours for the sixth time with 4–0–15, but, nevertheless, it clinched the B.A.R. for the eighteenth time with a record average of 26.665 m.p.h. Carol Barton finished second in the competition and Denise third.

Before the end of the year I was extremely pleased when Eileen Gray was elected President of the British Cycling Federation, a richly deserved honour. Her Presidency has been no sinecure, for she has made her presence felt over many years at U.C.I. meetings. As these words are being written she is entering upon her last year in office, having declared her intention to retire at the end of 1985. There have been few harder workers for the sport, and women's bike-racing world-wide owes her a debt of gratitude for the way she has always fought for the girls at the highest level. One of her dreams came true in 1984 when at last one women's cycling event was held at the Los Angeles Olympics. Present indications are that there could be more in 1988.

At the beginning of 1977 Denise left the Morley club. She was now engaged to a promising young roadman, Steve Thomas of the East Bradford, and it was his club that she joined. Not an unnatural thing to do, and in the circumstances probably for the best. I tried to keep matters on an even keel at home, which was not always easy and, meanwhile, my form of the previous year was returning.

The world championships were to be held in Venezuela this year, and for a time I toyed with the idea of trying for selection. With this in mind I entered for an inter-cities track meeting at Leicester where I realised I was no longer happy with a smaller fixed gear and the change of riding position for the track. In the pursuit victory went to Denise and I was fourth; I realised that I had lost my greatest pursuiting skills even if only the best girls in the country could beat me. I had changed my training routine at the suggestion of Val Rushworth, the B.C.F. ladies coach, and had reduced my mileage, although I have always felt happiest putting in plenty of miles in training – usually 100-mile stints. It is the only time I have not followed my own training routine, but, although it had not seemed to work at Leicester, I decided to persevere with the new regime a little longer.

At the end of June I defended the 25-mile title on a course between Kidderminster and Worcester on a very hard day, and I was successful with a slow time for me of 1–0–18. Denise was second, over five minutes behind, and I was pleased that at the age of forty I could still beat everyone in a time trial by big margins, thereby answering those who were wondering how much longer I could carry on. I made it a unique double a week later when I rode in the veterans, 25-mile title race and recorded the fastest time with 59–47 among the many superfast male 'vets'.

Still hankering after riding a decent pursuit I rode in the W.C.R.A. championships at Birmingham's Salford Park, where I found some of my old track form. I was the fastest of the qualifiers with 4–24.1 and went through to win the final with 4–26, beating Margaret Thompson (née Gordon-Smith) by nearly five seconds with Denise taking third place. I began to think that I might have another shot at the national title a few weeks later, but before then I took my nineteenth 50-mile title and then, in the 50-mile at the Harrogate Festival, finished with a time of 1–53–30, just two minutes outside my record.

The atmosphere at home had been smouldering for a long time and when

Denise and I arrived at Leicester for the national track championships I was not really in the best frame of mind for a pursuit series. I qualified fourth fastest behind Margaret Thompson, Denise and Cathie Swinnerton. I improved in the quarter-finals to beat Josie Randall while Denise moved into the 'semis' with a much faster time. Maggie Thompson was in fine form and she disposed of Swinnerton in one semi-final, and another little bit of cycling history was enacted when Denise and I met in the other semi-final. With mixed emotions I took my place at the start; it was our first confrontation in a pursuit championship and, for once, my ragged nerves showed.

I made a poor start and Denise was away to a 'flyer'. I rode as hard as I could, but she pulled steadily away, and my old power was no longer there. I was physically fit enough but had no answer to my daughter's polished performance. Under other circumstances the race could have been a happy sporting occasion with a 'what-the-hell-who-wins' attitude but, as it was, it was four minutes and some seconds of purgatory. Trembling I returned to the riders' enclosure and began to pull on my tracksuit. Then somebody was standing in front of me, and I looked up. Denise came into my arms and we hugged and wept, oblivious of the 'bikies' around us and the crowd in the stand. I felt very proud of her when I watched her line up later for the final against Maggie Thompson. It would have made a fairy-tale ending to the day if Denise had won the gold medal, but as I have previously said, life isn't like that. Thompson took a splendidly-earned gold medal and the Burtons had to be satisfied with silver and bronze, for I had beaten Swinnerton in the ride-off for third place.

I had missed the 100-mile championship because of the pursuits at Leicester, and still needed a passable '100' time to retain the B.A.R. title. I rode in the Yorkshire Century promotion early in September and it was a ghastly day of gale winds and driving rain, with a terrible 26-mile slog at the finish. My time was 4–29–40, the slowest I had recorded for years, but it was enough to clinch the Best All-rounder title for the nineteenth time.

By this time we had moved house and were living at Harrogate, and I had also left Nim's employment. I was temporarily not working, and although the season was finished I was still in training for a reason I will recount later. I decided one Monday late in November to take a ride in the Dales. I had been over to Ingleton and on the return run, scorching towards Skipton with a tail wind I passed a snack bar in a lay-by, wavered for a moment, but decided I wasn't thirsty and continued. If I had stopped, then probably what subsequently happened would have been avoided. I pressed on toward Gargrave and on a fast downhill run a car came towards me. Unexpectedly, the driver turned across the road and I had no chance of avoiding him. The light was good and I was wearing bright colours but, in the classic motorist's way, he just hadn't seen me.

I regained consciousness in ward 16 of Airedale Hospital near Keighley, a handsome young doctor hovering over me. 'You have had a very bad cycling accident,' he told me. 'You have broken a leg in two places, the other leg is badly bruised and swollen, we have had to put fifty-six stitches in your head, your ear has been almost torn off and we have had to sew it back. Also your shoulder blade is broken.'

I squinted at him, unable to see out of one eye which, as I discovered later, appeared to have had the attentions of Mohammed Ali. 'Fifty-six stitches,' I muttered. 'Pity it wasn't fifty-seven – it would have equalled the number of teeth on my chain-wheel.' No doubt he thought I was rambling.

I lay in bed day after day, surrounded by cards and flowers from well-wishers. The other women in the ward were amazed at the large number of visitors I had – mainly young male cyclists – and I told them that the secret was to buy a bike! Inevitably I had to consider my cycling future. There was no reason why the broken bones should not heal satisfactorily – but what effect would the accident have on my racing? I was forty and it would be understandable if I retired from competition. There seemed no more mountains to climb, but then I remembered that I would like my total of B.A.R. wins to be a nice sounding twenty-one. It seemed important to have a goal, something to make my mind transcend the physical difficulties.

My peace of mind was not helped by the right leg having to be re-set, and I chafed at the inactivity for three weeks until I told the doctors it was time I went home. Dr Tim Stahl supported me in this and, after discussions with the medical staff, he took over my case. I went home complete with crutches and decided that my first race of the season would be our own club promotion on the 22nd April. It seemed optimistic, not to say foolhardy, but I was determined. We obtained a rowing machine and a stationary exercise bike and day after day I exercised until my sweat-soaked body could take no more. Gradually I took on more and more domestic tasks which was not easy on crutches with a broken shoulder. I used to carry the shopping in a pack on my back, and one day in Marks and Spencer's I bent down to retrieve a crutch which I had dropped, completely forgetting that I was wearing the pack. The contents shot out over my head all over the place! It was a bit of a 'Casey's Court' situation, and I could not stop laughing.

Knowing the history of my previous knee trouble, Dr Stahl was worried about the effect the 'pot' would have on my right knee, so he cut the plaster down. His knowledge and attention were superb. The Falcon Cycle Company had arranged a pre-season training camp in February in Majorca for racing cyclists. One place had been made available to a Falcon dealer who passed over his opportunity to me – a very kind gesture. Now the question arose of whether I could make the journey.

I had a shock one night when I woke with a great deal of pain from my throbbing leg. Charlie phoned Tim Stahl who recommended him to saw off the plaster. He set to work with a small saw, having to stop from time to time when I felt sick. Eventually he managed it, to reveal my calf, red raw and covered with pus. I had been building up the muscle so much with my exercises that it had no room to move freely within the plaster.

Dr Stahl was not too keen on the Majorca trip, but relented when he saw how enthusiastic I was, and fixed me up with a covering that was rather like a farmer's gaiter. I promised him that I would not ride the bike without it. I thought that it would be an exceptional opportunity to ride the bike in clement weather away from the icy roads of England. Before going I tried the training rollers fixed to a racing bike and, getting the feel of things again, I was optimistic that I could meet my April deadline.

Taking my riding fairly gently in Majorca, I gradually built up from the slower training runs to the longer, faster efforts. The lads dropped me on the climbs, but by the end of the two weeks I was beginning to feel that I could face the season. But there was another journey to make. Shortly before my accident I had accepted an invitation from America to ride one of their classic stage races, which is why I had still been training in November. Subsequently I had written and told them of my accident, regretting that I would not be able to compete. The reply came back that they would still like me to make the trip and help with the promotional side of the race. It was a great opportunity to put in some more build-up miles in a good climate.

Mrs K.K. Hall was the organiser, and she fixed up for me to stay in Tucson with Colin and Margaret Laing, an English couple with two boys who had emigrated to America about six years earlier. They made me very welcome and comfortable. Colin had run a bike business before emigrating, so I was in a cycling milieu from the start. Accidents seem to follow me around. After I had been in Tucson about ten days Colin was knocked off his bike and broke his leg, which made things difficult for the family because of the bike shop they had to run. I was glad that I was there because I was able to help out in various ways, in between times training sixty to seventy miles a day. Before the stage race there was a separate one-day race which I decided to ride, just to test myself out. I had no idea what my form would be like, but I stayed with the main bunch all the way, and when it came to a sprint for the line I eased off, not tempting fate too much. I had stayed with many of the best riders in the world, an achievement which had hardly seemed possibly only a few weeks earlier.

On the 22nd April I met my deadline, and faced the timekeeper in the Morley '25' when I was the fastest girl with a time of 1-0-3. My form continued throughout the season, my eyes fixed on the national '25' which I hoped to win for the twentieth time. For once I was no longer favourite. Shirley Killingbeck had been inside the hour a week or two earlier and it was thought that, at forty-one and because of my accident, I would not quite make it. The following week the headline in *Cycling* read: 'Beryl Burton just won't be beaten', – I had retained the title with a time of 1-1-5 with Denise second in 1-3-34 and Killingbeck back in fifth. It was a personal triumph. None of my time-trial wins has given me greater satisfaction, and what had seemed an impossible dream at the beginning of the year had come true. I set my sights on another win in the B.A.R.

The next big hurdle came at the beginning of July. A new championship at ten miles had been instituted, and here was a distance, comparatively short, at which I could surely be beaten. I was determined that I would be the first winner of this title. On a cold showery day I won from a field of 118 with 24-45 and Denise was joint second with Carole Gandy, seventeen seconds behind. It was a tough race for me to win, and I kept up the pressure later in the month when I took the 50-mile championship again in spite of my leg aching. Denise again rode to a silver medal so we had now finished first and second in three championships. My leg did not feel quite right, though, in that I wasn't getting full power on my right side.

The 100-mile championship in Yorkshire gave me another win with a time of 4-15-22 on a day of heavy rain and murky visibility. I punctured and had to ride on a flat tyre for a mile, but I still had nearly thirteen minutes in hand from Mavis Ross. Denise had mechanical trouble and finished fourth, otherwise I think she would have been among the medals. A week later I won the Nunbrook Wheelers '50' well inside two hours, again with a puncture, and later in the month I beat my own twelve-year-old record at fifteen miles by twelve seconds. In September I recorded 55–19 in the Ferryhill Wheelers '25' and a week after that, 1–55–1 in the Clifton '50' effectively clinching the B.A.R. Less than a year earlier the possibility of racing again had seemed dubious and the chances of retaining the B.A.R. even more remote. But, I now needed only one more win to make it twenty-one.

The following January I received the British B.A.R. Trophy for the twentieth time along with my four championship gold medals. John Woodburn was the men's champion and Alf Engers was presented with a gold medal from *Cycling* for the first over-30 m.p.h. time trial. Denise was now married and had become Denise Thomas, and she took fourth place in the B.A.R. The following month I again received the C.A. Rhodes Memorial Award. The citation read: 'Her determination at the age of forty to overcome the effects of her injuries and maintain her position as the dominant force in women's time-trial sport is an outstanding example of true Yorkshire grit and courage and does her great credit.'

In the early part of the 1979 season I rode a number of '10s' and '25s' with success and vowed I would take the gold medal at the latter distance for the twenty-first time. It was a triumph for the older girls that day, for behind me came Shirley Killingbeck and Ann Illingworth for the place medals. Later in the month I made the first defence of the 10-mile title, and on a Midlands course was successful with 22–50. Again it had been thought that this was a race I might not win, many of the up-and-coming young girls being very fast at the distance, but I was determined and fit that day, winning from Ann Collingwood and Ann Illingworth. The 50-mile title race two weeks later was promoted by the Kettering Amateur C.C. on a stiff course made harder by the gusting wind, and the last few miles were exceptionally hard. It took me 2 hours 3 minutes 18 seconds to win this gold, with Shirley second and Ann Illingworth of Hainault taking yet another third place. Now, like me, very much a veteran, Shirley was having a wonderful season after making a comeback to the sport from a twelve-year absence. Now my collection of 'golds' at the '50' distance matched that of the '25' – twenty-one – and it was the sixtieth title win in time trials.

I decided to miss the 100-mile championship, worried about my knees which were still giving me some trouble and feeling that one ride at the distance would be enough for the season. Accordingly I entered the Yorkshire Cycle Federation promotion where I felt that I should be able to turn out a decent time for the B.A.R. In a strong men's field I finished sixth with 4–7–19, the winner being Len Orrick of Coventry C.C. in less than four hours. I kept trying to improve my average, turning out a '56' ride in the Knaresborough '25', nearly as fast as one I had done earlier in the season in the West Kent race, and the season finished for me with the Yorkshire Clarion event – another win and the conclusion of a successful B.A.R. campaign with an average of 25.228 m.p.h. I had achieved my aim of carrying this off for the twenty-first time.

If I had any regrets about the year it was that Denise, busy in setting up her new home, had not taken part in competition, but I think she was already being beset by problems which later overtook her. We were entering a new decade, and for more than the past two I had been at the top. Could I continue with my suspect knees and niggling back? I decided to let the winter months go by and wait and see. I had been out of racing for a few weeks late in 1979 with a touch of pleurisy which had caused me anxiety, and now I felt jaded and ready for a break.

In racing terms 1980 was almost a serene year. I won the championship titles at 10, 25, 50 and 100 miles and retained my Best All-rounder title for the twenty-second year with an average of 25.732 m.p.h., the best for four years. I was working on a farm again, doing the things I like in the open air. I was actually something of a wreck in athletic terms. I suffered with my knees, my back ached, and now my breathing was not too good, perhaps because of the pleurisy the previous year. But, once on a bike I was transformed, and this had decided me to keep racing during this season.

Much earlier in this story I referred to Bill Long, President of the Australian Cycling Council and owner of the famous Melbourne track, and his suggestion of a racing trip to Australia. This particular dream had now come true. It was to be no ordinary racing trip but one surrounded by controversy in Australia. I was invited to participate in the famous classic, the 161-mile Melbourne to Warrnambool Handicap, in its eighty-fifth year. Previously a professional race, it had become pro-am for the first and, I believe, only time, and some top amateurs were expected to ride. Bike racing among Australian women is not particularly strong, and nobody expected a woman to take part, particularly a 'pommie'! Representations against my inclusion were made to the B.C.F. from certain quarters in Australia, but the B.C.F. stood firm and gave me clearance to ride providing I did nothing to jeopardise my amateur status. 'Who wants women?' . . . 'She'll never finish' . . . 'She should stay at home in the kitchen!' . . . 'Cycling's no sport for women' were some of the quotes from the Australian he-men who resented my appearance.

As usual, my unceremonious departure from Heathrow contrasted greatly with the attention I received from the media when I arrived in Melbourne on the 23rd September. June Long looked after me superbly and, as in South Africa, I was able to concentrate on riding a bike without worrying about domestic chores. After breakfast I would relax for a while and then go for a training session of eighty to a hundred miles, have a rest and a snack, followed by some form of relaxation before dinner. In the evening I found myself giving T.V., radio and press interviews. The climate suited me, my breathing improved and I felt I was carrying over my form from the end of the English season.

Occasionally Bill would arrange for me to have a training companion and one day Hilton Clarke, who had ridden for Australia in the Olympic Games, turned up to accompany me. We had a really good, strenuous session, but, on the way home, Hilton hit a bump in the road, lost control and fell full against me. I did a somersault and crashed to the ground. Poor Hilton, who was not injured, was distraught as he picked me up. I was in a great deal of pain and seething at the bad luck which so often seemed to intervene before an important race. I was taken to hospital and X-rayed, and, surprisingly, no bones seemed to be broken. However, I had a large swelling on my forehead, a chunk of hair missing, my legs, ankles and one shoulder were badly lacerated and I had a giant black eye. In a worse condition, however, was my left hand which had a deep gash across the back and was swollen to king-sized proportions. To this day I carry a purple scar as a reminder.

Training was out of the question for some days, and I tried to salvage what I could by riding the Long's home trainer. I could not grip or even hold the bars very well, and the lacerations on my legs were painful, but so much attention had been paid to my proposed participation in the Handicap that I felt that I should, in the words of that well-known Yorkshireman, the late Wilfred Pickles, 'Have a go!' To travel all that way and not ride, so long as I could get astride a bike, would have been a disappointment I could never have lived with.

The Warrnambool is a race over tough country and has its own difficulties. Riders are not allowed any support, and must carry their own food and drink and attend to any punctures or mechanical difficulties themselves. With the state of my hand I doubted whether I could cope with any such eventualities, and I could only hope that nothing would go wrong with the bike. I was having enough problems worrying about the rider! As the name of the race suggests, groups of riders are started according to the handicapper's view of their ability and form, the starting order being announced a week before the race, except that my starting position was not announced until about a day before which provoked much speculation. As the big day approached I grew more and more tense. A battered 43-year-old woman riding in a field of 203 tough, Aussie men, all but twenty-six of them professionals, seemed madness. In Harrogate it had been an intriguing idea, another challenge to take on. In Melbourne, with aching limbs and a swollen hand, the enormity of the task seemed too ridiculous to contemplate. The Lord Mayor of Melbourne, Councillor Jack Woodruff, granted me a civic reception, an honour that the city rarely bestowed, and it was he who set the riders on their way on the 11th October. The handicapper had not been kind to me for I was placed in a thirty-strong group which had only the top men on scratch behind, and the general consensus was that I had been severely treated. To me it was just one more hurdle, because now I had only one object and that was to finish this tough and famous race, and I told Bill Long before the start that come what may I would arrive in Warrnambool. My face was still a mess, which did not help my state of mind as I faced the T.V. people who interviewed me before the start, and one scribe of the press described me as 'the black and white minstrel show'.

Our group set off at a fast pace, and I did my share of the work for about forty-five miles with increasing pain as I tried to pull on the bars and I realised, as the group piled on the pressure, that this speed was just a little too much for me. The race is ridden 'eye-balls out' so as to catch up on the bunch somewhere on the road in front, each rider sharing the work. To get dropped from a group is considered a disaster as you are then on your own. But that did not bother me; I was a time triallist, used to making my own pace, and if I was just a little slower than these men, so be it – that is how I would ride. There were still nearly 120 miles to go, and I plugged on by myself, coming to a detour off the road where for some miles there was no surface, and at this point it began to rain. From somewhere up in the eighties the temperature dropped, and then dropped some more, and an icy cold gripped me as I went through small towns each with its crowd of people urging on the riders. From time to time I would catch up with a rider who would try to hold me and then drop back, and many among the favourites retired from the race as the conditions grew worse. Twice officials pulled alongside briefly and asked if I wanted to quit. I must have looked a sight with the rain dripping down my face, pinched with cold and the purple bruises standing out on my pale 'pommie' skin. Each time I replied, not very politely, that I was going on to Warrnambool.

One of the difficulties I had was that I was not able to reach into the back pocket of my racing jersey for food. Nor was I able to pull the drinking bottle from its cage since my bandaged hand could not take hold of anything and could not grip the bars strongly enough for me to reach with the other hand. All I had to eat during the race was a piece of rice-cake which another rider passed to me. I suppose I could have actually stopped for a few moments to pull something out from the pocket but stopping, unless I really have to, never occurs to me.

Over the final miles it was reminiscent of the Grand Prix des Nations of some years earlier as the crowds thickened, police lining the road and shouting encouragement at me, and I sped on toward the coastal town with a police escort behind, the occupants of the car sounding more excited than I was myself. At last the finish was in sight, a huge crowd roaring their heads off, and I crossed the line and let the bike run down carrying its cold and soggy rider to the conclusion of what, in essence, had been another long time trial. It had carried me faithfully and well without a moment's anxiety from Melbourne to Warrnambool in a time of 7–11–12, eighty-six minutes behind a tremendous and outstanding winner, former Olympic rider, John Hine. My time was, in fact, a little over four minutes slower than the winning time of the previous year, and I reckon that without my injuries and with slightly better weather I would have beaten that by a considerable margin. I felt that I had upheld the honour of British racing girls.

Bill Long was over the moon with my showing, as was Bill Quinn, head of the well-known cycle firm that had sponsored the race. Their faith in me had been justified, and I was presented with a gorgeous racing jersey in the Quinn colours, which is a treasured possession although, of course, I can never wear it as an amateur. I was quite fresh after the race and, as in the 'Nations', I was capable of racing for much longer. It had been another 'mind over matter' job for me. By all accounts, I really had not been in a condition to race such a distance but, mindful of the trouble a lot of people had gone to and the honour of finishing, I had kept going – in the coldest and wettest conditions anyone could remember. In the shower after the race I stood under the hot water for minutes before the warmth penetrated, and even in bed that night under piles of blankets I could still not get warm. So, a memorable trip, topped off by a visit to the fabulous Sydney Opera House, especially thrilling for me with my love of opera – even if I was unable to see a performance!

I returned from Australia to some steady winter riding and to enjoy Christmas and the New Year – my wounds were healing and I was able to contemplate a new season. Having won the B.A.R. twenty-two successive years it was not unnatural to think of trying to make it twenty-five, although realistically it seemed an impossible dream. In 1980 I had ridden almost automatically, without the enthusiasm of earlier years, and it was the prospect of the Australian trip that had kept my keenness alive during the later months of the season.

My mind turned again to the possibility of returning to the track. Checking the times that had been done at Leicester during the previous year I thought I could make a successful return to pursuiting provided that I could put in plenty of training and ride regularly on the Leicester track. I had no doubts that track-wise I was rusty, but I felt that I could return to my old pursuiting form with the right commitment. The problem was financial, and I seriously began to think of leaving the Morley club and seeking the help of a sponsored club. When this became known a number of well-known sponsored clubs made overtures, and I had to consider matters carefully. I was pulled in both directions: I needed help with my cycling expenses but I had to set this against my loyalty to my club, albeit a small one with only a handful of active members – no great interest in its affairs was taken outside the immediate confines of Morley and the little that was, was only kept alive by the reports in the two local weekly papers. I stayed with Morley; its pull was too strong. When my decision became known there was some acrimonious comment in the correspondence columns of *Cycling* the feeling being that I had received a goodly sum of money from some source or other which made me a personally sponsored rider. The fact is that I received a very modest sum from a private and anonymous donor *after* I had already made my decision and, welcome as this was, it no way matched the amounts available to many well-known riders in sponsored clubs.

The season began disastrously. In the Don Valley Wheelers 'two-up' '25' I was riding with Malcolm Cowgill when I touched his wheel and came down. I seemed to be uninjured so I remounted and continued. I then became aware of blood running from the end of my chin, covering my legs and bike. I asked Malcolm to see if he could spot where the blood was coming from. He turned pale and suggested we should stop, but there did not seem much point, and we continued to the finish. A careful check revealed a cut on my head, not a severe one, but one of those that somehow seem to bleed badly. It was not until the following day when I was stringing together some raspberry canes at work that I became aware of a pain in my side. I put up with this for a few more days but the pain did not ease. At Leeds Infirmary I had some X-rays and they told me I had two broken ribs! I struggled on with a few races, and then came further trouble. I had banged my hip joint in the Don Valley fall, which had not seemed anything to worry about at the time, but a large bruise had since developed, the skin had broken, and now I had a large suppurating mess on my hip. I travelled to Warwick for the Easter Bank Holiday and rode one event, but pulled out of another and returned home in low spirits. The mess on my hip was the size of a plate, and I could now hardly walk. In addition to my personal health problems, Denise was a cause for concern. Her marriage had not worked out and she was also desperately ill with the wasting disease, anorexia nervosa, which had reduced her weight to about five stones. Looking at her you could not imagine the power she had once had on a bike.

Continuing to race in spite of the slowly healing wound and my strapped ribs, I won the Icknield '10' and Becontree '25'. On the 14th June I won the '25' title for the twenty-third time with 57–17. Second that day was Mandy Jones with 59–5, with Shirley Killingbeck in third place. Jones, the girl from Lancashire, was my successor in international terms. The previous season she had won the national pursuit title and then taken third place in the world championship in Italy. Hope was high that she could pull off a gold for Britain on either the road or track and it seemed she was the rider most likely to dethrone me in a national championship time trial. Mandy was an aggresive rider on the road, outstanding among the other girls and, like me in earlier years, was finding that the ambition of others seemed to be simply to stay behind her wheel.

At the May Bank Holiday we made the trek south, where I clocked 22–6 in the Colchester Rovers '10' which was won by John Patston and then, two days later in the Southend and County Wheelers '25', won in a fast 56–56. My form was holding good for the 10-mile championship a week later in the Harrogate Festival. I felt very vulnerable to Mandy Jones at this the shortest of the championships, and we had a keen tussle. There was a strong headwind to the halfway turn where I had only five seconds in hand. Over the second part of the course I slammed in the top gear and gave it everything I had, running out the winner in 23–17 to Mandy's 23–44. I think the conditions favoured me. I knew that on a calmer day I would be hard put to it to beat her at the shorter distances. Nevertheless it was a satisfying four out of four title wins at ten miles and my sixty-fourth championship time-trial victory at this point, not counting the team wins.

Bad luck with illness continued to follow me when later in the year I started in the 50-mile title race which was held in Wales. While staying with friends the night before I had felt unwell, and was still feeling very ill when I came to the line. Charlie tried to persuade me not to start but, as usual, since I was capable of sitting on the bike I felt that I should try to defend the title. Perhaps it was something I had eaten, I don't know, but shortly after the halfway point I had to retire, unable to keep a straight line and feeling decidedly groggy. Happily, that particular piece of misfortune lasted only a few days.

The next challenge was the 100-mile title in North Nottinghamshire, and although I was deeply worried about Denise I tried to focus my mind on this. On the day Charlie was out to give me a feed, accompanied by Denise, who was now slowly recovering but still had the appearance of a starving waif. My peace of mind was not helped by the sight of the car stuck in a ditch, as I went past them at one point. Pulling into the verge Charlie had not noticed that the long grass hid a ditch and the car had dipped into it. All kinds of thoughts went through my mind as I raced along to achieve my eighteenth win. The time was 4–13–47 over eleven minutes clear of Shirley Killingbeck on a very hot, sticky day. Denise had at one point tried to hand up a drink to me, but the poor girl did not have the energy to run fast enough, and I could hardly concentrate on my racing worrying about the two most important people in my life. These are the details that race reports never carry. We are all human, with our individual worries and anxieties but, truly, I sometimes used to think that people in the sport thought I was some kind of automaton who just came out and did the rides and then retired to a castle in the sky until the next race.

In August I briefly lost one of my records when Judy Glover of the Nova C.C. beat my time in the Yorkshire Ladies 15-mile, but I had started at the end of the field and cracked it again, setting up new figures of 32–56. It was quietly satisfying to be setting new records at my time of life. I did a 1–58 in the Otley '50' and bettered my '100' for the year in the Yorkshire Century event with 4–12–52. I had the B.A.R. again for the twenty-third time with an average of 25.219 m.p.h., and to round off the season I captured another record when I rode the Braintree '30' in 1–8–36. I had not raced at this distance for a long time, and Ann Illingworth had taken my old record in this period. It was pleasing to take the record at the end of the season, and in Essex. (The reader who throughout has been closely following where I raced will have noticed how many of my best rides were in the south of England, and not on the notorious – if I can put it that way – Boro' courses.)

The next logical step was to try for the B.A.R. a twenty-fifth time, but was I crazy? I had no right to be racing and winning at my age! It meant yet another two seasons of hard slog and my body was beginning to protest. It would be so pleasant to contemplate some week-ends at home, without any pressure or travelling, and perhaps a steady ride in the Dales and an hour by the Wharfe at

Grassington watching the sunlight glinting on the river. Also important, it would be pleasant for Charlie not having to face driving to a race, possibly a long distance with Saturday night away from home, and for him to be out on his bike with me in the Yorkshire country-side, enjoying himself and recharging his batteries for the work-a-day world. In the end the pull of the greatest and toughest sport in the world was too great.

But I had to give up any idea of winning the B.A.R. again before the season started. My breathing trouble returned and the doctor told me I had a chest infection. I rode in the Yorkshire R.C. '25' on the Boro' on the 4th April and managed 1-0-52, and a week later rode in the Port Sunlight Wheelers Hilly '22'. My time in this was reasonable, but breathing during a race was still difficult. The following day I raced in the Cleveleys 10-mile and was beaten by Mandy Jones by over a minute. It did not surprise me that this class rider could beat me at ten miles, but the margin indicated that all was not well. Later in the month in the Central District Ladies '10' I was beaten by Barbra Collins. My breathing had become so bad that I was now using an inhaler before racing, the sort of thing used by asthma sufferers. This was on medical advice, although the bottom line of that advice was that I should not be cycling at all. There were objections from the kind of people who are never happy unless they can find something to complain about, and I started carrying a letter from the doctor to show to anyone who was interested. It saddens me that this great sport, like all other activities, has its quota of petty-minded folk whose main purpose in life seems to be sniping at other people.

By this time I was attending the chest clinic in Leeds, coughing and spluttering and spitting blood, and they diagnosed a form of asthma. My lungs were dilating, making it difficult to breathe out when making any kind of effort, and for good measure I had an allergy to grass! Any possibility of retaining my 10-mile title seemed to have disappeared, but against everybody's advice I came to the line to defend it on a Norfolk course early in May. I frankly thought I would do well to finish in the first ten, and my eventual second to Jones surprised me. I continued racing, my mind on the forthcoming '25' championship and the expected clash with Mandy. I had to admit to myself that the chances of an asthmatic 45-year-old were not good against one of the world's top riders. The confrontation did not materialise. Mandy was away racing in France, and even if that improved my chances there were still many keen young girls capable of toppling me. I had a confidence-boosting time of less than fifty-nine minutes in the Knaresborough race the week before, and travelled down to the Kent coast feeling I still had a chance. I retained the title, winning it for the twenty-fourth time in 1-1-2, nearly two minutes clear of Auriel Bu'lock and Carole Gandy, who tied for second place.

I then travelled to Essex again to ride the Southend and County Wheelers

'25' and amazed myself with a winning 55–29. I now had to set my mind to the '50' title race which took place during the Harrogate Festival week. In mid-week Mandy Jones gained a psychological win over me by winning with 55–28, beating me by 1 minute 22 seconds. On the morning of the '50' on the York–Hull road I felt terrible, wheezing all the way to the start and in my warming-up ride. I knew then it would be impossible to beat a rider with the class of Mandy Jones, but I could only try my best – even a second-place medal was looking doubtful. The Thursday before the race I had attended the chest clinic and I'm sure they would have been aghast if they had known that I was to race in a national championship a few days later. Jones was a splendid winner with a time of 2–1–37, beating me into second place by 2 minutes 2 seconds, (Friends on the course told me afterwards that they knew I was coming along the road before they saw me by the racket I was making with my breathing.) I feel sure I would not have beaten Mandy that morning even if my health had been better, for she went on to win the world road championship the following month at Goodwood. It was a brilliant and superb gold medal Mandy won that day in Sussex, when she dominated the race from the start. It was reminiscent of the way I had won my two world golds on the road, and British cyclists rejoiced. We had turned out not only a winner, but an outstanding winner. I don't know a lot about Mandy, but as far as I can judge she rides road races like I always used to. She doesn't always win, but she always make a go of a race. In this, unfortunately, she seems to be on her own. She goes fast from the start, and that's the only way to get the standard higher. I'd rather have raced hard and come last than sat in and come first. That isn't racing to me.

Slowly my breathing problem improved, and I plugged away as best I could, forcing my reluctant, wheezing body to answer the call week-end after week-end, riding out of instinct and determination, meanwhile anxiously watching the times being turned out by my adversaries. My attempt on my twenty-fourth B.A.R. seemed to be 'on' again. I managed another ride of less than two hours in the Yorkshire Ladies '50' and then had a morale-boosting win in the Leeds Wellington '25' when I beat Mandy with 58–28 to her 1–0–20. (This was before the world championships.) A few days before I had won the East Bradford '25' with 56–26 so I knew my best form was returning, but I was anxious about a good 100-mile time. I did not take part in the national race at the distance, June Pitchford taking the gold, and tried for a fast time in the Yorkshire Century event. My time was 4–23–6 – not bad, but not good enough; it placed me in second place in the B.A.R., and time was running out. I desperately needed some improvement if I was to win the B.A.R. again, and in the middle of the month made a 'do or die' two-pronged attack. On a Saturday I made another journey to Essex where the weather was warm but with a stiff breeze, and rode in the Unity '25'. I really tried that day in Essex and pulled out a 56–45, an improvement of five seconds, shaving a very minute sliver off the difference between Shirley Killingbeck and me. But Shirley had faster 50- and 100-mile times and, feeling somewhat despondent, Charlie and I travelled north for the North Midlands C.F. 100-mile the next day. There was still a '50' to come the following week, but I could not leave things until then so everything depended on my showing in the North Mids.

I reported to the timekeeper on a dull but reasonably calm morning, feeling tense and keyed up as I contemplated what was one of my most important rides. I just had to turn out a reasonable time, and Charlie and I reckoned that something inside 4–15 should be enough. For miles I was below this schedule; the effort of the previous day seemed to hang in my legs and at one point I felt ragged, my rhythm going to pieces, I had to pull myself together mentally. Mile after mile of Nottinghamshire roads went by and gradually my speed increased, and over the last few miles I knew I had accomplished a decent ride. The time was 4–14–37, and with it I moved to the top of the B.A.R. table.

The following week gave the final chance of any improvement, in the Harrogate Nova '50', and it was just as well that I had ridden the previous week in the Nottinghamshire race. It was a pig of a day and although I was the fastest woman, albeit with a slow time, June Pitchford came pretty close with a ride which was only about a minute slower. There was a howling headwind from the halfway turn to the finish, and long before the end I realised any improvement was out of the question and eased off a little over the final miles.

So there it was. Another Best All-rounder title – the twenty-fourth. Earlier in the year it had seemed an impossible task, but I had persevered, and I was looking ahead to the twenty-fifth. I just had to have a crack at it, but already my tired body was telling me another year might just be too much.

I wound down the season with a few more races and unexpectedly collected another record, or at least a share in one. Denise, gradually recovering from her illness, and also an accident which had put her in hospital for several days, was at this time working in Essex as a nursery nurse, the job she had been trained for, and riding for the time being with the famous Hainault club. Treating it as a bit of a lark we came together on the tandem to ride the Lincoln Wheelers race over ten miles, it being only the third time in my life that I had even ridden one. We 'nicked' together from the start and clocked 21–25 for a fifteen-second beating of the record – a happy finish to the season for Denise. I was still attending hospital and could only hope that I would have recovered from my disabilities by the start of the season, but I finished 1982 in style by winning the Yorkshire B.A.R. for the twenty-fifth time, receiving my trophy and a special award of a beautiful silver locket and chain at the Hotel Majestic in Harrogate, only a few minutes' walk from my home.

I faced the 1983 season with a heavy load on my shoulders. For twenty-four successive years I had been the women's Best All-rounder champion. I could easily rest on my laurels and not bother trying to win it again. Two dozen was a phenomenal number of wins, and perhaps I could leave it at that. But twenty-five? That was a nice-sounding number, a sort of silver jubilee. Could I pull it off? I decided to try.

My breathing problem improved during the winter and I hoped for a trouble-free season, putting in many training miles before the season opened. Alas, the old gremlin struck again. In April, only yards from my home, I was knocked down by a car. Three broken ribs and severe bruising to my back and legs. I wept with frustration. All the training had virtually been a waste of time. I knew the ribs would heal given time, but the blow to my poor back was worrying. I pulled out the exercise bike again and tried to retain some semblance of fitness indoors. When I felt fit enough I started riding – on Charlie's bike, since my own had been wrecked in the accident.

At the beginning of May, with ribs strapped and feeling, by my standards, very unfit, I rode in the Doncaster Wheelers '25' and was quite pleased with a time of 1–1–42, although I 'soft pedalled' somewhat. There was a tough test for me later in the month in the South Elmsall '10' with top girls Maria Blower and Barbra Collins riding. Even a very fit Beryl would have been hard put to it to beat these riders, and I was not too disappointed with my third-place time of just over twenty-four minutes. By the time of the championship I seemed reasonably fit again but was not expecting too much against the likes of Jones and Collins. The result was another win for Mandy, with Barbra second and me third. I was quite happy at taking a bronze to these super-fast, much younger girls, particularly as the winner was a world champion. Denise also rode, gradually clawing her way back not only to racing fitness but to good health generally.

In June the 25-mile championship was promoted by Swindon R.C. and I hoped for a good result, but my back was still causing some concern, aching and giving me restless nights. Worse, I was beginning to find that my legs seemed to be affected too. The power was no longer there, and I seriously thought of bringing the season to a premature close and forgetting about another B.A.R. On the day Mandy Jones was a fine new title-holder, but I managed second place. At long last a new name was to be inscribed on the trophy.

A week later it was a case of two 'crocks' – one old and one young – getting together for another tandem race in the Letchworth V.C. 25-mile. Denise and I enjoyed ourselves, and had the satisfaction of finishing third behind two all-male combinations with 54–41, only seventy-one seconds outside the record. Denise was beginning to regain her health and fitness although she was still far from being the girl who had taken a world bronze medal.

By the time of the Harrogate Festival my cycling form was good, but I was still troubled with my back and not realising my full power, so I suppose I should have not been too disappointed when Mandy Jones beat me again in the *Cycling* 25-mile, recording 58–33 to my 58–58. I faced the championship 50-mile with no more hope than gaining a place medal against Mandy, the rising young Essex star, Sue Fenwick, and several others. In the event I won through with a time of 2–1–31, beating Sue Fenwick by over three minutes. Mandy Jones retired at thirty-five miles when I was in the lead, and one can only speculate what would have happened if she had continued.

I was still very worried about my state of health. I was finding that I was not perspiring in the way I usually did but finishing rides with a feeling of dehydration. I was utterly down, both mentally and physically, and weary of racing. I realised that, remarkable as my performances might seem for a 46-year-old woman, I could do better if I was fully fit. I needed a good 100-mile time for the B.A.R., and having decided not to ride in the title race I rode in the Rutland C.C. event in Nottinghamshire. I had to stop for an unshipped chain, and also suffered a broken spoke, but nevertheless managed a satisfying 4–19–57. I had hoped for something faster but it was a hot, airless sort of day, which I found hard.

The dull, cooler conditions a week later in the East Bradford '25' were more to my liking, and the form flowed back into my legs with a 56–32, nearly two minutes clear of Christine Miller of Border City Wheelers, one of the sport's rising stars. The form held a week later in the Yorkshire Ladies '50' with 1–58–42, Christine Miller again runner-up. However, I was now very anxious about the B.A.R. Sue Fenwick had ridden a magnificent 4–9–23 100-mile in the south, and I knew it was going to be a nail-biting conclusion.

Then medical checks revealed why I had been struggling through my races. I was diagnosed as having spinal concussion and anaemia! I was told to stop riding a bike for the time being and forget racing forever. It was a hell of a decision to make. I had set my heart on the Best All-rounder for the twenty-fifth time. I had raced for over half the season already and acquitted myself pretty well and, in spite of the challenge from Fenwick, Killingbeck, Gandy and others, there was still just a chance I might pull it off. I decided to stick it out but, as on other occasions, so far as possible I kept the extent of my problems to myself. If I lost out it was to be on the road, not in the doctor's surgery, and if anybody beat me in the B.A.R. I was not going to have their merit diluted with excuses from me.

It was now a desperate battle to fight off Sue Fenwick, and I entered the Y.C.F. '100' anxiously seeking an improvement. It was a terrible day for me: not only was there a strong breeze but it was also quite warm, precisely the conditions I could have done without. Battling into the breeze, feeling hot with the strength draining from me, I knew I was not going to improve my previous best time and was doing myself no good. At fifty-one miles I called it a day, sitting disconsolately at the roadside waiting for Charlie to pick me up. Apart from the earlier time in Wales when I had retired feeling ill and the business with my knees in the 24-hour and following '100', it was the only occasion that I had pulled out of a race.

A week later I faced a real challenge in the Otley C.C. 50-mile with both Sue and Shirley riding, and I knew that if the conditions were good both would turn out fast times that could further dent my B.A.R. prospects. I just had to ride. Again it was warm, again it was breezy, again my legs no longer rammed against a high gear effectively. It was slog, slog, and more slog. I poured everything into the ride, ignoring the pain, the elastic legs, the rasping breath. My mind had to dominate my body, and thankfully it succeeded. Only over the final few miles did my rhythm go to pieces and somehow I forced myself to finish, but by that time the race was as good as over. I had clocked 1–56–33 and it was really the result that clinched the B.A.R. for me, although I could not know it at the time. It was certainly in my opinion one of my greatest rides although perhaps it does not stand out in the mind of anyone else. I had beaten Shirley by over three minutes and Sue by nearly four. I had put together a decent B.A.R. average, and the thought occurred to me that perhaps I should call a halt and let whatever I had managed to that point stand for the year. It was no more than a passing thought. I continued working, training and racing, still attending the hospital for treatment both for my back and the blood disorder and decided to ride the Yorkshire Century '100' later in the month. It was a disastrous day for me and once again I packed in a race about halfway when I realised that I was well down on what I required. I felt a little better shortly afterward when I was the fastest girl in our own club's '25' managing 1–0–26. I was still very anxious to improve my 100-mile time, and tried in the North Midlands C.F. on another difficult day. I went quite well in the earlier miles but in the long trek by Clumber Park in the middle of the course everything seemed to collapse about me and, again, I failed to finish a race.

The season was now moving to a climax. I was in the lead in the B.A.R.

thanks to that inspired spell when I had managed to pull out the fast '25' and '50' but the eighteen-year-old Fenwick and my old adversary, Killingbeck, were pressing hard and were capable of pulling out something right at the end. Wearily I dragged myself southwards for a final effort in the Redbridge '25' and the Viking '50', an undertaking I hardly relished. In the Redbridge I managed 1–0–27, third to Carole Gandy, also a B.A.R. contender, who had a time over a minute faster. The crunch came the following day – the Viking. Fenwick was riding, and it could prove disastrous if the day was fast and I could not produce anything approaching my best form. Feeling wretched I faced the timekeeper with a low morale and a foreboding that this was to be the day I would fail to take the B.A.R. Fenwick was going to turn out a 'flyer' on her home ground; she would produce the form that had given her the magnificent '100' time earlier in the season; I would fail dismally and retire utterly exhausted and beaten. 'Well', I told myself, 'at least you put up a fight.' It turned out to be a hard day. 'Just one more time, then you can rest,' I thought. 'Grit your teeth and go.'

The racing conditions were grim, and in that, perhaps, I was lucky because young Sue finished down the field, and Joan Morris of Mid-Shropshire Wheelers came second to my time of 2–9–32. Wearily I climbed off the bike, exhausted, and my mind empty of any emotion. It was not until we were halfway back to Yorkshire that I realised what I had accomplished. It had been a long haul for that sick little girl all those years ago in St James Hospital.

Twenty-five years at the top! If I never managed anything else in my life, never won another race, I had been number one for an incredible length of time. And for Charlie also it was a triumph. The loving care and immaculate preparation of my bikes, the constant driving at week-ends, the sacrifice of his own cycling and other interests – it had all been worth it. Whatever I had achieved could not have been done without him.

The *Yorkshire Evening Post*, consistent as usual, gave a passing mention in about three lines at the foot of a column to my achievement, and again I wondered what criteria sports editors apply in choosing what they write about.

I had my reward the following January at the fortieth R.T.T.C. dinner and prize presentation held in the Great Hall of the Assembly Rooms in Derby. Mary Peters, M.B.E., the Olympic pentathlon gold medallist, presented the prizes, and she was an apt choice, her bubbling personality and recognition of the effort required to be at the top in sport making her a success with the assembled cyclists. The Lord Mayor of Leeds (Councillor Martin J. Dodgson, J.P.) sent a civic greeting, and there was also a message of congratulation from the Minister for Sport, the Right Honourable Neil McFarlane. Among my awards was a beautiful gold necklace in an inscribed case presented by the Road Time Trials Council, something I shall always treasure. Best of all was the acclaim from all those who had ever faced a timekeeper. They knew the worth of what I had done. The chairman brought a halt to the standing ovation after nearly five minutes. Ian Cammish, bless him, had won the men's B.A.R. for the fourth successive year, a marvellous achievement in face of the competition, but graciously he took a back seat on that night. Charlie and I were carried shoulder-high round the hall by Phil Griffiths and others, and I had to fight back the tears.

In the early hours of the morning in a room at the Midland Hotel a small gathering which constituted just about all the active members of the Morley Cycling Club had a quiet party. They gave me a lovely cake in the form of a '25' and iced in the Morley colours; there was a racing wheel also decked out in the club colours and covered with orchids and a scripted message of congratulation; there were mince pies, cakes and chocolates and lots of other goodies. I sat on the floor and munched cake, drank apple juice and realised that this, really, was what it was all about. The fellowship of like-minded folk who, in their various ways, were part of the greatest sport in the world. They knew what it was like to push through a howling wind in pouring rain with a determination to finish; they knew the discomfort of standing and shivering in the road at a junction to point the way, not only for riders such as B.B. but for any novice junior who happened to be riding; they knew the tediousness of collecting entries and typing out start sheets; they knew that, for there to be a winner, there had to be losers – except that in this sport there are no losers. To be part of it gives you something nobody else has. Others may not fully understand – but if you are a cyclist you understand, don't you?

That night in Derby, that Silver Jubilee night, was the end of a road that had stretched for twenty-five years. I was approaching my forty-seventh birthday and hardly knew what I intended to try in the season ahead, but I went to bed with the words of Mandy Jones in my head. Accepting her own championship trophies she had made no speech but simply said 'Beryl, you are the greatest!' Coming from a great rider and world champion herself that was worth more than any gold medal.

Early in 1984 I travelled to Spain. I had the chance of renting an apartment for some weeks, and I took my bike for convalescence and training, if that does not sound too much of a contradiction. Utterly drained from my efforts at the end of the 1983 season, I needed to be away from any pressure, and to have some gentle riding in a decent climate, gradually building up to some sterner work. I had it in mind to return to road racing, so I altered my position on the bike as well as my style of training, and put in plenty of hilly work, gradually getting used to moving through the gears much more than I had been doing.

For the first time there was to be a women's Tour de France, and Britain was sending a team. I rather fancied being part of it. Optimistic perhaps at my age, but I considered that I had the stamina to ride consistently day after day, once I had adapted myself to the different tempo of road racing as distinct from time trials. Gradually I built myself into something like the Beryl of old, and returned to this country looking much better than when I had left, and ready for the fray once again. During my absence I had been awarded the C.A. Rhodes Award for the fourth time, and Charlie received this for me at the Yorkshire Cycling Federation dinner. I regretted having to miss this occasion, for the Rhodes award is something very close to my heart.

My first outing of the new season was in the Pendle Forest race over a 33-mile course in East Lancashire. It was a cold day, and I rode steadily with the group the whole way round, feeling a little apprehensive. Nobody broke away and Louise Garbutt of Charnwood R.C.C. won the uphill sprint. Denise, now back in Morley colours on her return to Yorkshire, took a good fifth place.

On Good Friday I recorded 25–36 in the City R.C. '10' at Hull and followed this on the Easter Monday with a ride in the Circuit of Nidderdale, a tough 27-mile time trial. Chris Miller was the fastest girl with 1–14–52, 1 minute 32 seconds faster than me, and I realised that I had to sharpen myself on the hills. In between these two trials I had ridden the Lyme road race in Staffordshire over a 33-mile course, again finishing in the bunch, still feeling my way, and being reasonably pleased with my form.

I then learned that I was on the short list of names for the Tour de France. All my training and thinking now became centred on the Tour, and any time trials I rode were almost incidental. In May Denise and I rode the Romar handicap race over forty-four miles of winding Cheshire lanes and we were almost on scratch, giving up to seven minutes to a large group. This was the stimulation I needed, because I was still not mentally attuned to road racing competition, and I stretched the others with me until we caught the leaders with about five miles to the finish. I wished there had been about another ten miles, but I had begun to show my strength, and was quite happy to finish well up in the large bunch sprinting for the line, being placed equal tenth with Denise.

I could not resist having another shot at the 10-mile championship and I was pleasantly surprised to take the silver, being beaten by only one second by international Barbra Collins. Following this I just had to ride the 25-mile title race to see if I could pull it off for the twenty-fifth time. The course, near Bournemouth, was covered with mist before the start, causing a delay. Again it was a tussle between Barbra and me. I had to fight every inch of the way, and was delighted with a winning time inside fifty-eight minutes, just four seconds in front of her.

Back to road racing in the national championship and I was pleased with the way things were going, finishing in the leading group, but I had to admit to myself that it was taking longer than I expected to feel at home racing in a bunch. But at the end of June, however, I turned out a fast 50-mile in 1-57-16, so I knew that my form and speed were still there to call on.

The team for the Tour de France was then announced, and I was not chosen. I was very disappointed. I have a fast recovery rate, my form was good, and I knew that I could race day after day in this prestigious race. The day before the team was due to leave somebody dropped out and Charlie received a phone call asking if I would be available. He phoned me at the farm where I was working and I told Charlie to phone back and say I was not. I had told the boss that I had not been picked in the team, and we had re-arranged some work schedules accordingly, so other people were involved in all this, and I was not going to muck them about. I understand, also, that I was not the first choice as replacement either. After non-selection I had mentally written off the Tour and I doubt if I could have motivated myself again at the eleventh hour.

In the following weeks I pulled out 'inside' rides in the '25' on two occasions, but by August I was feeling decidedly unwell. Perhaps it had something to do with missing the Tour de France. I felt that I was carrying a heavy weight on my shoulders but, even when I was just riding steadily to work, my legs seemed to have lost their strength. My doctor thought it was a virus infection of some kind, and I had numerous tests which did not seem to lead to a positive diagnosis. Consequently, I called a halt to my season; there seemed no point in struggling further and I had no goal to aim at anyway. I missed the Y.C.F. 100-mile when June Pitchford scorched round in 4-4-41 and sealed the B.A.R. for 1984. June had beaten me in my last race of the season a week earlier by over a minute in a '50', and it had been a struggle for me just to finish.

My health slowly improved during the following weeks and I managed some gentle riding by autumn, but for the remainder of the season the only excitement I had was helping in the 24-hour championship. Vincente Rodriguez, a Spaniard who wears the Morley colours with as much pride as any native-born Morleian, was riding and following the trail set by Nim Carline. I think in the future he will surprise some people.

As I contemplate the 1985 season and my approaching forty-eighth birthday I am on holiday again in Spain, feeling better than a few months ago. My bike is with me and I am putting in some steady miles. Last year was not a complete waste, with gold and silver championship medals, but that is already in the past and, as usual, I look forward to the next challenge. Exactly what that will be I'm not sure, but I would still like to have a ride in the Tour de France . . .

The Boro'

Yes, it is a fast course, a course where a fit rider can turn out a good time in the main, for two reasons. First, the surface is good. Second, and more important to my way of thinking, the road is such that a rider can concentrate on the ride. There are usually only two, occasionally three or four, 'fast' days on the Boro' in any one season in terms of climatic conditions. More often it is pretty hard, and the gradients can drag. It is a disappointment to many first-time riders unless he or she encounters one of the rare days I have mentioned. But the myth continues fostered by our own cycling press. In 1985 the Junior 25-mile championship was held in Yorkshire, but not on the Boro'. 'Too dangerous for the youngsters,' said the powers that be. Instead, they rode the Hull–York course, and encountered more hazards in one mile than twenty-five on the Boro' – I've raced enough times on both courses to say that with certainty.

As for the traffic flow, I have access to figures for the 1983 and 1984 seasons that would surprise many. The girls, usually riding before the men, can finish a '25' having encountered little more traffic than they would in their own street.

Having put in a defence of the Boro' I must say that, even at its best, it is not as fast as the Catterick or the E.72 courses.

Food fads, fancy diets and get-fit regimes

Stay clear of them all. Eat what you want. Obviously you should not load your stomach in the hours before a race, but if you fancy a large slab of cream-cake the day before, then enjoy it! Getting fit is all in the mind, if you are determined to be so then you will. That does not mean adopting a yoga-like trance and merely telling yourself 'I'm going to be fit.' Together with adopting the right mental attitude you must work. The way to get fit for cycling is on the bike. Miles – plenty of 'em!

Sponsored clubs

They are here, and those who do not like them must learn to live with them. Cycling is not the poor man's sport that many folk outside it still quaintly believe. If all the cash I have spent over the years just travelling to events was suddenly to appear in my bank account it would make the manager of that establishment smile – and me too! I have managed without help except for the unexpected 'little lift' to which I have previously referred. I have also, over the years, had some assistance with the loan of equipment, which I have always returned. The use of this did not place any cash in my handbag, it merely made the outflow from same somewhat less than it would have been. I have been grateful for this.

Hence, it is easy to see why riders gravitate to sponsored clubs, and my only fear is that this is causing an imbalance in the club world in which I learned my cycling and grew up. It is leading to a certain amount of acrimony. I do not pretend to know the way to obviate this, but I think the sport's hierachy will have to get to grips with it sooner or later.

Gearing

I have already stated that I train on low gears and race on high but to the novice or junior I can only say it might not work for you. But I would add this for teenagers – learn to 'twiddle' first before starting on higher gears. I time trial well forward in the saddle and use my arms and shoulders. Don't leave it all to your legs!

R.T.C. regulation 52

I have received my share of 'chatter' in connection with the above, as have others. It is not so long ago that one chap was telling an interested crowd at the finish of one event that he had seen Charlie tucked in behind me in the car shouting instructions through a loud-hailer! We fell about laughing at that one. I told Charlie I would buy him an eye-shade to accompany it then he could look like Cecil B. de Mille directing one of those old-time films! The fact is that Charlie was out on his bike that day and not even in the car while I was riding that event.

For quite a number of years early in my career we had no car, and Charlie and I rode out to races using 'digs' or Youth Hostels outside the county, and then Charlie would ride up the course. In my earlier '100s' and first 12-hours he packed in goodness knows how many miles charging round the vicinity of the course to give me a 'feed'. We did things the hard way then and I fail to see why he should not occasionally go 'up the road' now in a car – so long as he keeps strictly out of my way. If anybody says they have seen Charlie hovering either just in front or behind me during an event then it is either a case of mistaken identity – or they are deluding themselves.

It seems to me that the girls who have husbands/boy friends riding their bikes about ten yards behind them all round the course infringe the spirit if not the letter of this regulation.

Drugs

I have to suffer a headache for some time before even taking an aspirin, and I have the personal satisfaction of knowing that my successes have been achieved by means of training, strength of will and solid, Yorkshire grub. In my earlier years I came up against riders who had been 'doctored' for international races. Latterly there has been stringent testing, but some countries and riders are always one step ahead particularly, it seems, with the use of steroids. The latest ploy is taking an athlete's own blood and transfusing it back before the big race. Not strictly against the rules, apparently. The American cyclists who won Olympic gold medals at Los Angeles who were 'treated' in this way should hang their heads in shame. If any so-called doctor ever suggested mucking about with my blood like that he would feel my toe-end up his backside!

Regrets

Not taking the 'hour' record. And that '24'!

The thread which runs through Beryl's story is her iron will and determination always to give 100% of herself. Those who know her well realise that she has the competitive spirit to the nth degree. This is just as true of her personal life, where everything from the simplest task to important undertakings must be completed in the most thorough way possible.

This may suggest a woman handy to have around if something wants doing but of limited personality and outlook. Nothing could be further from the truth! I have been in her company when, inevitably, conversation has turned to cycling and she has steered the converstion away on to another topic. This is particularly so when people from outside the sport have been present. Listening to Beryl explaining, for example, how to grow raspberries or make chutney, or the merits of different operatic tenors, can be quite an education if your interests run in one of those directions.

One aspect of her personality that few people are aware of is her compassion for others, that shows in her visits to the sick and elderly and giving practical help – though it's hard to see how she manages the time! To hear her laughing at herself is a treat. Beryl would not laugh at somebody slipping on a banana skin until she was certain they were not hurt – but would laugh the loudest if it happened to her.

She has had her disappointments; they are part of cycling history, along with her triumphs. The failure to achieve what she had set out to accomplish in the 24-hour time trial is one of them, but always, without fuss, Beryl put them behind her. Within a few weeks of the '24', and in spite of difficulties, she was riding as well as ever.

This may lead the reader to assume that the old cliché that 'champions are born and not made' applies to Beryl. Physiologically, she certainly has an extremely low pulse rate which never ceases to amaze the doctors who have checked it over the years, and her muscles are the soft, sinewy cords of the champion cyclist, noticeable only at the time of supreme effort. Psychologically, her will to succeed has been amply demonstrated in her story, and it could be said that this also is part of the champion's make-up and a natural gift. Interestingly, Beryl herself will have none of this. She does not believe that champions are born and not made. She will perhaps go so far as to say that nature may help a little, depending upon what field one sets out to be a champion in, but the exploitation of any gifts one may have depends entirely upon the individual will. Manifestly, not everyone can be a world champion, but Beryl believes that everyone can achieve more than they thought possible if they apply their minds to it. Those close to her, knowing her state of health during the 1983 season, faced up early in the season to the probability that she would not lift the B.A.R. championship for the twenty-fifth successive year. She decided that she would push herself to the limit to achieve that goal, and that it was, indeed, possible.

Is there some element in her make-up that Beryl herself will not acknowledge that sets her apart and places her among the other sporting 'greats'? Nobody can say. Beryl pours scorn on the idea. She turns the old adage on its head. 'Champions are made, not born,' she says, and particularly those that 'make' themselves. Who can argue with her?

In the 1985 season Beryl continued with competition in time trials. Now at a time of life that has its own difficulties, she was not pleased with her performances. A sixth place in the 10-mile championship in which Denise took the bronze medal, and other good results, would have satisfied others in her situation. But B.B. knew her form was see-sawing. She could never tell from one week-end to the next how she was going to feel as she waited for the timekeeper's 'Go!'

Denise was now back in full flight. A brilliant second place in the five-stage international Tour de l'Aude in France gave her selection for the second women's Tour de France, with high hopes of a strong performance. Denise had built her season around this, and the cruel crash on the eve of the national championship road race resulting in frightful facial and back injuries was a bitter blow to the Burton family.

The gloom was lifted a little when on one of her better days Beryl showed that she was not finished with medal winning. In the 25-mile championship she took third place, to add a rare bronze to her collection.

An invitation to race in Texas in the Spenco 500-mile in November was perhaps the spur that Beryl needed. She began distance training, riding in time trials up to the 30-mile distance to keep a competitive edge, and by September a noticeable change had occured. The sparkle had returned to her eyes and there was a jauntiness in her step. On the 22nd September she clocked 59–20 in Essex, beating the B.A.R., her old adversary June Pitchford, by fifty-three seconds, on a day with a stiff headwind from the turn. The malaise which had afflicted her for over two years seemed at last to have lifted.

Her experience in Texas is almost worth another story. Suffice it to say that the hot, dry conditions turned unexpectedly cold with lashing rain. Ill-equipped for this sudden change in weather, ill-served by inexperienced support which had forgotten to bring along most of her food, even Beryl had no other choice but to pull out. She had covered 209 miles, and many professionals had left the race before her.

This disappointment, however, like every other adversity – and triumph – in her astonishing career, has been put firmly behind her; if there's one thing we can be sure of, it is that the world has not seen the last of Beryl Burton.

C.K.

Distance	Name	Club	Time						Year
10 miles	Beryl Burton	Morley C.C.			21 mins	25 secs			1973
15 miles	Beryl Burton	Morley C.C.			32 mins	57 secs			1981
25 miles	Beryl Burton	Morley C.C.			53 mins	21 secs			1976
30 miles	Beryl Burton	Morley C.C.	1 hr		8 mins	36 secs			1981
50 miles	Beryl Burton	Morley C.C.	1 hr		51 mins	30 secs			1976
100 miles	Beryl Burton	Morley C.C.	3 hrs		55 mins	5 secs			1968

Time	Name	Club	Distance	Year
12 hours	Beryl Burton	Morley C.C.	277.25 miles	1967
24 hours	Ann E. Mann	Hainault R.C.	438.16 miles	1983